LEAGUE

OF THE

HO-DE'-NO-SAU-NEE

OR

IROQUOIS

HO-DE'-NO-SAU-NEE

OR

PEOPLE OF THE LONG HOUSE

I. Gä-ne-ă'-ga-o-no', or People Possessors of the Flint
   MOHAWK NATION

II. O-nun'-dä-ga-o-no', or People on the Hills
   ONONDAGA NATION

III. Nun-da'-wä-o-no', or Great Hill People
   SENECA NATION

IV. O-na'-yote-kä-o-no', or Granite People
   ONEIDA NATION

V. Gwe-u'-gweh-o-no', or People at the Mucky Land
   CAYUGA NATION

VI. Dus-ga'-o-weh-o-no', or Shirt Wearing People
   TUSCARORA NATION

GÄ-WA-NASE-GEH.

Ä-NIK-HÄ-DÄ-GE-GA.

LEAGUE

OF THE

HO-DE'-NO-SAU-NEE

OR

IROQUOIS

By LEWIS H. MORGAN

NESCIT VOX MISSA REVERTI
HORACE *De Art. Poet.*, *v. 390*

TWO VOLUMES IN ONE

Published in the USA 1995 by JG Press
Distributed by World Publications, Inc.

The JG Press imprint is a trademark of JG Press, Inc.,
455 Somerset Avenue, North Dighton, Mass. 02764.

This edition published by special arrangement with
W.S. Konecky Associates.

ISBN: 1-57215-124-2

Printed and bound in the USA

TO

HÄ–SA–NO–AN'–DA

(ELY S. PARKER)

A SENECA INDIAN,

𝕿𝖍𝖎𝖘 𝖂𝖔𝖗𝖐,

THE MATERIALS OF WHICH ARE THE FRUIT OF
OUR JOINT RESEARCHES,

𝕴𝖘 𝕴𝖓𝖘𝖈𝖗𝖎𝖇𝖊𝖉:

IN ACKNOWLEDGMENT OF THE OBLIGATIONS, AND
IN TESTIMONY OF THE FRIENDSHIP OF

THE AUTHOR

Preface

TO encourage a kinder feeling towards the Indian, founded upon a truer knowledge of his civil and domestic institutions, and of his capabilities for future elevation, is the motive in which this work originated.

The present Iroquois, the descendants of that gifted race which formerly held under their jurisdiction the fairest portions of our Republic, now dwell within our limits as dependent nations, subject to the tutelage and supervision of the people who displaced their fathers. Their numbers, the circumstances of their past history and present condition, and more especially the relation in which they stand to the people of the State, suggest many important questions concerning their future destiny.

Born to an unpropitious fate, the inheritors of many wrongs, they have been unable, of themselves, to escape from the complicated difficulties which accelerate their decline. To aggravate these adverse influences, the public estimation of the Indian, resting, as it does, upon an imperfect knowledge of his character, and tinctured, as it ever has been, with the coloring of prejudice, is universally unjust.

The time has come in which it is befitting to cast away all ancient antipathies, all inherited opinions; and having taken a nearer view of their social life, condition and wants, to study anew our duty concerning them. Notwithstanding the embarrassments which have obstructed their progress, the obscurity in which they have lived, and the prevailing indifference to their welfare, they have gradually overcome many of the evils inherent in their social system, and raised themselves to a considerable degree of prosperity. Their present condition, when considered in connection with the ordeal through which they have passed, testifies to the presence of an element in their character which must eventually lead to important results. It brings before us the question of their ultimate reclamation, certainly a more interesting subject, in itself, than any other connected with the Indian. Can the residue of the Iroquois be reclaimed, and finally raised to the position of citizens of the State? To secure this end, at once so just and so beneficent, our own people have an important part to perform.

As this work does not profess to be based upon authorities, a question may arise in the mind of the reader, whence its materials were derived, or what reliance is to be placed upon its statements. The credibility of a witness is known to depend chiefly upon his means of knowledge. For this reason, it may not be inappropriate to state, that circumstances in early life, not necessary to be related, brought the author in frequent intercourse with the descendants of the Iroquois, and led to his adoption as a Seneca. This gave him favorable opportunities for studying minutely into their social organization, and the structure and principles of the ancient League. Copious notes were made from time to time, when leisure enabled him to prosecute his researches among them, until these had accumulated beyond the bounds of the present volume. As the materials increased in quantity and variety, the interest awakened in the subject finally induced the idea of its arrangement for publication.

The work properly commences with the second chapter. The first, being introductory, has no necessary connection with the residue, but was introduced to give to those unfamiliar with the civil history of the Iroquois, some preliminary information concerning the rise and decline of the League.

It remains for the author to acknowledge his obligations to Ely S. Parker, Hä-sa-no-an'-da, an educated Seneca Indian, to whom this volume is inscribed. He is indebted to him for invaluable

PREFACE

assistance during the whole progress of the research, and for a share of the materials.   His intelligence, and accurate knowledge of the institutions of his forefathers, have made his friendly services a peculiar privilege.

To Charles T. Porter, Esq.,   of New York, who has made extensive inquiries into the civil and domestic institutions of the Iroquois, and prosecuted them, in many instances, in connection with the author, he is indebted for many valuable suggestions and for some material.

ROCHESTER, N. Y., January, 1851.

GENERAL CONTENTS

VOLUME I

BOOK I
STRUCTURE OF THE LEAGUE

BOOK II
SPIRIT OF THE LEAGUE

VOLUME II

BOOK III
INCIDENT TO THE LEAGUE

VOWEL SOUNDS

ä as in arm

ă as in at

a as in ale

ĕ as in met

ō as in tone

Table of Contents

VOLUME I

BOOK I

STRUCTURE OF THE LEAGUE

CONTENTS

BOOK II

SPIRIT OF THE LEAGUE

CHAPTER I

CONTENTS

BOOK III

INCIDENT TO THE LEAGUE

CHAPTER I

CHAPTER II

CHAPTER III

CONTENTS

CHAPTER IV

List of Illustrations

VOLUME I

ILLUSTRATIONS

VOLUME II

ILLUSTRATIONS

ILLUSTRATIONS

VOLUME I

BOOK FIRST

STRUCTURE OF THE LEAGUE

GÄ-NO-SOTE
or
BARK HOUSE.

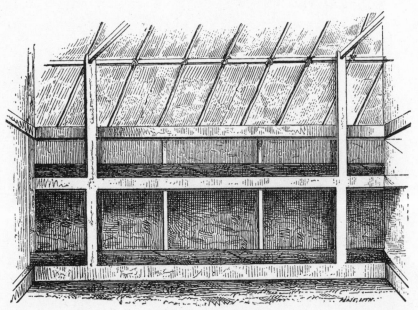

Interior View of
BARK HOUSE.

League of the Iroquois

BOOK I

STRUCTURE OF THE LEAGUE

Chapter I

Introductory Outline — Origin of the Iroquois — Formation of the League — Intercourse with Europeans — Wars with the Indian Nations — Wars with the French — Jesuit Missionaries — Number of the Iroquois — Fidelity to the English — Dispersion of the Nations — Present Condition — Future Prospects

AMONG the Indian nations whose ancient seats were within the limits of our republic, the Iroquois have long continued to occupy the most conspicuous position. They achieved for themselves a more remarkable civil organization, and acquired a higher degree of influence, than any other race of Indian lineage, except those of Mexico and Peru. In the drama of European colonization, they stood, for nearly two centuries, with an unshaken front, against the devastations of war, the blighting influence of foreign intercourse, and the still more fatal encroachments of a restless and advancing border population. Under their federal system, the Iroquois flourished in independence, and capable of self-protection, long after the New England and Virginia races had surrendered their jurisdictions, and fallen into the

3

condition of dependent nations; and they now stand forth in our Indian history, prominent alike for the wisdom of their civil institutions, their sagacity in the administration of the League, and their courage in its defence. When their power and sovereignty finally passed away, it was through the events of peaceful intercourse, gradually progressing to this result, rather than from conquest or forcible subjugation. They fell under the giant embrace of civilization, victims of the successful warfare of intelligent social life upon the rugged obstacles of nature; and in a struggle which they were fated to witness as passive and silent spectators.

As there is no connected history of the rise, progress, and decline of this Indian League, a brief general outline seems to be demanded, to refresh the mind of the reader, and to furnish a proper introduction to the following pages, which are devoted to an exposition of its structure, principles, and spirit. The eventful history of this interesting portion of our indigenous population furnishes ample materials for a separate work, the execution of which, it is to be hoped, will ere long be accomplished by capable hands.

At the era of Dutch discovery (1609), the Iroquois were found in the possession of the same territories between the Hudson and the Genesee rivers, upon which they afterwards continued to reside until near the close of the eighteenth century. At that time, the Five Nations, into which they had become subdivided, were united in a League; but its formation was subsequent to their establishment in the territories out of which the state of New York has since been erected.

Their remote origin, and their history anterior to the discovery, are both enshrouded with obscurity. Tradition interposes its feeble light to extricate, from the confusion which time has wrought, some of the leading events which preceded and marked their political organization. It informs us, that prior to their occupation of New York, they resided in the vicinity of Montreal, upon the northern bank of the St. Lawrence, where they lived in subjection to the Adirondacks, a branch of the Algonkin race, then in possession of the whole country north of that river. At that time, the Iroquois were but one nation, and few in number. From the Adirondacks they learned the art of husbandry, and while associated with them, became inured to the hardships of the war-path and of the chase. After they had multiplied in numbers and improved by experience, they made an attempt to secure the independent possession of the country they occupied; but having been, in the struggle, overpowered and vanquished by the Adirondacks, they were compelled to retire from the country, to escape extermination.

The period of their migration from the north cannot now be ascertained. Tradition informs us, that having ascended the St. Lawrence to Lake Ontario, and coasted its eastern shore to the mouth of the Oswego river, they entered through this channel the central parts of New York. Their first settlements, they believe, were located upon the Seneca river, where for a time they dwelt together. At a

subsequent day they divided into bands, and spread
abroad to found new villages.   One, crossing over
to the Mohawk, established itself at *Gä-né-ga-hä´-gä*,
below Utica, and afterwards became the Mohawk
nation.   This village, situated upon the south side
of the Mohawk river, in Herkimer county, is supposed to have been the oldest settlement of that
nation.   For some years the Oneidas and Mohawks
were one nation ; but one part of it having become
established at *Gä-no-a-lo´-häle*, east of the Oneida lake,
in time became independent.   The Onondagas planting themselves in the Onondaga valley and on the
hills adjacent, became also a separate nation.   In like
manner, the Cayugas and Senecas were many years
united, and resided upon the Seneca river ; but one
band of them having located themselves upon the east
bank of the Cayuga lake, grew up in time into a distinct nation ; while the residue, penetrating into the
interior of western New York, finally settled at *Nun-da-
wä´-o*, at the head of the Canandaigua lake, and there
formed the nucleus of the Seneca nation.

The Onondagas have a legend that they sprang out
of the ground on the banks of the Oswego river ; and
the Senecas have a similar legend, that they sprang
from the ground at *Nun-da-wä¹-o*.   By these legendary
inventions, they designed to convey an impression of
the remoteness of the period of their first occupation
of New York.

These several bands were, at first, obliged to contend with the various tribes whom they found in possession of the country.   After their expulsion, the
interests and pursuits of the five nations not only

6

became distinct, but the severance was followed by a gradual alienation, finally resulting in a state of open warfare, which continued for an unknown period. The project of a League originated with the Onondagas, among whom it was first suggested, as a means to enable them more effectually to resist the pressure of contiguous nations. The epoch of its establishment cannot now be decisively ascertained; although the circumstances attending its formation are still preserved by tradition with great minuteness. These traditions all refer to the northern shore of the Onondaga lake, as the place where the Iroquois chiefs assembled in general council, to agree upon the terms and principles of the compact, by which their future destinies were to be linked together. It is evident from their traditionary history, which is entitled to considerable credit, that they had long occupied the country before their necessities or increase of numbers made the League a feasible or desirable consummation. In relation to the period of its origin, there are some circumstances connected with their first intercourse with Europeans tending to show that it had subsisted about a century or a century and a half at the era of Dutch discovery; on the other hand, their principal traditions indicate a period far more remote.

After the formation of the League, the Iroquois rose rapidly in power and influence. It gave them additional strength by concentration of effort; a constant increase of numbers by the unity of the race; and a firmer establishment, through their more ample means for self-protection and foreign conquest. One of the first results of their federal system was a universal spirit of aggression; a thirst for military glory and political aggrandizement, which made the old forests of America resound with human conflicts from New England to the Mississippi, and from the northern confines of the great lakes to the Tennessee and the hills of Carolina. Unrecorded, except by tradition, is the narrative of the warlike achievements of this gifted and progressive race, who raised themselves, through the vicissitudes of incessant strife, to a general and acknowledged supremacy over these boundless territories. Without considering the terrible and ferocious characteristics of Indian warfare, it must be admitted that the empire which they reared over Indian nations, furnishes no slight evidence of their hardihood, courage, and sagacity.

With the first consciousness of rising power, they turned their long-cherished resentment upon the Adirondacks, who had oppressed them in their infancy as a nation, and had expelled them from their country, in the first struggle for the ascendency. This war raged for a long time with unceasing animosity, and was continued nearly fifty years after the commencement of French occupation, until the descendants of the ancient Adirondacks were almost totally extirpated. At the era of French discovery (1535), the latter nation appear to have been dispossessed of their original country, and driven down the St. Lawrence as far as Quebec. When Jacques Cartier first ascended this river in 1535, the country about Quebec was in the possession of a people speaking the Algonkin language, doubtless the Adirondacks, while the site of Montreal was occupied by a nation speaking the Huron tongue, of which the language of the Iroquois is a branch. After the permanent occupation of Canada by the French, in 1607, the Adirondacks became their allies ; but the protection of the former was insufficient to shield them against the hostile visitations of their hereditary enemy.

A new era commenced with the Iroquois upon the establishment of the Dutch trading-post at Orange, now Albany, in 1615. The principal Indian nations upon the north were the Hurons and Adirondacks ; upon the west, the Eries, Neuter Nation, Miamis, Ottawas, and Illinois ; upon the south, the Shawnees, Cherokees, Catawbas, Susquehannocks, Nanticokes, Delawares, and some lesser tribes ; and upon the east, the Minsi and New England Indians. Some of these nations had been subdued and made tributary. At this time, the Iroquois had grown up into a populous and powerful confederacy and were rapidly advancing to a general supremacy in the north-eastern section of the continent. No Indian race east of the Mississippi had reached such a position of authority and influence, or were bound together by such enduring institutions. Firmly established upon the territory of New York, and above the danger of displacement from adjacent nations, they had already entered upon that career of conquest which they afterwards prosecuted with such signal success.

Friendly relations were established between the Iroquois and the Dutch, which continued without interruption until the latter surrendered their possessions upon the Hudson to the English, in 1664.

During this period, a trade sprang up between them in furs, which the Iroquois exchanged for European fabrics, but more especially for firearms, in the use of which they were afterwards destined to become so expert. The English, in turn, cultivated the same relations of friendship which had been commenced with them by the Dutch. A " covenant chain " was established between them, which the Iroquois, with singular fidelity, preserved unbroken, until the independence of the American states terminated the jurisdiction of the English over the country.

It was otherwise, however, with the French. From the first to the last, they encountered the uncompromising and inveterate enmity of the League. As early as 1609, Champlain, having ascended through the lake which now bears his name into lake George, accompanied by the Adirondacks, fell in with a war-party of the Mohawks, numbering about two hundred, and an engagement ensued between them on the western shore of the lake. ' This was the first battle between the Iroquois and the Europeans, and the first time the former heard the sound of firearms, by the marvellous power of which they were then easily vanquished. The French having allied themselves with the Adirondacks and Hurons, given them arms and assistance, and incited them against the Iroquois, a spirit of hatred was aroused against them, which never ceased to burn until the final subjugation of Canada by the English, in 1760. Besides this alliance with their ancient enemies, the French were more inclined to resort to intimidation in their intercourse with the Iroquois, than to conciliation and forbearance.

In addition to these errors of policy, was the deep and abiding interest taken by the latter in the country about Montreal, which in ancient times had been the home of their fathers, which had been the theatre of their first military success, and which they had long continued to hold by the slender tenure of Indian conquest.   As the rival colonies of France and England were for many years nearly equally balanced, the enmity and power of the Hode'nosaunee were sufficient to turn the scale against the former.   To this Indian League, France must chiefly ascribe the final overthrow of her magnificent schemes of colonization in the northern part of America.

With the possession of firearms commenced not only the rapid elevation, but absolute supremacy of the Iroquois over other Indian nations.   In 1649–50, after a number of sanguinary conquests, the Hurons were overthrown and their power in Canada was destroyed.   In 1651, they expelled the Neuter Nation from the Niagara peninsula, and established a permanent settlement at the mouth of that river.   They nearly exterminated, in 1654, the Eries, who occupied the south side of lake Erie and from thence east to the Genesee, and thus possessed themselves of the whole area of western New York, and the northern part of Ohio.   About the year 1670, after they had finally completed the dispersion and subjugation of the Adirondacks, they acquired possession of the whole country between lakes Huron, Erie, and Ontario, and of the north bank of the St. Lawrence, to the mouth of the Otawas river, near Montreal.   On the north shore of lake Ontario they founded several villages, in the nature of colonial towns, to maintain possession of the conquered territory.

They also made constant inroads upon the New England Indians, who, after their partial subjugation by the English, were unable to cope with the formidable Iroquois. About the year 1670, they compelled them to break up many of their settlements, and flee for safety and protection to the borders of the English plantations. The name of the Iroquois had then become a terror among Indian nations. " I have been told," (says Colden) " by old men in New England, who remembered the time when the Mohawks made war on their Indians, that as soon as a single Mohawk was discovered in their country, their Indians raised a cry from hill to hill, a Mohawk! a Mohawk! upon which they fled like sheep before wolves, without attempting to make the least resistance."

In 1680, the Senecas with six hundred warriors invaded the country of the Illinois, upon the borders of the Mississippi river, while La Salle was among the latter, preparing to descend that river to the sea. So great was the dread and consternation of the Illinois, that they were inclined to abandon their villages, and retire from the country, to escape the fury of the conquering foe. At various times, both before and after this period, the Iroquois turned their warfare against the Cherokees upon the Tennessee, and the Catawbas in South Carolina, frequently returning from their distant expeditions with numerous captives, to grace the narrative of their invasions. Of these inroads they still preserve many traditions. All the intermediate country between the Allegany and the Tennessee acknowledged their authority, and the latter river became their southern boundary. War parties of the League also made irruptions into the country of the Miamis, others penetrated into the peninsula of Michigan, and still others were seen upon the distant shores of lake Superior. No distant solitude or rugged fastness was too obscure or difficult to escape their visitation; no enterprise was too perilous, no fatigue too great for their courage and endurance. The fame of their achievements resounded over the continent.

On the south-east, also, they extended their conquests. As early as 1607, Captain John Smith, the founder of Virginia, encountered a band of the Iroquois, in several canoes, upon the upper part of the Chesapeake bay, then on their way to the territories of the Powhattan confederacy. The Shawnees, Nanticokes, Unamis, Delawares, and Minsi were vanquished one after another, and reduced to the condition of dependent nations. Even the Canarese Indians, in their sea-girt home upon Long Island, found no protection against their attacks. In fact, they traversed the whole country from the St. Lawrence to the Tennessee, and from the Atlantic to the Mississippi.

For three quarters of a century, from the year 1625 to the year 1700, the Iroquois were involved in an almost uninterrupted warfare. At the close of this period, they had subdued and held in nominal subjection all the principal Indian nations occupying the territories which are now embraced in the states of New York, Delaware, Maryland, New Jersey, Pennsylvania, the northern and western parts of Virginia, Ohio, Kentucky, Northern Tennessee, part of Illinois, Indiana and Michigan, a portion of the New England states, and the principal part of Upper Canada. Over many of these nations, the haughty and imperious Iroquois exercised a constant supervision. If any of them became involved in domestic difficulties, a delegation of chiefs went among them and restored tranquillity, prescribing at the same time their future conduct. Some of these nations, like the Delawares, they prohibited from going out to war, having denationalized them by taking from them all civil powers. According to the Indian notion, they were made women, and were henceforth to confine themselves to pursuits appropriate to the Indian female. Such was the general awe and fear inspired by their warlike achievements, that they dictated to Indian nations their own terms of intercourse, and insisted upon the fulfilment of their requirements. In the conquered territories they often established settlements or colonies of their own people, to exercise a species of superintendence over their acquired possessions.

The multitude of independent tribes into which the generic stocks of the continent had become subdivided, and their want of concert and unity were extremely favorable to the career of conquest pursued by the Iroquois. In their disunited condition, they could but feebly resist the concentrated energies secured to the latter through the League.

About the year 1700, the Iroquois reached their culminating point. They had reared a formidable Indian power, so far as its sway over the aborigines was concerned, and in comparison with any Indian power which had risen north of the Aztec monarchy. Having established their dominion securely against all races of Indian lineage, and strengthened the bonds of union among themselves beyond the power of civil dissensions, they would seem to have prepared themselves for a still higher progress, through the pursuits of peace; but a different and more deadly enemy than the Indian had already stretched out its arms to enfold them in its withering embrace.

During the same period, or rather from about the year 1640 to the year 1700, a constant warfare was maintained between the Iroquois and the French, interrupted occasionally by negotiations and brief intervals of peace. As the former possessed both banks of the St. Lawrence, and the circuits of lakes Erie and Ontario, they intercepted the fur trade, which the French were anxious to maintain with the western nations. Upon this trade much of the prosperity of the new colony depended, for it furnished the chief article of export, and yielded the most profitable returns. But the war parties of the League ranged through these territories so constantly, that it was impossible for the French to pass in safety through the lakes, or even up the St. Lawrence above Montreal. Their traders were captured, and the rich furs of the west not only became the spoil of the victors, but the traders themselves were often led into captivity, and perhaps to the stake. So great was the fear of these sudden attacks, that both the traders and the missionaries were obliged to ascend the Otawas river to near its source, and from thence to cross over to

the Sauit St. Marie, and the shores of lake Superior.
For these reasons the French were extremely anxious,
either to detach the Iroquois from the English and
gain their alliance, or to reduce them to subjection by
conquest. They tried each successively, and in both
were equally defeated. The untractable and politic
Iroquois were averse to the former, and too powerful
for the latter. On numerous occasions the ambassa-
dors of the League were at Montreal and Quebec, to
negotiate with them for the adjustment of difficulties,
and the exchange of prisoners; in some of which
negotiations, the terms of a peace, or at least of an
armistice, were agreed upon; but these respites from
warfare were of short duration. The ravages committed upon the settlements of the French were so
frequent and so devastating as to place the colony in
imminent peril. But for the constant supplies from
the mother country, the French power in Canada
would inevitably have been overthrown at several
different periods prior to 1700.

To retaliate for these frequent inroads, and to prevent their recurrence, the country of the Iroquois was
often invaded by the French. On several occasions
they drew out the whole force of the colony, to devas-
tate the villages of the League; but after the most
toilsome expeditions into the heart of the wilderness
of New York, they returned without having accomplished sufficient to reward them for the fatigues and
perils of the enterprise. The Iroquois invariably retired into the depths of the forest, leaving nothing but
their deserted tenements and fields of corn to await
the invader. In this manner the unwearied persever-

ance and indomitable courage of the French were rendered futile against such an evanescent adversary.

In 1665, M. Courcelles, governor of Canada, led a strong party into the country of the Mohawks; but the hardships they encountered rendered it necessary for them to return, without accomplishing their purpose. The next year, M. De Tracy, viceroy of New France, with twelve hundred French and six hundred Indians, renewed the invasion with better success. He captured *Te-ä-ton-ta-lo'-ga*, one of the principal villages of the Mohawks, situated at the mouth of the Schoharie creek; but after destroying the town, and the stores of corn, which they found in caches, they were obliged to retire without meeting an opposing force. Again, in 1684, M. De La Barre, then governor of Canada, entered the country of the Onondagas with about eighteen hundred men. Having reached Hungry bay, on the east shore of lake Ontario, a conference was had with a delegation of Iroquois chiefs, headed by Garangula, the celebrated Onondaga orator. After they had exchanged recriminations and mutual defiance, a species of armistice was finally agreed upon, and thus the expedition ended.

A more successful enterprise was projected and carried into execution, in 1687, by M. De Nonville, then governor of Canada. Having raised a force of two thousand French and six hundred Indians, he embarked them in a fleet of two hundred bateau and as many birch bark canoes. After coasting lake Ontario from Kingston to Irondequoit bay, in the territory of the Senecas, he landed at the head of this bay, and found himself within a few miles of the principal villages of the Senecas, which were then in the counties of Ontario and Monroe. The nearest village was *Gä-o-sä-ga'-o*, near Victor, in the county of Ontario, and the next *Gä-nun-dă'-gwa*, at the foot of the Canandaigua lake. Taking the trail which led directly to these villages, De Nonville marched upon the first. After repulsing a body of five hundred Senecas, with whom he had a sharp engagement, he took and destroyed the town, which had been deserted by its inhabitants. Meeting with no further opposition, as the Senecas had retired into the interior, he marched southward as far as *Da-yo-de-hok'-to*, a village situated at the bend of the Honeoye outlet, west of Mendon, in the county of Monroe. This was the largest village of the Senecas, according to the official statement of De Nonville, and was the place selected for the execution of the *acté*, by which they took formal possession of the country of the Seneca-Iroquois, in the name of France. Four villages, with their extensive fields of corn then growing, were burned and devastated, after which the French army retired.

To retaliate for this invasion, a formidable party of the Iroquois, in the fall of the same year, made a sudden descent upon fort Chambly, on the Sorel river, near Montreal. Unable to capture the fort, which was resolutely defended by the garrison, they ravaged the settlements adjacent, and returned with a number of captives. About the same time, a party of eight hundred attacked Frontenac, on the site of Kingston, and destroyed and laid waste the plantations and establishments of the French without the fortification. In July of the ensuing year, the French were made to feel still more sensibly the power of their revenge.   A band of twelve hundred warriors, animated with the fiercest resentment, made a descent upon the island of Montreal. They had covered their plans with such secrecy, and advanced with such celerity, that the inhabitants had no admonition of their approach.   Their first intimation of impending danger was the fearful onset of the Iroquois.   Unprepared, and without the means of resistance, they were overpowered and slain in every direction.   All that were without the fortifications fell under the rifle or the relentless tomahawk.   Their houses were burned, their plantations ravaged, and the whole island covered with desolation.   About a thousand of the French, according to some writers, perished in this invasion, or were carried into captivity.   When the work of destruction was completed, the Iroquois retired, bearing with them the spoils of the island, and about two hundred prisoners.

Overwhelmed by this sudden disaster, the French destroyed their forts at Niagara and Frontenac, and thus yielded the whole country west of Montreal to the possession of the Iroquois.   At this critical period Count Frontenac again became governor of Canada, and during the short residue of his life devoted himself, with untiring energy, to restore its declining prosperity.   War had now commenced between the English and French, which drew his first attention to the defence of Quebec against the attack of the English ; but after this had been successfully resisted, he again sought to chastise the fierce enemy who had so long disputed with the French the possession of

Canada. In the winter of 1692–3, he sent a detachment of six hundred French and Indians against the Mohawks; which, after travelling through the dense forests upon snow-shoes, and encountering almost insurmountable obstacles, finally reached in safety the vicinity of the Mohawk villages. They surprised and captured three of these, took three hundred prisoners, and returned with the loss of thirty men. Again, in 1696, Count Frontenac conducted an expedition in person against the Onondagas and Oneidas, with a thousand French and as many Indians. Having ascended the St. Lawrence in bateau and bark canoes, he coasted the eastern shore of the lake, to the mouth of the Oswego river. From thence he marched to the salt springs, near the site of Syracuse, and up the Onondaga valley to the principal village of the Onondagas. He found it, as usual, deserted, although fortified with palisades, and supplied with stores of corn. The village was then burned, and the growing corn, which was found in great abundance in the fields adjacent, was cut down with the sabre. A detachment was then sent against the Oneidas, under M. De Vaudreuil, by whom their fields also were laid waste, after which the French army returned to Canada.

This was the last French invasion of the territories of the Iroquois. A general peace soon followed, and continued without interruption, until the war of 1755, which finally resulted in the conquest of Canada by the English, in 1760.

From the commencement of English intercourse with the Iroquois, down to the independence of the American states, the covenant of friendship between them remained unbroken. The importance of conciliating this powerful confederacy was fully appreciated by the colonial authorities, especially during the infancy of the English establishments. Unwearied pains were taken by them to secure and retain their favor and confidence. Each successive governor announced his arrival to the Sachems of the League, and invited them to meet him in council, at an early day, to renew the "covenant chain." Each new alliance was cemented by presents, by mutual professions of kindness, and by assurances of mutual assistance. An intercourse sprang up between them in matters of trade, and in public affairs, which continued to increase, until councils with the Iroquois became nearly as frequent as the sessions of the provincial legislature. Independent of the profitable trade in furs, with which they enriched their commerce, they felt the necessity of interposing the power of the Indian League, as a barrier to French progress, not only towards their own settlements, but also towards the west. The French were constantly striving to open an extensive fur trade with the western nations, and for its necessary protection, to extend their possessions up the St. Lawrence, and upon the northern shores of Lake Ontario. With the exclusive navigation of this river and lake, they would have obtained nearly the absolute control of this important trade; under the powerful stimulus of which, the strength and prosperity of the French colony would have risen with such rapidity as to threaten the security of the English possessions. Both ·the English and the French were fully aware of the important part the Iroquois were destined to bear in the drama of colonization; but the former, by their superior advantage of position, and from their greater dependence upon the forbearance of the League, were induced to pursue a course of policy which gained their unchangeable friendship. The French would inevitably, if unopposed by them, have possessed themselves of the greater part of New York, and, perhaps, have established their empire so firmly, that the united forces of the English colonies would have been unable to effect their displacement. At one period, the French had pushed their settlements up Lake Champlain, until both sides of the lake, as far up as the foot of Lake George, were covered with French grants.

A reference, at least, to the missionary efforts of the French, while in the occupation of Canada, ought not to be omitted. While the English entirely neglected the spiritual welfare of the Indians, the French were unremitting in their efforts to spread Christianity among them. The privations and hardships endured by the Jesuit missionaries, and the zeal, the fidelity and devotion, exhibited by them, in their efforts for the conversion of the Indian, are unsurpassed in the history of Christianity. They traversed the forests of America alone and unprotected; they dwelt in the depth of the wilderness, without shelter, and almost without raiment; they passed the ordeal of Indian captivity, and the fires of the torture; they suffered from hunger and violence; but in the midst of all, they never forgot the mission with which they were intrusted. The fruits of these labors of

Christian devotion are yet visible among the descendants of the ancient Iroquois : for the precepts spread abroad among them by the missionaries are still in the Indian mind, and many of them have been incorporated by them into their own religious system. The intercourse of the French Jesuits with the Iroquois furnishes, in some respects, the most pleasing portion of their history.

In 1715, the Tuscaroras, having been expelled from North Carolina, turned to the north, and sought a home among the Iroquois, on the ground of a common origin. That they were originally descended from the same stock is sufficiently evinced by their language. They were admitted into the League as a constituent member, and a portion of the Oneida territory assigned to them as their future home. After this event, the Iroquois, who had before been styled by the English the " Five Nations," were known by them under the name of the " Six Nations."

With this brief and barren outline of prominent events, the civil history of the Iroquois, prior to 1760, is dismissed.

It is difficult to form a correct estimate of their number; the opinions of those having the best opportunities of judging have been so various. La Hontan placed them at seventy thousand. The estimate made by Colonel Coursey, at Albany, in 1677, gave them about fifteen thousand ; but it is known that his means of judging were very imperfect. Bancroft estimates them, including the Tuscaroras, at seventeen thousand. Calculations made at a later day, after they had greatly declined in number, allowed them ten thousand. This was substantially the estimate of Sir William Johnson, in 1763. There is a tradition among the Senecas, that at the period of their highest prosperity and numbers, they took a census of their nation, by placing a kernel of white flint corn for each Seneca, in a corn husk basket, which, from the description of its size, would hold ten or twelve quarts. Taking the smallest size, and making the estimate accordingly, it will give us the number of Senecas alone at 17,760. At the present time there are about seven thousand Iroquois within the United States and Canada, who have continued to preserve their lineage and nationality through all their vicissitudes. This appears from the reports of the Indian Department, and from other sources of information.

It is well understood, that the decline of the Iroquois commenced with their first intercourse with Europeans. The possession of firearms, and their use in Indian warfare, the introduction of ardent spirits among them, with its train of frightful excesses, and their incessant conflicts with the French, and with Indian nations, were calculated to waste them away with great rapidity. In 1750, from these various causes, they had become diminished about one half. Another and a prominent cause of the decline of the Iroquois, was the large numbers induced, at various times, to emigrate to the banks of the St. Lawrence, under the influence of the Jesuit missionaries, and who, by placing themselves under French protection, became the enemies of their kindred and of the League. The most successful colony of this descrip-

tion was that established by the Abbé Picquet at
Swe-gắ-che, on the site of Ogdensburg, in 1749. The
first year, he constructed a fort of palisades, and commenced with six Iroquois families; in the second
year, the number of families had increased to eighty-
seven, and in the third, to 396. Such was the influx
from the territories of the League to the new missionary establishment, that, in 1754, the number of
inhabitants in their three villages, at and near *Swe-
gắ-che*, were estimated by the French at three thousand.
This band were afterwards known as the "Praying
Indians," from their conversion to Christianity. Their
descendants now reside upon the St. Regis reservation,
in the county of St. Lawrence.

The period of their greatest prosperity, and of their
highest numbers, was evidently about the year 1650,
shortly after the commencement of their intercourse
with Europeans. At that time, their total population
may be safely placed at twenty-five thousand. A
higher estimate would be better supported by such
data as the case affords, than a lesser one; although
the impression of later writers seems to be the contrary. An approximation to the relative strength
of the several nations of the League, upon this basis,
may be made by the following apportionment: To
the Senecas, ten thousand; to the Cayugas, three
thousand; to the Onondagas, four thousand; to the
Oneidas, three thousand; and to the Mohawks, five
thousand. A century later, their total population was
probably about half this number, the Mohawks having
wasted away the most rapidly.

A few brief observations upon the modern transactions of the Iroquois will close this outline. From the close of the French war until the commencement of the American Revolution, was a time of general peace. The Revolution placed them in a position of great difficulty, as the Continental congress negotiated to secure their neutrality, and the English to obtain their assistance. Their sympathies, as was anticipated, were strongly enlisted in favor of their ancient ally, with whom, for upward of a century, they had maintained an unbroken friendship. They were thoroughly English in sentiment. Having no motive of self-interest to engage them on either side, neutrality was the true policy of the League ; more especially, as the final success of the American arms might lead to the forfeiture of their country, if they enlisted against them. In the end, the appeals and the appliances of the English were found irresistible ; and, placing their country and the homes of their fathers in the event of the struggle, the people of the Long House went out for the last time in battle array, not to peril their lives for themselves, but to keep the " covenant chain " with a transatlantic ally.

When the question of declaring for the English came before the council of sachems and chiefs, the Oneidas alone resisted the measure, as unwise and inexpedient. Their opposition defeated the war measure, as an act of the League, unanimity being a fundamental law in the legislation of the Iroquois. But the course of events had, at this time, greatly impaired and weakened the confederacy. Their power and numbers had wasted away ; their political existence, as an independent people, was drawing to its close; and it was found impossible, under the pressure of circumstances, to adhere to the ancient principles of the League. It was finally determined, that each nation might engage in the war upon its own responsibility; so that, ultimately, the Mohawks, Onondagas, Cayugas and Senecas took up the rifle for the English. The border wars of the Revolution, in which the Iroquois participated, and the devastations which they committed in the valleys of the Mohawk and Susquehanna, and their tributaries, are too familiar to require a recital. Their irruptions into the border settlements were so frequent, and the track of their invasions was marked with such desolation, that the American congress were obliged to send against them a powerful detachment, to lay waste their villages, and to overawe them with the fear of final extirpation. General Sullivan, in 1779, led an army of four thousand men into the Seneca territory, which he penetrated as far as the Genesee, at that time the centre of their population. After destroying their principal towns, their fruit orchards, and stores of grain, he returned to Pennsylvania; having first sent a detachment into the Cayuga territory to ravage their settlements.

The treaty of peace between Great Britain and the United States, in 1783, made no provision for the Iroquois, who were abandoned in adversity by their ally, and left to make such terms as they could with the successful republic. A few years afterwards a general peace was established with the northwestern Indian nations, including the Iroquois, all of whom had, more or less, become involved in the general controversy. With the restoration of peace, the political transactions of the League were substantially closed. This was, in effect, the termination of their political existence. The jurisdiction of the United States was extended over their ancient territories, and from that time forth they became dependent nations.

During the progress of the Revolution, the Mohawks abandoned their country and removed to Canada, finally establishing themselves partly upon Grand river, in the Niagara peninsula, and partly near Kingston, where they now reside upon two reservations secured to them by the British government.

The Oneidas, notwithstanding their friendly position during the war, in the end fared little better than their Mohawk brethren. A rapid influx of population, the tide of which set to the westward with the restoration of peace, soon rendered their possessions valueless. Negotiations were immediately commenced by the State for the purchase of their lands, which they yielded from time to time in large grants, until their original possessions were narrowed down to one small reservation. In these negotiations, as well with the other Iroquois nations as with the Oneidas, the policy of the State of New York was ever just and humane. Although their country, with the exception of that of the Oneidas, might have been considered as forfeited by the event of the Revolution, yet the government never enforced the rights of conquest, but extinguished the Indian title to the country by purchase, and treaty stipulations. A portion of the Oneida nation emigrated to a reservation on the river Thames, in Canada, where about four hundred of them now reside.

Another and a larger band removed to Green Bay, in Wisconsin, where they still make their homes to the number of seven hundred. But a small part of the nation have remained around the seat of their ancient council-fire. One hundred and twenty-six, according to the census of the last year, are now dwelling near Oneida castle, in the county of Oneida, and have become fully habituated to an agricultural life.

Perhaps, in the result, the Onondagas have been the most fortunate nation of the League. They still retain their beautiful and secluded valley of Onondaga, with sufficient territory for their comfortable maintenance, even with the limited production of Indian husbandry. After the Revolution, they granted their lands to the State by treaty, with the exception of the tract they now occupy, the proceeds, as in other cases, being invested by the government for their benefit. About a hundred and fifty Onondagas now reside with the Senecas; another party are established on Grand river, in Canada, and a few have removed to the west. The total number still remaining at Onondaga is about two hundred and fifty.

Over the fate of the Cayugas a feeling of regret and sympathy is awakened, as having been even less fortunate than their unfortunate kindred. This nation has become literally scattered abroad. Immediately after the Revolution, the tide of population began to press upon them, and hem them in on every side, to such a degree that they were obliged wholly to surrender their domain. In the brief space of twelve years after the first house of the white man was erected in Cayuga county (1789) the whole nation was uprooted and gone. In 1795, they ceded, by treaty, all their lands to the State, with the exception of one reservation, which they finally abandoned about the year 1800. A portion of them removed to Green Bay, another to Grand river, and still another, and a much larger band, settled at Sandusky, in Ohio, from whence they were removed by government, a few years since, into the Indian Territory, west of the Mississippi. About one hundred and twenty-five still reside among the Senecas, in western New York, and yet retain their name and lineage, and have their separate chiefs. Those west of the Mississippi, and those residing with the Senecas, divide between them the State annuity of $2,300, which was secured to them upon the sale of their former possessions.

The Tuscaroras, after removing from the Oneida territory, finally located near the Niagara river, in the vicinity of Lewiston, on a tract given to them by the Senecas, where about three hundred of them now reside.

After the displacement of the Cayugas, the flow of population, still advancing westward with constantly augmenting force, next began to press upon the broad domains of the Senecas. They passed through the same ordeal to which the other nations had been subjected, by means of which they were speedily induced to grant away their lands, not by townships and counties, but from river to river, reserving here and there a small oasis, sufficient to rescue a favorite village with its burial-place. Their wide-spread territories were in a few years narrowed down, to gratify the demands of the white man, until the residue of the Senecas are now shut up within three small reservations, the Tonawanda, the Cattaraugus and the Allegany, which, united, would not cover the area of one of the lesser counties of the State. To embitter their sense of desolation as a nation, the " preemptive right " to these last remnants of their ancient possessions is now held by a company of land speculators, the Ogden Land Company, who, to wrest away these few acres, have pursued and hunted them for the last fourteen years, with a degree of wickedness hardly to be paralleled in the history of human avarice. Not only have every principle of honesty, every dictate of humanity, every christian precept been violated by this company, in their eager artifices to despoil the Senecas ; but the darkest frauds, the basest bribery, and the most execrable intrigues which soulless avarice could suggest, have been practiced, in open day, upon this defenceless and much-injured people. The natural feelings of man, and the sense of public justice are violated and appalled at the narration of their proceedings. It is no small crime against humanity to seize the firesides and the property of a whole community, without an equivalent, and against their will ; and then to drive them, beggared and outraged, into a wild and inhospitable wilderness. And yet this is the exact scheme of the Ogden Land Company ; the one in which they have long been engaged, and the one which they still continue to prosecute. The Georgia treaty with the Cherokees, so justly held up to execration, is a white page, compared with the treaties of 1838 and 1842, which were forced upon the Senecas. This project has already, however, in part, been defeated, by the load of iniquity which hung upon the skirts of these treaties; and it is to be hoped, for the credit of humanity, that the cause of the Indian will yet triumph, and that the residue of the Senecas will be permitted to dwell in peace in the land of their nativity.[1]

The census of last year fixes the number of Senecas upon their then reservations, in western New York, at two thousand seven hundred and twelve. A small band, after the Revolution, emigrated to Grand river, where they now have a miniature of the ancient League, and another removed to Sandusky, and from thence into the Indian Territory. Those at present within the State are rapidly improving in their social and moral condition; as also, it is believed, are those residing upon Grand river, in Canada, where there are now about seven hundred Mohawks, besides five hundred near Kingston, four hundred Onondagas, seven hundred Cayugas, three hundred Tuscaroras, and two hundred Senecas and Oneidas.

From the sales of the lands of the Iroquois, at various times, large sums of money have accrued, which have been invested by the State and national governments for their benefit; and the interest arising from the same is now paid over and distributed among them semi-annually. The Senecas alone have an

---

[1] The Buffalo Reservation, which made the fourth reserved tract, and was the most valuable, has fallen into the hands of the Ogden Company, but not so much by virtue of the treaties as by skilful management. It contains forty-nine thousand acres of land bordering the corporate limits of the city of Buffalo, and was supposed to be worth over a million of dollars. For the land, and its farming improvements, the Company paid the Senecas about one hundred thousand dollars.

annual income from these sources, amounting to $18,000.

There are still residing in the State of New York about four thousand Iroquois. The several fragments of the nations yet continue their relationships and intercourse with each other, and cling to the shadow of the ancient League. At intervals of one or two years, they assemble in general council to raise up, with their primitive forms and ceremonies, sachems to fill vacancies occasioned by death or deposition. These councils are summoned and conducted, in all respects, as they were wont to be in the days of Indian sovereignty. They still cherish the remembrance of their fathers, and the institutions which they transmitted to them, with religious affection. In each nation, also, with the exception of the Oneidas and Tuscaroras, the larger portion of the people continue to adhere to their ancient faith and worship; celebrating their religious festivals after the original method, and preserving, in their social intercourse, the habits and the customs of their ancestors. It is another singular fact, in connection with their history, that since their adoption of agricultural pursuits, as the exclusive source of subsistence, their further decline has been arrested, and they are now increasing in numbers. In many respects they have become an interesting portion of our population, yielding many hopes of their future elevation. The policy of the State towards them has ever been enlightened, humane and just, the government seizing upon every opportunity to promote their welfare, to protect their interests, and to extend to them facilities for education.

It is a pleasing and a proud reflection, that there is a universal spirit of kindness, sympathy and benevolence towards the Iroquois, among the people of New York. They would shield them in their defenceless condition, stimulate their efforts for social improvement, encourage their aspirations for a higher life, and finally, when they have become sufficiently advanced in agricultural life, raise them to the condition of citizens of the State.

The materials for the preceding chapter were drawn from the following sources : Colden's Hist. Five Nations ; Charlevoix's Hist. New France ; Smith's Hist. N. Y. ; Macauley's Hist. N. Y. ; Doc. Hist. N. Y. ; Morse's Hist. Am. Rev. ; Bancroft's Hist. U. S. ; Warburton's Conquest of Canada ; Marshall's Nar. De Nonville's Exped. ; Schoolcraft's Notes on the Iroquois ; Doc's of the Indian Department ; MSS. Treaties with the Iroquois, State Dep. Alby. ; Traditions of the Onondagas, Tuscaroras, Senecas and Cayugas.

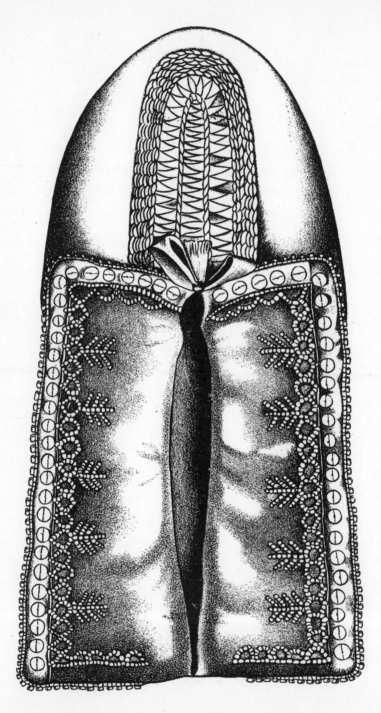

AH-TÄ-QUÄ-O-WEH OR MOCCASIN FOR MALE.

Chapter II

OUR Indian geography, excluding lines of lati-
tude, descriptions of soil and climate, and
precise territorial limits, confines itself to the
external features of the country, and to the period
when the hemlock and the maple, the pine and the
oak, interlocked their branches in endless alternation,
spreading out from river to river, and from lake to
lake, in one vast, continuous, interminable forest.

As the aboriginal, or poetic period of our territorial history recedes from us, each passing year both
deepens the obscurity upon the Indian's footsteps,
and diminishes the power of the imagination to recall
the stupendous forest scenery by which he was surrounded. To obtain a glance at the face of nature
during the era of Indian occupation, the wave of improvement must be rolled backward, not only displac-
ing, in its recession, the city and the village which have
sprung up in the wilderness; but restoring, also, by a
simultaneous effort, the original drapery of nature,
when clothed in her wild attire.[1]

[1] In those forest days, the graceful swan folded her wings in unmo-
lested seclusion upon our inland lakes ; but with the departure of the
Indian, she spread them again, and followed him. They sat upon the

Surrounded by all the grandeur of this forest scenery, the Indian constructed his *Gä-no'-sote*, or Bark House, upon the winding stream, or on the margin of the lake; and, one of the multitudinous inhabitants of the forest, he passed his days and years in sylvan pursuits, unless he went forth upon the war-path in quest of adventure or renown.

Between the Hudson and lake Erie, our broad territory was occupied by the *Ho-de'-no-sau-nee*, or Iroquois, scattered far and wide, in small encampments, or in disconnected villages. Their council-fires, emblematical of civil jurisdiction, burned continuously from the Hudson to Niagara. At the era of Dutch discovery (1609), they had pushed their permanent possession as far west as the Genesee; and shortly after, about 1650, they extended it to the Niagara. They then occupied the entire territory of our State west of the Hudson, with the exception of certain tracts upon that river below the junction of the Mohawk, in the possession of the River Indians, and the country of the Delawares, upon the Delaware river. But both these had been subdued by the conquering Iroquois, and had become tributary nations.

The villages of the Mohawks were chiefly located in the valley of the Mohawk, upon the south side of the river. Around and near the Oneida lake were the principal villages of the Oneidas. The Onondagas were established in the valley of the river of that name, and upon the hills adjacent. On the east shore of the

water in pairs, and not in flocks. It is said they still frequent the small lakes in the wild regions of northern New York. The American swan (Cygnus Americanus) was called by the Senecas *Ah-weh'-ah-ah.*

Cayuga lake, and upon the ridge to the eastward, were the settlements of the Cayugas. In the counties of Ontario and Monroe were found the principal villages of the Senecas, the most populous nation of the League. These were their chief localities at the era of their discovery. At a later period, in the progress of their intercourse and warfare with the whites, many of their ancient settlements were abandoned, and new ones established. This was especially the case with the Senecas, until their villages, at various periods, have been sprinkled over the whole area of western New York.

This territory, lying between the Hudson and lake Erie, and embracing the most valuable portions of our State, constituted the Home Country of the Iroquois, as distinguished from other territories upon the north, south, east and west, which they held in subjection by conquest, and occupied only in the season of the hunt. At the era of their highest military supremacy, about the year 1660, the Iroquois, in their warlike expeditions, ranged unresisted from New England to the Mississippi, and from the St. Lawrence to the Tennessee. They held under their dominion the greater part of these vast territories by the slender tenure of Indian conquest. But New York was their hereditary country, the centre of their power, and the seat of their council-fires. Here were their villages, their fields of maize and tobacco, their fishing and hunting grounds, and the burial-places of their fathers. The Long House, to which they likened their political edifice, opened its eastern door upon the Hudson, while the western looked out upon Niagara. At the epoch of their discovery, this fair domain was the patrimony of the Iroquois, the land of their nativity, if not of their remote origin, and they had defended it against hostile bands with a patriotism as glowing as such a fair possession could inspire in the heart of man. They were not insensible to the political advantages afforded by their geographical position. It was their boast that they occupied the highest part of the continent. Situated upon the head-waters of the Hudson, the Delaware, the Susquehanna, the Ohio and the St. Lawrence flowing in every direction to the sea, they held within their jurisdiction as it were, the gates of the country, and could, through them, descend at will upon any point. At the same time, lake Ontario, and the mountains upon the north, and the range of the Alleganies upon the south gave to their country itself an isolation which protected them, in a great measure, against the external pressure of migratory bands; while the lakes and streams, which in so remarkable a manner intersected every part of the Long House, and whose head-waters were separated only by short portages, and its continuous valleys, divided by no mountain barriers, offered them every facility for the most rapid intercommunication. They themselves declared that "their country possessed many advantages superior to any other part of America."

A boundary line would seem at first to be a difficult problem in Indian geography. But a peculiar custom of our predecessors has divested this subject of much of its embarrassment, and enabled us to ascertain with considerable certainty the territorial limits of the nations of the League. The Iroquois rejected all natural boundaries, and substituted longitudinal lines. This appears to have resulted from the custom of establishing themselves upon both banks of the streams upon which they resided. Having no knowledge of the use of wells, they were accustomed to fix their habitations upon the banks of creeks, and easily forded rivers, or in the vicinity of copious springs. Inland lakes were never divided by a boundary line; but the line itself was deflected, that the entire circuit of each lake might be possessed by a single nation. The natural limits which rivers and lakes might furnish having thus been disregarded, and straight lines substituted, the inquiry is freed from some of its difficulties, and greater certainty is given to their boundaries, when certain points upon them are decisively ascertained.

After the expulsion of the Neuter Nation (*Je-go'-sä-sa*) from the borders of the Niagara river, in 1651,[1] and of the Eries (*Gä-quä'-ga-o-no*) from the country between the Genesee and lake Erie in 1655,[2] the Senecas, who before these periods had resided east of the Genesee, extended their jurisdiction over the whole area between the Seneca lake and lake Erie. On the east, their territory joined that of the Cayugas. The line of boundary between them, which is well authenticated, commenced at the head of Sodus bay, on lake Ontario, and running south, nearly upon the

---

[1] Charlevoix, v. i. p. 377. The Neuter Nation were known to the Iroquois as the "Cat Nation;" the word itself (*Je-go'-sä-sa*) signifying "a wild cat." Charlevoix has assigned this name to the Eries (v. ii. p. 62).

[2] Ib. v. ii. p. 62.

longitude of Washington, crossed the Clyde river near the village of that name, and the Seneca river about four miles east of its outlet from the Seneca lake. Continuing south, and inclining a little to the east, the line ran near the lake at its head, and having crossed the Chemung river east of Elmira, it passed into Pennsylvania.

The territory of the Cayugas lay upon both sides of the Cayuga lake, and extended to the eastward so as to include the Owasco. As the Senecas were the hereditary "Door-keepers" of the Long House, in their figurative way of designating each other, they were styled the first fire; and so on to the Mohawks, who were the fifth. Between the Cayugas and Onondagas, who were the third fire, the limital line is not as well defined; as the latter claimed farther to the westward than the boundary assigned. It commenced on lake Ontario, near the mouth of the Oswego river, and on its west side, and passing between the Cross and Otter lakes, continued south into Pennsylvania, crossing the Susquehanna west of Owego.

On the boundary line between the Onondagas and Oneidas, the most prominent point was the Deep Spring (*De-o-song'-wa*) near Manlius, in the county of Onondaga. This spring not only marked the limital line between them, but it was a well known stopping-place on the great central trail or highway of the Iroquois, which passed through the heart of their territories from the Hudson to lake Erie. From the Deep Spring, the line ran due south into Pennsylvania, crossing the Susquehanna near its confluence with the Chenango. North of this spring the line was deflected to the west, leaving in the Oneida territory the whole circuit of that lake. Crossing the *She-u'-kä*, or Oneida outlet, a few miles below the lake, the line inclined again to the east, until it reached the meridian of the Deep Spring. From thence it ran due north, crossing the Black river at the site of Watertown, and the St. Lawrence to the eastward of the Thousand Islands.

The testimony of the Iroquois concerning this boundary line is confirmed by facts contained in existing treaties. At the treaty of Fort Schuyler, the Oneidas, after ceding " all their lands to the people of the state of New York forever," reserved, in addition to their principal reservation, " a convenient piece of land at the fishing-place in the Oneida river, about three miles from where it issues from the Oneida lake, and to remain as well for the Oneidas and their posterity, as for the inhabitants of the said State to land and encamp upon." [1] In the same treaty it appears, that the Deep Spring was upon the west boundary of the Oneida reservation.[2]

[1] Vide Treaty of Fort Schuyler, September 22, 1788. MSS. State Department, Albany.

[2] Judge Jones of Utica, in 1846, in a letter in the author's possession, speaks of this spring as follows : " Near the summit of what was formerly called the Canaseraga hill, near where now runs the road from Chittenango to Manlius, is a large, well-known ever-living spring, familiarly known as the 'Big Spring.' The excavation, whether made by Omnipotence, or by human hands, may be fifteen feet in diameter, and several feet deep, with sloping sides, easy of descent, and in the bottom is a reservoir ever full. What is quite singular is, that the water runs in at the lower, and disappears at the upper side of the reservoir. This spring, while the old woods were its shade, and the wild deer descended to taste its limpid waters, was long the favorite meeting-place between the Oneidas and Onondagas. Here for ages had the old men of the two

The Tuscaroras, upon their expulsion from North Carolina, in 1712, turned to the north, and sought the protection of the *Ho-de'-no-sau-nee*, on the ground of generic origin. They were admitted into the League as the Sixth nation, and were ever afterwards regarded as a constituent member of the confederacy, although never admitted to a full equality.

A portion of the Oneida territory was assigned to them, lying upon the Unadilla river on the east, the Chenango on the west, and the Susquehanna on the south. Whether they occupied entirely across the southern skirt of the Oneida territory, as their boundary is run upon the accompanying map, is a matter of doubt, as the Oneidas might thereby have cut off their southern possessions in Pennsylvania and Virginia. To these southern lands the Tuscaroras had no title, and it is probable that their territorial rights, which were never absolute, were restricted between the Unadilla and the Chenango. The Oneidas, as the original owners of this tract, were made a party, with the Tuscaroras, to the treaty of Fort Herkimer, in 1785, by which it was ceded to the State.[1] The Tuscaroras were partially scattered among the other nations, although they continued to preserve their nationality. They had some settlements at a later day near the Oneida lake, a village at the inlet of the Cayuga, and one in the valley of the Genesee, below Avon. At a subsequent period, the Senecas gave

nations met to rehearse their deeds of war; here the young braves met in friendly conclave. . . . This was the boundary between the nations."

[1] Vide Treaty of Fort Herkimer, June 28, 1785. MSS. State Dep.

them a tract upon the Niagara river, where they afterwards removed; and their descendants still occupy a reserved portion of this land, near Lewiston, in the county of Niagara.

There were two other small bands, or remnants of tribes, located within the territories of the Oneidas; the Mohekunnuks, situated a few miles south of Oneida castle, and the New England Indians, south of Clinton. For these lands they also were indebted to the generosity of the Oneidas, to whom, as refugees, they applied for "a place to spread their blankets;" and their possessions were subsequently secured to each band by treaty.

Of the several boundaries, that between the Oneidas and the Mohawks is the most difficult to establish; there being a disagreement between the line of boundary as given by the Iroquois, and that indicated, although imperfectly, by existing treaties. According to their own evidence, and it is the safest authority, this line came down from the north near the west boundary of Herkimer county, and, crossing the Mohawk about five miles below Utica, continued south into Pennsylvania. On the other hand, it appears from various treaties with the Oneidas, that they sold lands to the State on both sides of the Mohawk, as low down as Herkimer and the German Flats, and also on the Mohawk branch of the Delaware, as far east as Delhi. After the departure of the Mohawks, the Oneidas might have asserted claims against the State, which they would not against their brethren; so also the State may have preferred to include these lands, to prevent all future disputation.

The upper castle of the Mohawks, *Gä-ne-ga-hä'-gä*,[1] was situated in the town of Danube, Herkimer county, nearly opposite the junction of the West Canada creek with the Mohawk. From these facts, the boundary given may be regarded as the most reliable. The territory of the Mohawks extended to the Hudson and lake Champlain on the east, with the exceptions before mentioned, and northward to the St. Lawrence.

Such were the territorial divisions between the several nations of the League. In their hunting excursions they were accustomed to confine themselves to their own domains : which, to a people who subsisted, in part, by the chase, was a matter of some moment. Upon their foreign hunting grounds, which were numerous and boundless, either nation was at liberty to encamp. By establishing these territorial limits between the nations of the League, the political individuality of each was continued in view.

In intimate connection with our Indian geography are the Trails, or forest highways of the Iroquois. A central trail passed through the State from east to west, intersected at numerous points by cross trails, which passed along the banks of the lakes and rivers. It commenced at the site of Albany on the Hudson, and having touched the Mohawk at Schenectady, it followed up this river to the carrying-place at Rome. From thence, proceeding westward, it crossed the Onondaga valley, the foot of the Cayuga and of the Seneca lakes, the Genesee valley

---

[1] This was, doubtless, the oldest village of the Mohawks ; as it is the one from which the nation takes its name. It is *Gä-ne-ä'-gä* in the Seneca dialect.(42)

AH TA QUA O WEH or **MOCCASON**
Embroidered with porcupine quills

at Avon, and finally came out upon the Buffalo creek, at the site of Buffalo. This route of travel was so judiciously selected, that after the country was surveyed, the turnpikes were laid out upon the Indian highway, with slight variations, through the whole length of the State. This trail not only connected the principal villages of the Iroquois, but established the route of travel into Canada on the west, and over the Hudson on the east. The pursuits of trade, and the development of the resources of the country in modern times have shown this to be one of the great natural highways of the continent. It appears now to be indicated by the geographical features of the territory ; but as extensive intercourse was necessary to its discovery, the establishment of this great route of travel furnishes evidence of a more general intercourse of the Iroquois with the east and west, than has ever been ascribed to them.

Upon the banks of the Susquehanna and its branches, the sources of which are near the Mohawk, and upon the banks of the Chemung and its tributaries, which have their sources near the Genesee, were other trails, all of which converged upon Tioga, at the junction of these two principal rivers. They became thus gathered into one, which, descending the Susquehanna, formed the great southern trail into Pennsylvania and Virginia.

For centuries upon centuries, and by race after race, these old and deeply worn trails had been trod by the red man. From the Atlantic to the Mississippi, and from the northern lakes to the Mexican gulf, the main Indian routes through the country were as accurately and judiciously traced, and as familiar as our own. On many of these distant foot-paths the Iroquois had conducted warlike expeditions, and had thus become practically versed in the geography of the country. Within their immediate territories, they were quite as familiar with the geographical features, the routes of travel, the lakes, and hills and streams, as we ourselves have since become.

In the accompanying map, an attempt has been made to restore the geographical names of the Iroquois, as they stood at the period of its date (1720). Many of our own names have their radices in the dialects of the Iroquois; and as to such names, this map is designed to furnish an index of their origin and signification. Our geography is as yet incomplete in the christening of some of the features of nature, while some of the names in actual use might be profitably exchanged for the aboriginal; in both of which cases such a map will at least offer a choice. The date given to it introduces some anachronisms, which will be obvious to the critical eye; but these do not furnish a sufficient reason for an earlier, or a later date. The descendants of the Iroquois have preserved, with great fidelity, the names of their ancient localities; and have bestowed them upon our cities and villages as they have successively appeared. It is but a fit tribute to our Indian predecessors, to record the baptismal names of our rivers, lakes and streams, and also of their ancient sites.

An effort has been made to furnish these names

in the particular dialect of the nation within whose
territories the places or objects named were situated;
and, with a few exceptions, this has been accomplished.
The nations spoke different dialects of a common
language; and although they could understand each
other with readiness, the distinctions between them
were very decisive. These dialectical differences are
more strongly marked in their geographical names
than in the body of the several dialects themselves;
furnishing, perhaps, the principal reason why these
names are written so variously. Thus the Iroquois
name of Buffalo, in the Seneca dialect is, *Do-sho'-weh*,
in Cayuga *De-o-sho'-weh*, in Onondaga *De-o-sa'-weh*, in
Oneida *De-ose'-lole*, in Mohawk *De-o-hose'-lole* and
in Tuscarora *Ne-o-thro'-rä*. For the same purpose,
and in the same order, the variations in the name
of Utica may be cited: *Nun-da-dä'-sis, Nun-da-dä'-ses,
None-da-dä'-sis, Ya-nun-da-dä'-sis, Yo-none-dä'-sis, Ya-
nun-nä'-rats*. The resemblances in these examples are
nearer than they are usually found. In the transition of these names from the unwritten dialects of
the Iroquois into our language, they lose much of
their euphony, and the force of their accent. It
would therefore be difficult to judge of the language
itself from these specimens. That entire accuracy
has been attained in the spelling of these words is
not expected. Indeed, many of their elementary
sounds, in the manner, and in the combination in
which they use them, it is impossible to express
with our letters. But they are as nearly accurate,
as the frequent repetition of each name by the native
speaker, that the sound of each syllable might be

obtained, together with a careful revision of the whole, would enable the author to make them. In the Appendix A. 1, will be found a table, containing a list of all the names upon the map, arranged by counties, with the signification of each. As the county lines are dotted on the map, it will be easy to refer to any locality.

The trails *(Wä-ä-gwen'-ne-yuh)*, or highways of travel pursued by our predecessors, are also traced upon the map.[42] Among the number will be found the great central trail from the site of Albany to that of Buffalo, which is traced minutely from point to point, throughout its whole extent.

It remains to notice the origin and signification of the names of the several nations. After the formation of the League, the Iroquois called themselves the *Ho-de'-no-sau-nee*, which signifies "the people of the long house." It grew out of the circumstance, that they likened their confederacy to a long house, having partitions and separate fires, after their ancient method of building houses, within which the several nations were sheltered under a common roof. Among themselves they never had any other name. The various names given to them at different periods were entirely accidental, none of them being designations by which they ever recognized themselves.

The Senecas called themselves the *Nun-da-wä'-o-no*, which signifies "the great hill people." *Nun-da-wä'-o*, the radix of the word, means "a great hill," and the terminal syllables, *o-no*, convey the idea of "people." This was the name of their oldest village, situated upon a hill at the head of the Canandaigua lake, near Naples, where, according to the Seneca fable, they sprang out of the ground.

Gué-u-gweh-o-no, the name of the Cayugas, signifies "the people at the mucky land;" the root of the word literally meaning "the mucky land." It doubtless referred to the marsh at the foot of the Cayuga lake, near which their first settlement was, in all probability, established.

O-nun-dä'-ga, the origin of the name of the Onondagas, signifies "on the hills;" hence the name they gave themselves, *O-nun-dä'-ga-o-no*, is rendered "the people on the hills." It appears from various authors, that their principal village, at the era of their discovery, was on one of the eminences overlooking the Onondaga valley.

The Oneidas have been so long distinguished as "the people of the stone," that it is perhaps venturesome to suggest a change. *O-na-yote'-kä*, however, the radix from which their name is derived, signifies not only "a stone," but one of the species known to us as granite. In the Seneca dialect, it means this particular rock; hence the propriety of rendering literally their national name, *O-na-yote'-kä-o-no*, "the granite people." [1]

There is doubt about the signification of the name of the Mohawks, *Gä-ne-ä'-ga-o-no*, from the fact that the Oneidas, Onondagas and Senecas have lost its meaning. But the Mohawks render the root of the word, "the possessor of the flint," without being able to give any further explanation. It is to

[1] The original Oneida Stone, now in the cemetery at Utica, is said to be a boulder of granite.

be observed, however, that the word as given by the latter, *Gä-ne-ga-hä'-gä*, has one syllable more than the corresponding word in Seneca, which may account for the loss of its signification. In a report enumerating our Indian nations, ascribed to M. De Joncaire, is the following passage bearing upon this subject: "The Mohawks have for a device of the village *a steel and a flint*."[1] The possession of such a novelty may have been, at an early day, sufficient to change not only the name of the village, but also of the nation.

The name of the Tuscaroras, *Dus-ga-o'-weh*, is rendered "the shirt-wearing people;" and was a name adopted before their emigration from Carolina, and after the commencement of their intercourse with the whites. All of the preceding names are given in the Seneca dialect to preserve uniformity; as not only the terminations, but the radices themselves are different in the several dialects.

The geographical names, the courses of the trails, and the locations of the villages of the Iroquois, will be more particularly considered in a subsequent chapter.

[1] Doc. Hist. N. Y., v. i. p. 22.

GA-KA or BREECH CLOTH.

Chapter III

THE social history and political transactions of the Indian are as easily enveloped in obscurity, as his footsteps through the forest are obliterated by the leaves of autumn. Nation upon nation, and race after race have sprung up and hastened onward to their fall; and neither the first nor the last could explain its origin, or number the years of its duration.

From this general uncertainty of knowledge which surrounds our Indian races, we turn with some degree of encouragement to the Iroquois, the last in the order of succession which exercised dominion over the territories out of which New York was erected. We stand with them in many interesting relations. Having flourished side by side with our early population, the events of their decline became interwoven with our civil affairs; and having finally yielded up their sovereignty, from the rulers of the land, they became dependent nations, dwelling under the protection of the government which displaced them.

To the Iroquois, by common consent, has been assigned the highest position among the Indian races of the continent living in the hunter state. In legislation, in eloquence, in fortitude and in military sagacity they had no equals. "No frightful solitude in the wilderness, no impenetrable recess in the frozen north" was proof against their courage and daring. Space offered no protection, distance no shelter from their war parties, which ranged equally the hills of New England, the declivities of the Alleganies, the prairies of the Mississippi, and the forests of the Tennessee. In the establishment of a League for the double purpose of acquiring strength and securing peace, their capacity for civil organization, and their wisdom in legislation were favorably exhibited. During the expansion of the power of the Iroquois, from the commencement of the seventeenth to the middle of the eighteenth centuries, there sprang up among them a class of orators and chiefs, unrivalled among the red men for eloquence in council, and bravery upon the war-path. In a word, the League of the Iroquois exhibited the highest development of the Indian ever reached by him in the hunter state.

Many circumstances thus unite to invest its history with permanent interest. An analysis of its civil and domestic institutions will exhibit all the elements of Indian society, and of Indian life, throughout the republic. From the higher legislation of the Iroquois, and the increased weight and diversity of affairs under the League, there resulted a fuller manifestation of the Indian character than is to be found in any other race except the Aztec. Their institutions contain the sum and substance of those of the whole Indian family. While, however, their political events have been diligently collected and arranged, the government which they constructed, the social ties by which they were bound together, and the motives and restraints by which they were influenced have scarcely been made subjects of inquiry, and never of extended investigation. The League of the Iroquois, dismembered and in fragments, still clings together in the twilight of its existence, by the shreds of that moral faith, which no political misfortunes could loosen, and no lapse of years could rend asunder. There are reasons for this spectacle, which no mere alliance of nations can explain, and which history has hitherto failed to reach. It is not the purpose of this work to narrate their political events; but to inquire into the structure and spirit of the government, and the nature of the institutions, under and through which these historical results were produced.

In entering upon such a theme of inquiry as an Indian organization, there are some general considerations which press upon the attention, and which are worthy of previous thought. By the formation of societies and governments, mankind are brought largely under the influence of the social relations, and their progress has been found to be in exact proportion to the wisdom of the institutions under which their minds were developed. The passion of the red man for the hunter life has proved to be a principle too deeply inwrought, to be controlled by efforts of legislation. His government, if one was sought to be established, must have conformed to this irresistible tendency of his mind, this inborn sentiment; otherwise it would have been disregarded. The effect of this powerful principle has been to enchain the tribes of North America to their primitive state. Another effect of this principle, and still more fatal to their political prosperity, is to be found in the repeated subdivisions of the generic stocks of the continent, by which all large accumulations of numbers and power, in any race or nation, have been prevented. Whenever a hunting-ground became too thickly populated for the easy subsistence of its occupants, a band, under some favorite chief, put forth, like the swarm from the parent hive, in quest of a new habitation; and in course of time became independent. We have here the true reason, why the red race has never risen, nor can rise above its present level. The fewness of the generic stocks, the unlimited number of independent tribes, and their past history establish the correctness of this position.

It is obvious that the founders of the League were aware of the enfeebling effects of these repeated subdivisions, and sought, by the counter principle of federation, to arrest the evil. They aimed to knit the whole race together under such a system of relationships, that, by its natural expansion, an Indian empire would be developed, of sufficient magnitude to control surrounding nations, and thus secure an exemption from perpetual warfare. We must regard it, therefore, as no ordinary achievement, that the legislators of the Iroquois united the several tribes into independent nations, and between these nations established a perfect and harmonious union. And beyond this, that by a still higher effort of legislation, they succeeded in so adjusting the confederacy, that as a political fabric composed of independent parts, it was adapted to the hunter state, and yet contained the elements of an energetic government.

It is another singular feature, in connection with Indian organizations, that their decline and fall are sudden, and usually simultaneous. A rude shock from without or within but too easily disturbs their inter-relations; and when once cast back upon the predominating sentiment of Indian life, the hunter inclination, a powerful nation rapidly dissolves into a multitude of fragments, and is lost and forgotten in the undistinguished mass of lesser tribes. But the League of the Iroquois was subjected to a severer test. It went down before the Saxon, and not the Indian race. If it had been left to resist the pressure of surrounding nations, living, like the Iroquois themselves, a hunter life, there is reason to believe that it would have subsisted for ages; and perhaps, having broken the hunter spell, would have introduced civilization by an original and spontaneous movement.

Of the Indian character it is an original peculiarity, that he has no desire to perpetuate himself in the remembrance of distant generations, by monumental inscriptions, or other erections fabricated by the art and industry of man. The Iroquois would have passed away without leaving a vestige or memorial of their existence behind, if to them had been intrusted the preservation of their name and deeds. A verbal language, a people without a city, a government without a record, are as fleeting as the deer and the wild fowl, the Indian's co-tenants of the forest. With the departure of the individual, every vestige of Indian sovereignty vanishes. He leaves but the arrow-head upon the hillside, fit emblem of his pursuits; and the rude pipe and ruder vessel entombed beside his bones — at once the record of his superstition, and the evidence of his existence. If the red man had any ambition for immortality, he would intrust his fame to the unwritten remembrance of his tribe and race, rather than to inscriptions on columns in his native land, or other monument more durable than brass, which neither wasting rain, nor raging wind, nor flight of time could overthrow.[1]

Since this race must ever figure upon the opening pages of our territorial history, and some judgment be passed upon them, it becomes our duty to search out their government and institutions, and to record with impartiality their political transactions; lest, in addition to the extinguishment of their Council Fires, we subject their memory, as a people, to an unjust and unmerited judgment.

Upon an extended examination of their institutions, it will become apparent, that the League was established upon the principles, and was designed to be but an elaboration, of the Family Relationships. These relations are older than the notions of society or government, and are consistent alike with the hunter, the pastoral and the civilized state. The several nations of the Iroquois, united, constituted one Family, dwelling together in one Long House; and these ties

---

[1] Compare the sentiments of Pericles, —

ʼΑνδρῶν γὰρ ἐπιφανῶν πᾶσα γῆ τάφος, καὶ οὐ στηλῶν μόνον ἐν τῇ οἰκείᾳ σημαίνει ἐπιγραφῇ. ἀλλὰ καὶ ἐν τῇ μὴ προσηκούσῃ ἄγραφος μνήμη παρ᾽ ἑκάστῳ τῆς γνώμης μᾶλλον ἢ τοῦ ἔργου ἐνδιαιτᾶται,

THUCYD., Lib. 2, c. 43.

with those of Horace, —

Exegi monumentum ære perennius, *
Regalique situ pyramidum altius ;
Quod non imber edax, non Aquilo impotens
Possit diruere, aut innumerabiles
Annorum series, et fuga temporum.

HOR., Lib. 3, Ode 30.

* See Vol. II. p. 161.

of family relationship were carried throughout their civil and social system, from individuals to tribes, from tribes to nations, and from the nations to the League itself, and bound them together in one common, indissoluble brotherhood.

In their own account of the origin of the League, the Iroquois invariably go back to a remote and uncertain period, when the compact between the Five Nations was formed, its details and provisions were settled, and those laws and institutions were established, under which, without essential change, they afterwards continued to flourish. If we may trust their testimony, the system under which they confederated was not of gradual construction, under the suggestions of necessity; but was the result of one protracted effort of legislation. The nations were, at the time, separate and hostile bands, although of generic origin, and were drawn together in council to deliberate upon the plan of a League, which a wise man of the Onondaga nation had projected, and under which, he undertook to assure them, the united nations could elevate themselves to a general supremacy. Tradition has preserved the name of *Da-gä-no-we'-dä* as the founder of the League, and the first lawgiver of the *Ho-de'-no-sau-nee*. It likewise points to the northern shore of the *Gä-nun'-ta-ah*, or Onondaga lake, as the place where the first council-fire was kindled, around which the chiefs and wise men of the several nations were gathered, and where, after a debate of many days, its establishment was effected.

Their traditions further inform us, that the confederacy, as framed by this council, with its laws, rules, inter-relationships of the people and mode of administration, has come down through many generations to the present age, with scarcely a change ; except the addition of an inferior class of rulers, called chiefs, in contradistinction to the sachems, and a modification of the law in relation to marriage. Without entering here upon any inquiry to show the probable accuracy of their traditions, it will be sufficient to investigate the structure of the government, as it stood in its full vigor at the commencement of the last century, and to deduce the general principles upon which it was founded.

The central government was organized and administered upon the same principles which regulated that of each nation, in its separate capacity ; the nations sustaining nearly the same relation to the League, that the American states bear to the Union. In the former, several oligarchies were contained within one, in the same manner as in the latter, several republics are embraced within one republic. To obtain a general conception of the character of a government the ruler, or ruling body, or bodies, as the case may be, would be the first object of attention ; and when their powers and tenure of office are discovered, the true index is obtained to the nature of the government. In the case of the *Ho-de'-no-sau-nee*, the organization was externally so obscure as to induce a universal belief that the relations between ruler and people were simply those of chief and follower — the earliest and lowest political relation between man and man ; while, in point of fact, the Iroquois had emerged from this primitive state of society, and had organized a systematic government.

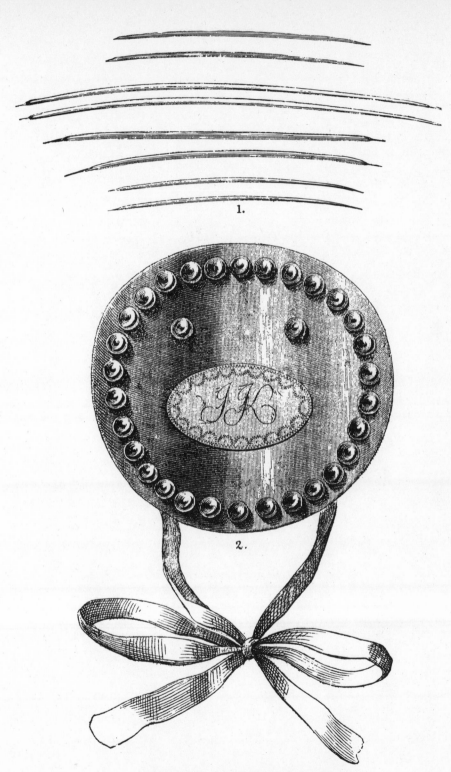

1. O-HA-DA or PORCUPINE QUILL
2. GÄ-NO-SÄ or CONCH SHELL BREAST PLATE

At the institution of the League, fifty permanent sachemships were created, with appropriate names; and in the sachems who held these titles were vested the supreme powers of the confederacy. To secure order in the succession, and to determine the individuals entitled, the sachemships were made hereditary, under limited and peculiar laws of descent. The sachems themselves were equal in rank and authority, and instead of holding separate territorial jurisdictions, their powers were joint, and co-extensive with the League. As a safeguard against contention and fraud, each sachem was " raised up," and invested with his title by a council of all the sachems, with suitable forms and ceremonies. Until this ceremony of confirmation or investiture, no one could become a ruler. He received, when raised up, the name of the sachemship itself, as in the case of titles of nobility, and so also did his successors, from generation to generation. The sachemships were distributed unequally between the five nations, but without thereby giving to either a preponderance of political power. Nine of them were assigned to the Mohawk nation, nine to the Oneida, fourteen to the Onondaga, ten to the Cayuga and eight to the Seneca. The sachems, united, formed the Council of the League, the ruling body, in which resided the executive, legislative and judicial authority. It thus appears that the government of the Iroquois was an oligarchy, taking the term, at least, in the literal sense, " the rule of the few; " and, while more system is observable in this than in the oligarchies of antiquity, it seems, also, better calculated, in its framework, to resist political changes.

This specimen of Indian legislation is so remarkable, that a table of these sachemships, with their division into classes, indicating certain inter-relations, hereafter to be explained, is inserted in the Seneca dialect.

Titles or Sachemships of the Iroquois, founded at the institution of the League; which have been borne by their Sachems in succession, from its formation to the present time.

GÄ-NE-Ä'-GA-O-NO, OR MOHAWK NATION.

I. 1. Da-gä-e'-o-gă.[1]   2. Hä-yo-went'-hä.[2]   3. Da-gä-no-we'-dä.[3]

II. 4. So-ä-e-wä'-ah.[4]   5. Da-yo'-ho-go.[5]   6. O-ä-ä'-go-wä.[6]

III. 7. Da-an-no-gä'-e-neh.[7]   8. Sä-da'-gä-e-wä-deh.[8] 9. Häs-dä-weh'-se-ont-hä.[9]

O-NA-YOTE'-KAH-O-NO, OR ONEIDA NATION.

I. 1. Ho-däs'-hä-teh.[10]   2. Ga-no-gweh'-yo-do.[11]   3. Da-yo-hä'-gwen-da.[12]

II. 4. So-no-sase'.[13]   5. To-no-ä-gă'-o.[14]   6. Hä-de-ä-dun-nent'-hä.[15]

III. 7. Da-wä-dä'-o-dä-yo.[16]   8. Gä-ne-ä-dus'-ha-yeh.[17] 9. Ho-wus'-hä-da-o.[18]

---

[1] This name signifies "Neutral," or "the Shield."   [2] "Man who combs."   [3] "Inexhaustible."   [4] "Small speech."   [5] "At the forks." [6] "At the great river."   [7] "Dragging his horns."   [8] "Even tempered." [9] "Hanging up rattles."   The Sachems of the first class belonged to the Turtle Tribe, of the second to the Wolf Tribe, and of the third to the Bear Tribe.

[10] "A man bearing a burden."   [11] "A man covered with cat tail down."   [12] "Opening through the woods."   [13] "A long string." [14] "A man with a headache."   [15] "Swallowing himself."   [16] "Place of the echo."   [17] "War club on the ground."   [18] "A man steaming himself."   The sachems of the first class in the Oneida nation belonged to the Wolf Tribe, of the second to the Turtle Tribe, and of the third to the Bear Tribe.

O-NUN-DAH'-GA-O-NO, OR ONONDAGA NATION.

I. 1. To-do-dä-ho.[1] 2. To-nes'-sa-ah. 3. Da-ät-ga-dose.[2]

II. 4. Gä-neä-dä'-je-wake.[3] 5. Ah-wä'-ga-yat.[4] 6. Da-ä-yat'-gwä-e.

III. 7. Ho-no-we-nä'-to.[5]

IV. 8. Gä-wǎ-nä'-san-do.[6] 9. Hä-e'-ho.[7] 10. Ho-yo-ne-ä'-ne.[8] 11. Sa-dä'-quä-seh.[9]

V. 12. Sä-go-ga-hä'.[10] 13. Ho-sa-hä'-ho.[11] 14. Skä-no'-wun-de.[12]

GUE'-U-GWEH-O-NO, OR CAYUGA NATION.

I. 1. Da-gä'-ǎ-yo.[13] 2. Da-je-no'-dä-weh-o. 3. Gä-dä'-gwä'-sa. 4. So-yo-wase'. 5. Hä-de-äs'-yo-no.

II. 6. Da-yo-o-yo'-go. 7. Jote-ho-weh'-ko.[14] 8. De-ä-wate'-ho.

III. 9. To-dä-e-ho'. 10. Des-gä'-heh.

NUN-DA-WAH'-O-NO, OR SENECA NATION.

I. 1. Gä-ne-o-di'-yo.[15] 2. Sä-dä-gä'-o-yase.[16]

II. 3. Ga-no-gi'-e.[17] 4. Sä-geh'-jo-wä.[18]

III. 5. Sä-de-a-no'-wus.[19] 6. Nis-hä-ne-a'-nent.[20]

IV. 7. Gä-no-go-e-dä'-we.[21] 8. Do-ne-ho-gä'-weh.[22]

---

[1] "Tangled." This was the most dignified title in the list. It belonged to the Bear Tribe. [2] "On the watch," Bear Tribe. This sachem and the one before him were hereditary counsellors of *To-do-dä'-ho*.

[3] This word signifies "Bitter body." The title belonged to the Snipe Tribe. [4] Turtle Tribe. [5] This sachem was the hereditary keeper of the Wampum, Wolf Tribe. (83) [6] Deer Tribe. [7] Deer Tribe. [8] Turtle Tribe. [9] Bear Tribe. [10] Signifies "Having a glimpse," Deer Tribe. [11] "Large mouth," Turtle Tribe. [12] "Over the creek," Turtle Tribe.

[13] "Man frightened." [14] "Very cold." The tribes of the Cayuga sachems were as follows: 1 Deer, 2 Heron, 3 and 4 Bear, 5 and 7 Turtle, 8 Heron, 9 and 10 Snipe.

[15] "Handsome lake," Turtle Tribe. [16] "Level heavens," Snipe Tribe. [17] Turtle Tribe. [18] "Great forehead," Hawk Tribe. [19] "Assistant," Bear Tribe. [20] "Falling day," Snipe Tribe. [21] "Hair burned off," Snipe Tribe. [22] "Open door," Wolf Tribe.

These titles or names were hereditary in the several tribes of which each nation was composed. When an individual was made a sachem, upon the death or deposition of one of the fifty, his name was " taken away," and the name of the sachemship held by his predecessor was conferred upon him. Thus, upon the demise of the Seneca sachem who held the title *Gä-ne-o-di'-yo*, a successor would be raised up from the Turtle tribe, in which the sachemship was hereditary, and after the ceremony of investiture, the person would be known among the Iroquois only under the name of *Gä-ne-o-di'-yo*. These fifty titles, excepting two, have been held by as many sachems, in succession, as generations have passed away since the formation of the League.

The Onondaga nation, being situated in a central position, were made the keepers both of the Council Brand, and of the Wampum, in which the structure and principles of their government, and their laws and treaties were recorded. At stated periods, usually in the autumn of each year, the sachems of the League assembled in council at Onondaga, which was in effect the seat of government, to legislate for the common welfare. Exigencies of a public or domestic character often led to the summoning of this council at extraordinary seasons, but the place was not confined to Onondaga. It could be appointed in the territory of either of the nations, under established usages. Originally the object of the general council was to raise up sachems to fill vacancies. In the course of time, as their intercourse with foreign nations became more important, it assumed the charge of all matters which concerned the League. It declared war and made peace, sent and received embassies, entered into treaties of alliance, regulated the affairs of subjugated nations, received new members into the League, extended its protection over feeble tribes, in a word, took all needful measures to promote their prosperity, and enlarge their dominion.

Notwithstanding the equality of rights, privileges and powers between the members of this body of sachems, there were certain discriminations between them, which rendered some more dignified than others. The strongest illustration is found in the Onondaga sachem, *To-do-dä'-ho*, who has always been regarded as the most noble sachem of the League. As an acknowledgment of his eminence, two of the Onondaga sachems were assigned to him as hereditary counsellors. The great respect and deference paid by the Iroquois to this title, has led to the vulgar error, that *To-do-dä'-ho* was the king or civil head of the confederacy. He possessed, in fact, no unusual or executive powers, no authority which was not equally enjoyed by his compeers; and when the light of tradition is introduced, to clear up the apparent anomaly, it will be seen that the reverence of the people was rather for the title itself than for the person who held it, as it was one of their illustrious names. At the establishment of the League, an Onondaga by the name of *To-do-dä'-ho* had rendered himself a potent ruler, by the force of his military achievements. Tradition says that he had conquered the Cayugas and the Senecas. It represents his head as covered with tangled serpents, and his look, when

63

angry, as so terrible that whoever looked upon him fell dead. It relates that when the League was formed, the snakes were combed out of his hair by a Mohawk sachem, who was hence named Hä-yo-went'-hä, "the man who combs." *To-do-dä'-ho* was reluctant to consent to the new order of things, as he would thereby be shorn of his absolute power, and be placed among a number of equals. To remove these objections in some measure, and to commemorate his magnanimity, the first sachemship was named after him, and was dignified above the others by special marks of honor; but such, however, as were in perfect consistency with an equal distribution of powers among all the sachems as a body. Down to the present day, among the Iroquois, this name is the personification of heroism, of forecast, and of dignity of character; and this title has ever been regarded as more illustrious than any other in the catalogue of Iroquois nobility.

To several other of these officers or names, particular duties were affixed at the institution of the League. For example: the Senecas were made the door-keepers of the Long House; and having imposed upon *Do-ne-ho-gä'-weh*, the eighth sachem,[13] the duty of watching the door, they gave to him a sub-sachem, or assistant, to enable him to execute this trust. This sub-sachem was raised up at the same time with his superior, with the same forms and ceremonies, and received the name or title which was created simultaneously with that of the sachemship. It was his duty to stand behind the sachem on all public occasions, and to act as his runner or attendant, as well as in the capacity of a counsellor. *Ho-no-we-nă'-to*, the Onondaga sachem who was made the keeper of the wampum, had also a sub-sachem, or assistant. Several other sachems, to whom special responsibilities were confided, were allowed sub-sachems, to enable them to fulfil their duties, or perhaps as a mark of honor. All of these special marks of distinction were consistent with perfect equality among the sachems, as members of one ruling body, in the administration of the affairs of the League. When their method of legislating is considered, this fact will appear with greater distinctness.

The several sachems, in whom, when united in general council, resided the supreme powers of the League, formed, when apart in their own territories, the ruling bodies of their respective nations. When assembled as the Council of the League, the power of each sachem became co-extensive with the government, and direct relations were created between all the people and each individual ruler; but when the sachems of a nation were convened in council, all its internal affairs fell under their immediate cognizance. For all purposes of a local and domestic, and many of a political character, the nations were entirely independent of each other. The nine Mohawk sachems administered the affairs of that nation with joint authority, precisely in the same manner as they did, in connection with their colleagues, the affairs of the League at large. With similar powers, the ten Cayuga sachems regulated the domestic affairs of their nation.

As the sachems of each nation stood upon a perfect equality, in authority and privileges, the measure of influence was determined entirely by the talents and address of the individual. In the councils of the nation, which were of frequent occurrence, all business of national concernment was transacted; and, although the questions moved on such occasions would be finally settled by the opinions of the sachems, yet such was the spirit of the Iroquois system of government, that the influence of the inferior chiefs, the warriors, and even of the women would make itself felt, whenever the subject itself aroused a general public interest.

If we seek their warrant for the exercise of power in the etymology of the word *Ho-yar-na-gó-war*, by which the sachems were known as a class, it will be found to intimate a check upon, rather than an enlargement of their authority; for it signifies, simply, "counsellor of the people," a beautiful as well as appropriate designation of a ruler. But within their sphere of action, their powers were highly arbitrary in ancient times.

Next to the sachems, in position, stood the Chiefs, an inferior class of rulers, the very existence of whose office was an anomaly in the oligarchy of the Iroquois. Many years after the establishment of the League, even subsequent to the commencement of their intercourse with the whites, there arose a necessity for raising up this class. It was an innovation upon the original framework of the confederacy, but it was demanded by circumstances which could not be resisted. The office of chief, *Hä-seh-no-wä'-neh*, which is rendered "an elevated name," was made elective, and the reward of merit; but without any power of descent, the title terminating with the individual. No limit to the number was established. The Senecas, still residing in New York, number about two thousand five hundred, and exclusive of the eight sachems, they have about seventy chiefs. At first their powers were extremely limited, and confined to a participation in the local affairs of their own nation, in the management of which they acted as the counsellors and assistants of the sachems, rather than in the capacity of rulers. But they continued to increase in influence, with their multiplication in numbers, and to encroach upon the powers of the sachems, until at the present time, when the League is mostly dismembered, and their internal organization has undergone some essential changes, they have raised themselves to an equality, in many respects, with the sachems themselves. After their election, they were raised up by a council of the nation; but a ratification, by the general council of the sachems, was necessary to complete the investiture. The tenure of this office still continues the same.

The powers and duties of the sachems and chiefs were entirely of a civil character, and confined, by their organic laws, to the affairs of peace. No sachem could go out to war in his official capacity, as a civil ruler. If disposed to take the war-path, he laid aside his civil office, for the time being, and became a common warrior. It becomes an important inquiry, therefore, to ascertain in whom the military power, was vested. The Iroquois had no distinct class of war-chiefs, raised up and set apart to command in time of war; neither do the sachems or chiefs appear to have possessed the power of appointing such persons as they considered suitable to the post of command. All military operations were left entirely to private enterprise, and to the system of voluntary service, the sachems seeking rather to repress and restrain, than to encourage the martial ardor of the people. Their principal war-captains were to be found among the class called chiefs, many of whom were elected to this office in reward for their military achievements. The singular method of warfare among the Iroquois renders it extremely difficult to obtain a complete and satisfactory explanation of the manner in which their warlike operations were conducted. Their whole civil policy was averse to the concentration of power in the hands of any single individual, but inclined to the opposite principle of division among a number of equals; and this policy they carried into their military as well as through their civil organization. Small bands were, in the first instance, organized by individual leaders, each of which, if they were afterwards united upon the same enterprise, continued under its own captain, and the whole force, as well as the conduct of the expedition, was under their joint management. They appointed no one of their number to absolute command, but the general direction was left open to the strongest will, or the most persuasive voice.

As they were at war with all nations not in their actual alliance, it was lawful for any warrior to organize a party, and seek adventures wherever he pleased to direct his steps. Perhaps some chief, filled

with martial ardor, planned an inroad upon the Cherokees of the south ; and, having given a war-dance,
and thus enlisted all who wished to share the glory
of the adventure, took the war-path at once, upon
his distant and perilous enterprise. In such ways as
this, many expeditions originated ; and it is believed
that a great part of the warlike transactions of the
Iroquois were nothing more than personal adventures,
or the daring deeds of inconsiderable war-parties.
Under such a state of things, a favorite leader, possessed of the confidence of the people from his warlike achievements, would be in no want of followers,
in the midst of a general war; nor would the League
be in any danger of losing the services of its most
capable military commanders. To obviate the dangerous consequences of disagreement, when the several
nations were prosecuting a common war, and their
forces were united into one body, an expedient was
resorted to for securing unanimity in their plans, in
the establishment of two supreme military chieftaincies. The two chieftains who held these offices were
designed rather to take the general supervision of the
affairs of war, than the actual command in the field,
although they were not debarred from assuming it,
if they were disposed to do so. These war-chiefships
were made hereditary, like the sachemships, and vacancies were filled in the same manner. When the
Senecas, at the institution of the League, were made
the door-keepers, these chieftaincies were assigned to
them, for the reason that being at the door, they
would first take the war-path to drive back the invader. The first of these was named *Ta-wan'-ne-*

ars,[1] "needle breaker," and the title made hereditary in the Wolf tribe; the second was named *So-no'-so-wä*, "great oyster shell," and the office assigned to the Turtle tribe. To these high chieftains, as the Iroquois now affirm, was intrusted the supreme command of the forces of the League, and the general management of its military affairs.

During the Revolution, Tä-yen-dä-na'-ga, Joseph Brant, commanded the war-parties of the Mohawks; and, from his conspicuous position and the high confidence reposed in him, rather than from any claim advanced by himself, the title of military chieftain of the League has been conceded to him by some writers. But this is entirely a mistake, or rather, a false assertion, which is expressly contradicted by all of the Iroquois nations, including the Mohawks themselves.

It is, perhaps, in itself singular, that no religious functionaries were recognized in the League. This is shown by the fact, that none were ever raised up by the general council of sachems, to fill a sacerdotal office. There was, however, a class in each nation, styled *Ho-nun-de'-unt*, "keepers of the faith," who were regularly appointed to officiate at their festivals, and to take the general supervision of their religious affairs.

To the officers above enumerated, the administration of the League was intrusted. The congress of sachems took the charge of all those matters

---

[1] Governor Blacksnake, who now resides upon the Allegany reservation, and is upwards of a hundred years of age, now holds this title.

which pertained to the public welfare. With them resided the executive, legislative and judicial authority, so far as they were not possessed by the people; although their powers in many things appear to have been rather advisory than executive. The chiefs, from counsellors and intermediaries between the sachems and the people, increased in influence, until they became rulers with the sachems themselves, thus widening and liberalizing the oligarchy. In all matters of war, the power appears to have resided chiefly with the people, and its prosecution to have been left to private adventure. If several bands united, they had as many generals as bands, who governed their proceedings by a council, in which, as in civil affairs, unanimity was a fundamental law. The two high military chieftains had rather the planning and general management of the campaign, than the actual conduct of the forces. Running through their whole system of administration, was a public sentiment, which gave its own tendency to affairs, and illustrated to a remarkable degree, that the government rested upon the popular will, and not upon the arbitrary sway of chiefs.

From whatever point the general features of the League are scrutinized, it must be regarded as a beautiful, as well as a remarkable structure — the triumph of Indian legislation. When the possessions of the Iroquois were enlarged by conquest followed by occupation, it was an expansion, and not a dismemberment of the confederacy, one of its leading objects being the absorption of contiguous nations. To the Eries and to the Neuter nation, according to tradition, the Iroquois offered the alternative of admission into the League, or extermination; and the strangeness of this proposition will disappear, when it is remembered that an Indian nation regards itself as at war with all others not in actual alliance. Peace itself was one of the ultimate objects aimed at by the founders of this Indian oligarchy, to be secured by the admission, or subjugation of surrounding nations. In their progressive course, their empire enlarged, until they had stretched their chain around the half of our republic, and rendered their names a terror from the hills of New England to the deepest seclusions upon the Mississippi; when the advent of another race arrested their career, and prepared the way for the gradual extinguishment of their council-fires, and the desolation of the Long House.

With a mere confederacy of Indian nations, the constant tendency would be to a rupture, from remoteness of position and interest, and from the inherent weakness of such a compact. In the case under consideration, something more lasting was aimed at, than a simple union of the five nations, in the nature of an alliance. A blending of the national sovereignties into one government was sought for and achieved by these forest statesmen. The League made the *Ho-de'-no-sau-nee* one people, with one government, one system of institutions, one executive will. Yet the powers of the government were not so entirely centralized that the national independencies disappeared. This was very far from the fact. The crowning feature of the League, as a political structure, was the perfect independence and individuality of the national sovereignties, in the midst of a central and embracing government, which presented such a cemented exterior that its subdivisions would scarcely have been discovered in the general transactions of the League.

How these ends were attained we have yet to examine.

The government sat lightly upon the people, who, in effect, were governed but little. It secured to each that individual independence, which the *Ho-de'-no-sau-nee* knew how to prize as well as the Saxon race; and which, amid all their political changes, they have continued to preserve.

Chapter IV

THE division of a people into tribes is the
most simple organization of society.

Each tribe being in the nature of a family,
the ties of relationship which bind its individual
members together are indispensable, until they are
rendered unnecessary by the adoption of a form
of government, and the substitution of other ties,
which answer the same ends of protection and
security.

When a people have long remained in the tribal
state, it becomes extremely difficult to remove all
traces of such organic divisions by the substitution
of new institutions.   In the tribes of the Jews,
this position is illustrated. Among the Greeks also,
especially the Athenians, the traces of their original
divisions never entirely disappeared. Solon substituted classes for tribes, but subsequently Cleisthenes
restored the tribes, retaining however the classes, and
increased the number; thus perpetuating this early
social organization of the Athenians among their civil
institutions. The Athenian tribe was a group of
families, with subdivisions; the Roman tribes, estab-

lished by Romulus, the same. On the other hand, the Jewish tribes embraced only the lineal descendants of a common father; and its individual members being of consanguinity, the tribe itself was essentially different from the Grecian. The Iroquois tribe was unlike them all. It was not a group of families; neither was it made up of the descendants of a common father, as the father and his child were never of the same tribe. In the sequel, however, it will be discovered to be nearest the Jewish; differing from it, as from all other similar institutions of the old world, chiefly in this, that descent followed, in all cases, the female line.

The founders of the Iroquois Confederacy did not seek to suspend the tribal divisions of the people, to introduce a different social organization; but on the contrary, they rested the League itself upon the tribes, and through them, sought to interweave the race into one political family. A careful exploration of those tribal relationships which characterize the political system of the Iroquois, becomes, therefore, of importance. Without such knowledge as this will afford, their government itself is wholly unmeaning and inexplicable.

In each nation there were eight tribes, which were arranged in two divisions, and named as follows : —

Wolf,	Bear,	Beaver,	Turtle.
Deer,	Snipe,	Heron,	Hawk.

These animals are common to all latitudes between Louisiana and Montreal, and hence in themselves are incapable of throwing any light upon the land, or locality in which the race originated.[1] These names had doubtless an emblematical signification, which reached beyond the object itself. Of the origin of their tribal divisions but little is known, and to it, perhaps, but little importance attaches. Tradition declares that the Bear and the Deer were the original tribes, and that the residue were subdivisions.

Evidence of the existence of seven of the tribes at the establishment of the Oligarchy, is furnished in the distribution of the Onondaga and Seneca sachemships. The fourteen assigned to the former nation were divided between the Wolf, Bear, Beaver, Turtle, Snipe, and Deer tribes; while the eight belonging to the latter, were given to the Wolf, Bear, Turtle, Snipe, and Hawk, to the exclusion of the others, if they then existed; and in these several tribes they were made perpetually hereditary.

[1] Table exhibiting the scientific names of the animals adopted by the Iroquois as the emblems of their respective tribes. It follows the classification employed in the Nat. History of New York. The species have been determined from careful descriptions obtained of the Senecas.

Animal.	Seneca Name.	Order.	Family.	Genus.	Species.
Wolf.	Tor-yoh'-ne.	Carnivora.	Canidæ.	Lupus.	Occidentalis.
Bear.	Ne-e-ar'-gu-ye.	Carnivora.	Ursidæ.	Ursus.	Americanus.
Beaver.	Non-gar-ne'-e-ar-goh.	Rodentia.	Castoridæ.	Castor.	Fiber.
Turtle.	Gä-ne-e-ar-teh-go'-wä.	Chelonia.	Chelonidæ.	Chelonura.	Serpentina.
Deer.	Nä-o'-geh.	Ungulata.	Cervidæ.	Cervus.	Virginianus.
Snipe.	Doo-ese-doo-we'.	Grallæ.	Scolopacidæ.	Totanus.	Semipalmatus.
Heron.	Jo-äs'-seh.	Grallæ.	Ardeidæ.	Ardea.	Candidissima.
Hawk.	Os-sweh-gä-dä-gä'-ah.	Accipitres.	Falconidæ.	Falco.	Columbarius.

NOTE. Some doubt rests upon the Heron and the Snipe concerning the species. In the former case the choice lies between the Ardea Candidissima and the Ardea Leuce. In the latter, the large number of the species introduces a difficulty. The Semipalmatus corresponds most nearly with the description of the bird.

The division of the people of each nation into eight tribes, whether pre-existing, or perfected at the establishment of the Confederacy, did not terminate in its objects with the nation itself.[1] It became the means of effecting the most perfect union of separate nations "ever devised by the wit of man."   In effect, the Wolf tribe was divided into five parts, and one fifth of it placed in each of the five nations.   The remaining tribes were subjected to the same division and distribution.   Between those of the same name — or in other words, between the separated parts of each tribe — there existed a tie of brotherhood, which linked the nations together with indissoluble bonds. The Mohawk of the Wolf tribe recognized the Seneca of the Wolf tribe as his brother, and they were bound to each other by the ties of consanguinity. In like manner the Oneida of the Turtle or other tribe received the Cayuga or Onondaga of the same tribe, as a brother, and with a fraternal welcome. This relationship was not ideal, but was founded upon actual consanguinity.   In the eyes of an Iroquois, every member of his own tribe, in whatever nation, was as much his brother or his sister as if children of the same mother. This cross-relationship between the

1 The Senecas had eight tribes, the Cayugas eight, the Tuscaroras seven, the Onondagas eight, the Oneidas three, and the Mohawks three. The descendants of the ancient Oneidas and Mohawks affirm that their ancestors never had but three tribes, the Wolf, Bear, and Turtle. On old treaties with these nations now in the State Department, these titles appear as their only social divisions. But by the original laws of the League, neither of these tribes could intermarry. Hence there appears to have been a necessity for the existence originally of the remaining tribes, or some of them, to admit of the verity of this law in relation to marriage.

77

tribes of the same name, and which was stronger, if possible, than the chain of brotherhood between the several tribes of the same nation, is still preserved in all its original strength. It doubtless furnishes the chief reason of the tenacity with which the fragments of the League still cling together. If either of the five nations had wished to cast off the alliance, it must also have broken this bond of brotherhood. Had the nations fallen into collision, it would have turned Hawk tribe against Hawk tribe, Heron against Heron, brother against brother. The history of the *Ho-de'-no-sau-nee* exhibits the wisdom of these organic provisions ; for, during the long period through which the League subsisted, they never fell into anarchy, nor even approximated to dissolution from internal disorders.

With the progress of the inquiry, it becomes more apparent that the Confederacy was in effect a League of Tribes. With the ties of kindred as its principle of union, the whole race was interwoven into one great family, composed of tribes in its first subdivision (for the nations were counterparts of each other) ; and the tribes themselves, in their subdivisions, composed of parts of many households. Without these close inter-relations, resting, as many of them do, upon the strong impulses of nature, a mere alliance between the Iroquois nations would have been feeble and transitory.

In this manner was constructed the *League* of the *Ho-de'-no-sau-nee*, in itself an extraordinary specimen of Indian legislation. Simple in its foundation upon the family relationships, effective in the lasting vigor inherent in the ties of kindred, and perfect in its suc-

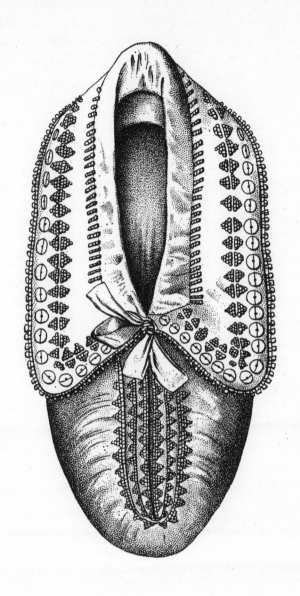

AH-TA-QUA-O-WEH OR MOCCASIN FOR FEMALE.

cess, in achieving a permanent and harmonious union of the nations, it forms an enduring monument to that proud and progressive race, who reared under its protection a wide-spread Indian sovereignty.

All the institutions of the Iroquois have regard to the division of the people into tribes. Originally with reference to marriage, the Wolf, Bear, Beaver, and Turtle tribes, being brothers to each other, were not allowed to intermarry. The four opposite tribes, being also brothers to each other, were likewise prohibited from intermarrying. Either of the first four tribes, however, could intermarry with either of the last four, the relation between them being that of cousins. Thus Hawk could intermarry with Bear or Beaver, Heron with Turtle; but not Beaver and Turtle, nor Deer and Deer. Whoever violated these laws of marriage incurred the deepest detestation and disgrace. In process of time, however, the rigor of the system was relaxed, until finally the prohibition was confined to the tribe of the individual, which, among the residue of the Iroquois, is still religiously observed. They can now marry into any tribe but their own. Under the original as well as modern regulation, the husband and wife were of different tribes. The children always followed the tribe of the mother.

As the whole Iroquois system rested upon the tribes as an organic division of the people, it was very natural that the separate rights of each should be jealously guarded. Not the least remarkable among their institutions, was that which confined the transmission of all titles, rights and property in the female line to the exclusion of the male. It is strangely unlike the canons of descent adopted by civilized nations, but it secured several important objects. If the Deer tribe of the Cayugas, for example, received a sachemship at the original distribution of these offices, the descent of such title being limited to the female line, it could never pass out of the tribe. It thus became instrumental in giving to the tribe individuality. A still more marked result, and perhaps a leading object of this enactment was the perpetual disinheritance of the son. Being of the tribe of his mother formed an impassable barrier against him; and he could neither succeed his father as a sachem, nor inherit from him even his medal, or his tomahawk. The inheritance, for the protection of tribal rights, was thus directed from the lineal descendants of the sachem, to his brothers, or his sisters' children, or, under certain circumstances, to some individual of the tribe at large; each and all of whom were in his tribe, while his children, being in another tribe, as before remarked, were placed out of the line of succession.

By the operation of this principle, also, the certainty of descent in the tribe, of their principal chiefs, was secured by a rule infallible; for the child must be the son of its mother, although not necessarily of its mother's husband. If the purity of blood be of any moment, the lawgivers of the Iroquois established the only certain rule the case admits of, whereby the assurance might be enjoyed that the ruling sachem was of the same family or tribe with the first taker of the title.

The Iroquois mode of computing degrees of consanguinity was unlike that of the civil or canon law;
but was yet a clear and definite system.   No distinction was made between the lineal and collateral
lines, either in the ascending or descending series.
To understand this subject, it must be borne in mind,
that of the grandparents one only, the maternal grandmother, necessarily was, and of the parents only the
mother, and, in the descending line, only the sisters'
children could be of the same tribe with the propositus, or individual from whom the degrees of relationship were reckoned.   By careful attention to this rule,
the reasons of the following relationships will be readily perceived.   The maternal grandmother and her
sisters were equally grandmothers; the mother and
her sisters were equally mothers; the children of a
mother's sisters were brothers and sisters; the children
of a sister were nephews and nieces; and the grandchildren of a sister were his grandchildren.   These
were the chief relatives within the tribe, though not
fully extended as to number.   Out of the tribe, the
paternal grandfather and his brothers were equally
grandfathers; the father and his brothers equally
fathers; the father's sisters were aunts, while, in the
tribe, the mother's brothers were uncles; the father's
sister's children were cousins as in the civil law; the
children of these cousins were nephews and nieces, and
the children of these nephews and nieces were his
grandchildren, or the grandchildren of the propositus.
Again: the children of a brother were his children,
and the grandchildren of a brother were his grandchildren; also, the children of a father's brother were

his brothers and sisters, instead of cousins, as under the civil law; and lastly, their children were his grandchildren.

It was the leading object of the Iroquois law of descent, to merge the collateral in the lineal line, as sufficiently appears in the above outline. By the civil law, every departure from the common ancestor in the descending series, removed the collateral from the lineal; while, by the law under consideration, the two lines were finally brought into one.[1] Under the civil law mode of computation, the degrees of relationship become too remote to be traced among collaterals; while, by the mode of the Iroquois, none of the collaterals were lost by remoteness of degree. The number of those linked together by the nearer family ties was largely multiplied by preventing, in this manner, the subdivision of a family into collateral branches. These relationships, so novel and original, did not exist simply in theory, but were actual, and of constant recognition, and lay at the foundation of their political as well as social organization.

The succession of the rulers of the League is one of the most intricate subjects to be met with in the political system of the Iroquois. It has been so diffi-

---

[1] The following are the names of the several degrees of relationship recognized among the *Ho-de'-no-sau-nee*, in the language of the Senecas :

Hoc-sote',	Grandfather.	Hoc-no'-seh,	Uncle.
Uc-sote',	Grandmother.	Ah-geh'-huc,	Aunt.
Hä'-nih,	Father.	Hä-yan-wän-deh',	Nephew.
Noh-yeh',	Mother.	Kä-yan-wän-deh',	Niece.
Ho-ah'-wuk,	Son.	Dä-ya-gwä'-dan-no-dä,	Brothers and Sisters.
Go-ah'-wuk,	Daughter.	Ah-gare'-seh,	Cousin.
Kä-yä'-dä,	Grandchildren.		

cult to procure a satisfactory exposition of the enactments by which the mode of succession was regulated, that the sachemships have sometimes been considered elective, at others as hereditary. Many of the obstacles which beset the inquiry are removed by the single fact, that the title of sachem was absolutely hereditary in the tribe to which it was originally assigned, and could never pass out of it but with its extinction. How far these titles were hereditary in that part of the family of the sachem who were of the same tribe with himself, becomes the true question to consider. The sachem's brothers, and the sons of his sisters were of his tribe, and, consequently, in the line of succession. Between a brother and a nephew of the deceased, there was no law which established a preference; neither between several brothers, on the one hand, and sons of several sisters on the other, was there any law of primogeniture; nor, finally, was there any positive law, that the choice should be confined to the brothers of the deceased ruler, and the descendants of his sisters in the female line, until all these should fail, before a selection could be made from the tribe at large. Hence, it appears, so far as positive enactments were concerned, that the office of sachem was hereditary in the particular tribe in which it ran; while it was elective, as between the male members of the tribe itself.[1]

[1] Laws of succession somewhat similar existed among the Aztecs. " The sovereign was selected from the brothers of the deceased prince, or, in default of them, from his nephews, thus the election was always restricted to the same family. * * * The scheme of election, however defective, argues a more refined and calculating policy than was to have been expected from a barbarous nation." — Prescott's Conquest of Mexico, vol. i. p. 23.

In the absence of laws, designating with certainty the individual upon whom the inheritance should fall, custom would come in and assume the force of law, in directing the manner of choice, from among a number equally eligible. Upon the decease of a sachem, a tribal council assembled to determine upon his successor. The choice usually fell upon a son of one of the deceased ruler's sisters, or upon one of his brothers — in the absence of physical and moral objections; and this preference of one of his near relatives would be suggested by feelings of respect for his memory. Infancy was no obstacle, it involving only the necessity of setting over the infant a guardian, to discharge the duties of a sachem until he attained a suitable age. It sometimes occurred that all the relatives of the deceased were set aside, and a selection was made from the tribe generally; but it seldom thus happened, unless from the great unfitness of the near relatives of the deceased.

When the individual was finally determined, the nation summoned a council, in the name of the deceased, of all the sachems of the League; and the new sachem was raised up by such council, and invested with his office.

In connection with the power of the tribes to designate the sachems, should be noticed the equal power of deposition. If, by misconduct, a sachem lost the confidence and respect of his tribe, and became unworthy of authority, a tribal council at once deposed him; and, having selected a successor, summoned a council of the League to perform the ceremony of his investiture.

Still further to illustrate the characteristics of the

tribes of the Iroquois, some reference to their mode of bestowing names would not be inapt.[1] Soon after the birth of an infant, the near relatives of the same tribe selected a name. At the first subsequent council of the nation, the birth and name were publicly announced, together with the name and tribe of the father, and the name and tribe of the mother. In each nation the proper names were so strongly marked by a tribal peculiarity, that the tribe of the individual could usually be determined from the name alone. Making, as they did, a part of their language, they were all significant. When an individual was raised up as a sachem, his original name was laid aside, and that of the sachemship itself assumed. In like manner, at the raising up of a chief, the council of the nation which performed the ceremony, took away the former name of the incipient chief and assigned him a new one, perhaps, like Napoleon's titles, commemorative of the event which led to its bestowment. Thus, when the celebrated Red-Jacket was elevated by election to the dignity of a chief, his original name, *O-te-ti-àn'-i*, "always ready," was taken from him, and in its place was bestowed *Sä-go-ye-wät'-hä*, "keeper awake," in allusion to the powers of his eloquence.

Each tribe in the nation thus formed a species of separate community. The members were all of consanguinity, and their relationships easily traced. In like manner those of the same tribe in each of the

---

[1] Like the ancient Saxons, the Iroquois had neither a prenomen, nor a cognomen; but contented themselves with a single name. The name of an individual was often changed at different periods of life, as when the youth became a warrior; and again, at the approach of age.

other nations were their consanguinii, and their relationships, near and remote, were also traceable. As two tribes were necessarily joined in each family, there was a perfect diffusion of tribes throughout the nation, and throughout the League. In this manner the race of the Iroquois, although consisting of different nations, was blended into one people. The League was in effect established, and rested for its stability, upon the natural faith of kindred.

It now remains to define a tribe of the *Ho-de'-no-sau-nee*. From the preceding considerations it sufficiently appears, that it was not, like the Grecian and Roman, a circle or group of families; for two tribes were necessarily represented in every family; neither, like the Jewish, was it constituted of the lineal descendants of a common father; on the contrary, it distinctly involved the idea of descent from a common mother; nor has it any resemblance to the Scottish clan, or the Canton of the Switzer. In the formation of an Iroquois tribe, a portion was taken from many households, and bound together by a tribal bond.

The wife, her children, and her descendants in the female line, would, in perpetuity, be linked with the destinies of her own tribe; while the husband, his brothers and sisters, and the descendants of the latter, in the female line, would, in like manner, be united to another tribe, and held by its affinities. Herein was a bond of union between the several tribes of the same nation, corresponding, in some degree, with the cross-relationship founded upon consanguinity, which bound together the tribes of the same emblem in the different nations.

The Iroquois claim to have originated the idea of a division of the people into tribes, as a means of creating new relationships by which to bind the people more firmly together. It is further asserted by them, that they forced or introduced this social organization among the Cherokees, the Chippeways, (Massasaugas) and several other Indian nations, with whom, in ancient times, they were in constant intercourse. The fact that this division of the people of the same nation into tribes does not prevail generally among our Indian races, favors the assertion of the Iroquois. On the other hand, the laws of descent, at least of the crown, among the Aztecs, dimly shadows forth the existence of a similar social organization, which may have been reproduced among the Iroquois, or preserved through a remote affinity of blood. At all events, it was the life and strength of the League.

Of the comparative value of these institutions, when contrasted with those of civilized countries, and of their capability of elevating the race, it is not necessary here to inquire. It was the boast of the Iroquois that the great object of their confederacy was peace — to break up the spirit of perpetual warfare, which had wasted the red race from age to age. Such an insight into the true end of all legitimate government, by those who constructed this tribal league, excites as great surprise as admiration. It is the highest and the noblest aspect in which human institutions can be viewed; and the thought itself — universal peace among Indian races possible of attainment — was a ray of intellect from no ordinary mind. To consummate such a purpose, the Iroquois nations were to be concentrated into one political fraternity; and in a manner effectively to prevent offshoots and secessions. By its natural growth, this fraternity would accumulate sufficient power to absorb adjacent nations, moulding them, successively, by affiliation, into one common family. Thus, in its nature, it was designed to be a progressive confederacy. What means could have been employed with greater promise of success than the stupendous system of relationships, which was fabricated through the division of the *Ho-de'-no-sau-nee* into tribes? It was a system sufficiently ample to enfold the whole Indian race. Unlimited in their capacity for extension, inflexible in their relationships, the tribes thus interleagued would have suffered no loss of unity by their enlargement, nor loss of strength by the increasing distance between their council-fires. The destiny of this League, if it had been left to work out its own results among the red races exclusively, it is impossible to conjecture. With vast capacities for enlargement, and remarkable durability of structure, it must have attained a great elevation, and a general supremacy.

It is apparent from the examination of such evidences as can be discovered, that the several Iroquois nations occupied positions of entire equality in the League, in rights, privileges and obligations. Such special immunities as were granted to either, must be put down to the chances of location, and to the numerical differences at the institution of the Confederacy; since they neither indicate an intention to establish an unequal alliance, nor exhibit the exercise of privileges by either nation, inconsistent with the principle of political equality, on which the League was founded.

The sources of information, from which this conclusion is drawn, are to be found in the mass of Iroquois traditions, and in the structure of the Confederacy itself. Those traditions which reach beyond the formation of the League, are vague and unreliable, while all such as refer to its establishment assume a connected and distinctive form. It follows that confidence may be reposed in such inferences as are derived from these traditions, and corroborated by the internal structure of the government, and by the institutions of the League.

There were provisions apparently vesting in certain nations superior authority, which it is desirable to introduce and explain. The most prominent was the unequal distribution of sachemships, indicating an unequal distribution of power : the Onondagas, for example, having fourteen sachems, while the Senecas, by far the most powerful nation in the Confederacy, were entitled to but eight. It is true, *ceteris paribus*, that a larger body of sachems would exercise a greater influence in general council ; but it will appear, when the mode of deciding questions is considered, that it gave no increase of power, for each nation had an equal voice, and a negative upon the others.

By another organic provision, the custody of the " Council Brand," and also of the " Wampum," into which the laws of the League " had been talked," was given by hereditary grant to the Onondagas. This is sufficiently explained by their central position, which made the council-fire in the Onondaga valley, in effect, the seat of government of the League. It was equally a convenience to all, and does not necessarily involve a preference enforced by superior power.

The *To-do-dä-ho* was likewise among the Onondaga sachems. Upon this point it has heretofore been stated that the higher degree of consideration attached to this title resulted exclusively from the exalted estimation in which the original *To-do-da-ho* was held, on account of his martial prowess and achievements.

An apparent inequality between the nations of the League is also observable in the award of the two highest military chieftains to the Senecas. It will be sufficient, on this difficult feature in the system of the Iroquois, to note that when they constructed their political edifice, the Long House, with its door opening upon the west, they admitted the supposition that all hostile onsets were to be expected from that direction; and on placing the Senecas as a perpetual shield before its western portal, these war-captains were granted, as among the means needful for its protection.

The Mohawks were receivers of tribute from subjugated nations. This hereditary privilege must be placed upon the same footing with the preceding. It may, perhaps, indicate that the nations upon their borders were in subjection.

Unequal terms in a Confederacy of independent nations would not be expected. True wisdom would dictate the principle of equality, as the only certain foundation on which a durable structure could be erected. That such was the principle adopted by the legislators of the Iroquois, is evinced by the equality of rights and immunities subsisting between the sachems of the League. Their authority was not limited to their own nation, but was co-extensive with the Confederacy. The Cayuga sachem, while in the midst of the Oneidas, could enforce from them the same obedience that was due to him from his own people; and when in general council with his compeers, he had an equal voice in the disposal of all business which came before it. The special privileges enumerated, and some others which existed, were of but little moment, when compared with the fact that the nations were independent, and that each had an equal participation in the administration of the government.

At the epoch of the League, the several nations occupied the territory between the Hudson and the Genesee, and were separated by much the same internal boundaries, as at the period when they yielded up their sovereignty. From geographical position, or from relative importance, or yet, for the mere purpose of establishing between the nations relationships similar to those existing between the tribes, certain rules of precedence, and national ties, were constituted between them. The nations were divided into two classes, or divisions; and when assembled in general council were arranged upon opposite sides of the " council-fire." On the one side stood the Mohawks, Onondagas and Senecas, who, as nations, were regarded as brothers to each other, but as fathers to the other nations. Upon the other side were the Oneidas and Cayugas, and at a subsequent day, the

Tuscaroras, who, in like manner, were brother nations to each other, but children to the first three. These divisions were in harmony with their system of relationships, or more properly formed a part of it. They may have secured for the senior nations increased respect, but they involved no idea of dependence in the junior, or inequality in civil rights.

When the nations were enumerated, the Mohawks were placed first, but for what reason is not precisely understood. In the councils of the Confederacy they were styled *Da-gä-e-o'-gä*, which became their national epithet. It was a term of respect, and signifies " neutral," or, as it may be rendered, " the shield." Its origin is lost in obscurity.

The Onondagas were placed next in the order of precedence, and were addressed in council by the appellation *Ho-de'-san-no-ge-tä*. This term signifies " name-bearer," and was conferred in commemoration of the circumstance that the Onondagas bestowed the names upon the fifty original sachems. This was a privilege of some moment, as these " names " were to descend from generation to generation, upon the successive rulers of the *Ho-de'-no-sau-nee*.

Next in order stood the Senecas, justly proud of their national designation, *Ho-nan-ne-ho'-ont*, or " the door-keeper." To them, as elsewhere remarked, belonged the hereditary guardianship of the door of the Long House.

The Oneidas occupied the fourth place in the Iroquois order of precedence, and originally had no appellation by which they were distinguished. At a subsequent and quite modern period, the epithet

Ne-ar-de-on-dar-go'-war, or "Great Tree," was conferred upon them by their confederates. This name was seized upon from some occurrence at a treaty with the people of *Wastow*, or Boston.

Of the five original nations, the Cayugas were placed last in the enumeration. They were designated in council by the appellation, *So-nus'-ho-gwä-to-war*, signifying "Great Pipe." Tradition refers this epithet to the incident that the leading Cayuga chief in attendance at the council which established the League smoked a pipe of unusual dimensions and workmanship.

The admission of the Tuscaroras having been long subsequent to the formation of the League, they were never received into an equal alliance with the other nations. After their disastrous overthrow, and expulsion from North Carolina, they turned towards the country of the Iroquois, and were admitted about the year 1715, as the sixth nation, into the Confederacy. But they were never allowed to have a sachem, who could sit as an equal in the council of sachems. The five nations were unwilling to enlarge the number of sachemships founded at the institution of the League. For purposes of national government, however, they were organized like the other nations, with similar tribes, relationships, laws and institutions. They also enjoyed a nominal equality in the councils of the League, by the courtesy of the other five, and their sachems were "raised up" with the same ceremonies. They were not dependent, but were admitted to as full equality as could be granted them, without enlarging the framework of the Confederacy. In the councils of the League, they had no national designation.

At the establishment of the Confederacy, the office of chief, *Hä-seh-no-wä'-neh*, " an elevated name," was entirely unknown among the Iroquois. Their traditions, as elsewhere stated, affirm that this title was instituted long subsequent to the foundation of the fifty sachemships, and the full adjustment of the League. The necessity in which this office had its origin, and the illustration which it furnishes of a position elsewhere advanced, that all political institutions, as they unfold, progress from monarchy towards democracy, leads to the presentation of this subject in this place.

When the power of the *Ho-dé'-no-sau-nee* began to develop, under the new system of oligarchies within an oligarchy, there sprang up around the sachems a class of warriors, distinguished for enterprise upon the war-path, and eloquence in council, who demanded some participation in the administration of public affairs. The serious objections to the enlargement of the number of rulers, involving, as it did, changes in the framework of the government, for a long period enabled the sachems to resist the encroachment. In the progress of events, this class became too powerful to be withstood, and the sachems were compelled to raise them up in the subordinate station of chiefs. The title was purely elective, and the reward of merit. Unlike the sachemships, the name was not hereditary in the tribe or family of the individual, but terminated with the chief himself; unless subsequently bestowed by the tribe upon some other person, to preserve it as one of their illustrious names. These chiefs were originally invested with very limited powers, their principal office being that of advisers and counsellors of the sachems. Having thus obtained a foothold in the government, this class, to the number of which there was no limit, gradually enlarged their influence, and from generation to generation drew nearer to an equality with the sachems themselves.[1] By this innovation the government was liberalized, to the sensible diminution of the power of the sachems, which, at the institution of the League, was extremely arbitrary.

It is a singular fact, that none of the sachems of the Iroquois, save Logan,[2] have ever become distinguished in history; although each of the fifty titles or sachemships have been held by as many individuals, as generations have passed away since the foundation of the Confederacy. If the immortality of men, " worthy of praise," is committed to the guardianship of the Muse —

" Dignum laude virum Musa vetat mori,"

— the muse of tradition, if such a conception may be indulged, has been enabled, out of this long line of sachems, to record the deeds of none, save the military achievements of the first *To-do-dä'-ho*, the

---

[1] At the present time among the dismembered fragments of the Iroquois nations, the chiefs are found to be nearly, if not in all respects, upon an equality with the sachems, although the offices are still held by different tenures.

[2] Logan was one of the ten Cayuga sachems, but which of the ten names or sachemships he held, is not at present ascertained. His father, Shikellimus or *Shikalimo*, who is usually mentioned as a Cayuga sachem, was but a chief.

wisdom in legislation of the first *Da-gä-no-we'-dä*,[1] and the sacred mission of *Gä-ne-o-di'-yo*, who pretended to have received a revelation from the Great Spirit. The residue have left behind them no remembrances conferring special dignity upon the sachemships entrusted to their keeping.

The celebrated orators, wise men, and military leaders of the *Ho-de'-no-sau-nee*, are all to be found in the class of chiefs. One reason for this may exist in the organic provision which confined the duties of the sachems exclusively to the affairs of peace; and another may be that the office of chief was bestowed in reward of public services, thus casting it by necessity upon the men highest in capacity among them. In the list of those chiefs who have earned a place upon the historic page, as well as in the " unwritten remembrance " of their tribe and race, might be enumerated many who have left behind them a reputation which will not soon fade from the minds of men.

By the institution of this office, the stability of the government was increased rather than diminished.

---

[1] *Da-gä-no-we'-dä*, the founder of the confederacy, and *Hä-yo-went'-hä*, his speaker, through whom he laid his plans of government before the council which framed the League, were both " raised up " among the fifty original sachems, and in the Mohawk nation ; but after their decease these two sachemships were left vacant, and have since continued so.

Da-gä-no-we'-dä was an Onondaga, but was adopted by the Mohawks and raised up as one of their sachems. Having an impediment in his speech, he chose *Hä-yo-went'-hä* for his speaker. They were both unwilling to accept office, except upon the express condition that their sachemships should ever remain vacant after their decease. These are the two most illustrious names among the Iroquois.

In their own figurative enunciation of the idea, the chiefs served as braces in the Long House — an apt expression of the place they occupied in their political structure. It furnished a position and a reward for the ambitious, and the means of allaying discontent, without changing the ruling body. In this particular, the oligarchy of the Iroquois appears to have enjoyed some superiority over those of antiquity.

" In aristocratical governments," says Montesquieu, " there are two principal sources of disorder : excessive inequality between the governors and the governed, and the same inequality between the different members of the body that governs." [1] The government of the *Ho-de'-no-sau-nee* was exposed to neither of these difficulties. Between the people and the sachems, the chiefs formed a connecting link ; while the sachems themselves were perfectly equal in political privileges.

The unchangeable number of the rulers, and the stability of the tenure by which the office itself is held, are both sources of security in an oligarchy. To the former safeguard the Iroquois adhered so firmly, that upon the admission of the Tuscaroras, as the sixth nation of the League, they were unwilling to increase the original number of sachemships ; and the Tuscaroras have not to this day a sachem who is admitted to all the privileges of a sachem of the Confederacy. The latter is established by the career of *Sä-go-ye-wät'-hä*, the most gifted and intellectual of the race of the Iroquois, and, perhaps, of the whole

[1] Montesquieu, Spirit of Laws, lib. v. cap. 8.

Indian family. With all the influence which he exercised over the people by the power of his eloquence, and with all the art and intrigue which his capacity could suggest, he was never able to elevate himself higher than to the title of Chief. To attain even this dignity, it is said that he practiced upon the superstitious fears of the people. The Senecas themselves aver, that it would have been unwise to raise up a man of his intellectual power and extended influence to the office of sachem; as it would have concentrated in his hands too much authority. Nearly the same observations apply to the celebrated Joseph Brant, *Tä-yen-dä-na'-ga*, whose abilities as a military leader secured to him the command of the war parties of the Mohawks during the Revolution. He was also but a chief, and held no other office or title in the nation, or in the Confederacy. By the force of his character, he acquired the same influence over the Mohawks which *Sä-go-ye-wät'-hä* maintained over the Senecas by his eloquence. The lives of these distinguished chiefs, both equally ambitious, but who pursued very different pathways to distinction, sufficiently prove that the office of sachem was surrounded by impassable barriers against those who were without the immediate family of the sachem, and the tribe in which the title was hereditary.

Chapter V

Councils of the Iroquois — Influence of Public Sentiment — Oratory — Civil Councils — Unanimity — Mourning Councils — Wampum — Festivities — Religious Councils

IN an oligarchy, where the administrative power is vested in the members of the Ruling Body jointly, a Council of the Oligarchs becomes the instrumentality through which the will of this body is ascertained and enforced. For this reason the Councils of the Iroquois are important subjects of investigation. By them were exercised all the legislative and executive authority incident to the League, and necessary for its security against outward attack and internal dissensions. When the sachems were not assembled around the general council-fire, the government itself had no visible existence. Upon no point, therefore, can an examination be better directed, to ascertain the degree of power vested in the Ruling Body, and the manner in which their domestic administration and political relations were conducted. When the sachems were scattered, like the people, over a large territory, they exercised a local and individual authority in the matters of every-day life, or in national council jointly adjusted the affairs of their respective nations. Those higher and more important concernments, which involved the interests of the League, were reserved to the

99

sachems in general council. In this council resided the animating principle, by which their political machinery was moved. It was, in effect, the government.

The oligarchical form of government is not without its advantages, although indicative of a low state of civilization. A comparison of views, by the agency of a council, would at any time be favorable to the development of talent. It was especially the case among the Iroquois, in consequence of the greater diversity of interests, and the more extended reach of affairs incident to several nations in close alliance. Events of greater magnitude would spring up in the midst of a flourishing confederacy, than in a nation of inconsiderable importance; and it is demonstrated by the political history of all governments, that men develop intellect in exact proportion to the magnitude of the events with which they become identified. For these reasons, the League was favorable to the production of men higher in capacity than would arise among nations whose institutions and systems of government were inferior.

The extremely liberal character of their oligarchy is manifested by the *modus procedendi* of these councils. It is obvious that the sachems were not set over the people as arbitrary rulers, to legislate as their own will might dictate, irrespective of the popular voice; on the contrary, there is reason to believe that a public sentiment sprang up on questions of general interest, which no council felt at liberty to disregard. By deferring all action upon such questions until a council brought together the sachems of the League,

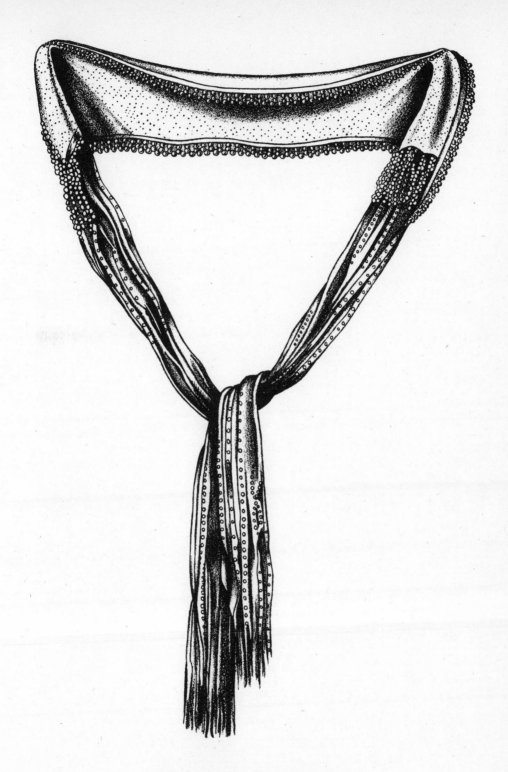

GÄ-GEH-TÄ or **BELT.**

attended by a concourse of inferior chiefs and warriors, an opportunity was given to the people to judge for themselves, and to take such measures as were necessary to give expression and force to their opinions. If the band of warriors became interested in the passing question, they held a council apart, and having given it a full consideration, appointed an orator to communicate their views to the sachems, their *Patres Conscripti*. In like manner would the chiefs, and even the women proceed, if they entertained opinions which they wished to urge upon the consideration of the council. From the publicity with which the affairs of the League were conducted, and the indirect participation in their adjustment thus allowed the people, a favorable indication is afforded of the democratic spirit of the government.

Oratory, from the constitutional organization of the council, was necessarily brought into high repute. Questions involving the safety of the race, and the preservation of the League, were frequently before it. In those warlike periods, when the Confederacy was moving onward amid incessant conflicts with contiguous nations, or, perchance, resisting sudden tides of migratory population, there was no dearth of those exciting causes, of those emergencies of peril, which rouse the spirit of the people, and summon into activity their highest energies. Whenever events converged to such a crisis, the council was the first resort; and there, under the pressure of dangers, and in the glow of patriotism, the eloquence of the Iroquois flowed as pure and spontaneous as the fountains of their thousand streamlets.

The Indian has a quick and enthusiastic appreciation of eloquence. Highly impulsive in his nature, and with passions untaught of restraint, he is strongly susceptible of its influence. By the cultivation and exercise of this capacity, was opened the pathway *to* distinction ; and the chief or warrior gifted with its magical power could elevate himself as rapidly, as he who gained renown upon the war-path. With the Iroquois, as with the Romans, the two professions, oratory and arms,[1] could establish men in the highest degree of personal consideration. To the ambitious Roman in the majestic days of the Republic, and to the proud Indian in his sylvan house, the two pursuits equally commended themselves ; and in one or the other alone, could either expect success.

It is a singular fact, resulting from the structure of Indian institutions, that nearly every transaction, whether social or political, originated or terminated in a council. This universal and favorite mode of doing business became interwoven with all the affairs of public and private life. In council, public transactions of every name and character were planned, scrutinized and adopted. The succession of their rulers, their athletic games, dances, and religious festivals, and their social intercourse, were all alike identified with councils. It may be said that the life of the Iroquois was either spent in the chase, on the war-path, or at the council-fire. They formed the three leading objects of his existence ; and it would be difficult to

---

[1] Duæ sunt artes quæ possunt locare homines in amplissimo gradu dignitatis ; una imperatoris, altera orationis boni : ab hoc enim pacis ornamenta retinentur : ab illo belli pericula repelluntur. — CICERO *Pro Muræna*, § 14.

determine for which he possessed the strongest predilection. Regarding them in this light, and it is believed they are not over-estimated, a narrative of these councils would furnish an accurate and copious history of the Iroquois, both political and social. The absence of these records, now irreparable, has greatly abridged the fulness, and diminished the accuracy of our aboriginal history.

The councils of the League were of three distinct kinds; and they may be distinguished under the heads of civil, mourning and religious. Their civil councils, *Ho-de-os'-seh*, were such as convened to transact business with foreign nations, and to regulate the internal administration of the Confederacy. The mourning councils, *Hen-nun-do-nuh'-seh*, were those summoned to " raise up" sachems to fill such vacancies as had been occasioned by death or deposition, and also to ratify the investiture of such chiefs as the nations had raised up in reward of public services. Their religious councils, *Gä-e-we'-yo-do Ho-de-os-hen'-dä-ko*, were, as the name imports, devoted to religious observances.

No event of any importance ever transpired without passing under the cognizance of one or another of these species of councils; for all affairs seem to have converged towards them by a natural and inevitable tendency. An exposition of the mode of summoning each, of their respective powers and jurisdictions, and of the manner of transacting business, may serve to unfold the workings of their political system, their social relations, and the range of their intellectual capacities.

The name *Ho-de-os'-seh*, by which the Iroquois designated a civil council, signifies "advising together." It was bestowed upon any council of sachems, which convened to take charge of the public relations of the League, or to provide for its internal administration. Each nation had power, under established regulations, to convene such a council, and prescribe the time and place of convocation.

If the envoy of a foreign people desired to submit a proposition to the sachems of the League, and applied to the Senecas for that purpose, the sachems of that nation would first determine whether the question was of sufficient importance to authorize a council. If they arrived at an affirmative conclusion, they immediately sent out runners to the Cayugas, the nation nearest in position, with a belt of wampum. This belt announced that, on a certain day thereafter, at such a place, and for such and such purposes, mentioning them, a council of the League would assemble. The Cayugas then notified the Onondagas, they the Oneidas, and these the Mohawks. Each nation, within its own confines, spread the information far and wide; and thus, in a space of time astonishingly brief, intelligence of the council was heralded from one extremity of their country to the other. It produced a stir among the people in proportion to the magnitude and importance of the business to be transacted. If the subject was calculated to arouse a deep feeling of interest, one common impulse from the Hudson to the Niagara, and from the St. Lawrence to the Susquehanna, drew them towards the council-fire. Sachems, chiefs and warriors, women, and

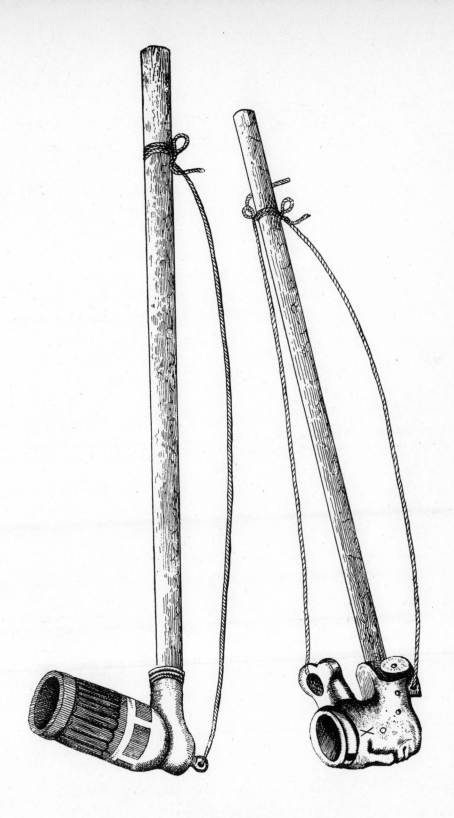

AH·SO·QUA·TA.

PIPES

even children, deserted their hunting grounds and woodland seclusions, and taking the trail, literally flocked to the place of council. When the day arrived, a multitude had gathered together, from the most remote and toilsome distances, but yet animated by an unyielding spirit of hardihood and endurance.

Their mode of opening a council, and proceeding with the business before it, was extremely simple, yet dilatory, when contrasted with the modes of civilized life. Questions were usually reduced to single propositions, calling for an affirmative or negative response, and were thus either adopted or rejected. When the sachems were assembled in the midst of their people, and all were in readiness to proceed, the envoy was introduced before them. One of the sachems, by previous appointment, then arose, and having thanked the Great Spirit for his continued beneficence in permitting them to meet together, he informed the envoy that the council was prepared to hear him upon the business for which it had convened. The council being thus opened, the representative proceeded to unfold the objects of his mission. He submitted his propositions in regular form, and sustained them by such arguments as the case required. The sachems listened with earnest and respectful attention to the end of his address, that they might clearly understand the questions to be decided and answered. After the envoy had concluded his speech, he withdrew from the council, as was customary, to await at a distance the result of its deliberations. It then became the duty of the sachems to agree upon an answer; in doing which, as would be expected, they passed through the ordinary routine of speeches, consultations, and animated discussions. Such was the usual course of proceeding in the Iroquois council. Variations might be introduced by circumstances.

At this place another peculiar institution of the *Ho-dé'-no-sau-nee* is presented. All the sachems of the League, in whom originally was vested the entire civil power, were required to be of " one mind," to give efficacy to their legislation. Unanimity was a fundamental law. The idea of majorities and minorities was entirely unknown to our Indian predecessors.

To hasten their deliberations to a conclusion, and ascertain the result, they adopted an expedient which dispensed entirely with the necessity of casting votes. The founders of the Confederacy, seeking to obviate as far as possible altercation in council, and to facilitate their progress to unanimity, divided the sachems of each nation into classes, usually of two and three each, as will be seen by referring to the table of sachemships. No sachem was permitted to express an opinion in council, until he had agreed with the other sachem or sachems of his class, upon the opinion to be expressed, and had received an appointment to act as speaker for the class. Thus the eight Seneca sachems, being in four classes, could have but four opinions ; the ten Cayuga sachems but four. In this manner each class was brought to unanimity within itself. A cross-consultation was then held between the four sachems who represented the four classes ; and when they had agreed, they appointed one of their number to express their resulting opinion, which was the answer of their nation. The several nations having, by this ingenious method, become of "one mind" separately, it only remained to compare their several opinions, to arrive at the final sentiment of all the sachems of the League. This was effected by a conference between the individual representatives of the several nations; and when they had arrived at unanimity, the answer of the League was determined.

The sovereignty of the nations, by this mode of giving assent, was not only preserved, but made subservient to the effort itself to secure unanimity. If any sachem was obdurate or unreasonable, influences were brought to bear upon him which he could not well resist; and it was seldom that inconvenience resulted from their inflexible adherence to the rule. When, however, all efforts to produce unanimity failed of success, the whole matter was laid aside. Farther action became at once impossible. A result, either favorable or adverse, having, in this way, been reached, it was communicated to the envoy by a speaker selected for the purpose. This orator was always chosen from the nation with whom the council originated, and it was usual with him to review the whole subject presented to the council in a formal speech, and at the same time to announce the conclusions to which the sachems of the Confederacy had arrived. This concluding speech terminated the business of the council, and the Indian diplomatist took his departure.

The war against the Eries, which resulted in the extermination or expulsion of that nation from the western part of this State, about the year 1654, was declared by the sachems of the Iroquois in general council. The French war, also, which they waged with such indomitable courage and perseverance for so many years, was resolved upon in the same manner. Their traditions record other struggles with Indian nations, some of which were engaged in by the League, and others either commenced or assumed by a nation separately. At the beginning of the American Revolution, the Iroquois could not agree in council to make war as a confederacy upon our confederacy. A number of the Oneida sachems firmly resisted the assumption of hostilities, and thus defeated the measure as an act of the League, for the want of unanimity. Some of the nations, however, especially the Mohawks, were so interlinked with the British, that neutrality was impossible. Under this pressure of circumstances, it was resolved in council to suspend the rule, and leave each nation to engage in the war upon its own responsibility.

In the councils of the Iroquois, the dignity and order ever preserved have become proverbial. The gravity of Nestor was exemplified by their sages, and more than the harmony of the Grecian chiefs existed among their sachems. In their elevation to the highest degree of political distinction ever reached by any Indian race, except the Aztec, the clearest evidence is presented of the wisdom and prudence with which these councils watched over the public welfare.

The succession of the Ruling Body, whether secured by election, or by laws of inheritance, is an event of deep importance to the people, whose personal security and welfare are to a large extent under the guardianship of their rulers. It seems to have been the aim of the *Ho-de'-no-sau-nee* to avoid the dangers of an hereditary transmission of power, without fully adopting the opposite principle of a free election, founded upon merit and capacity. Their system was a modification of the two opposite rules, and claims the merit of originality, as well as of adaptation to their social and political condition.

It is in accordance with the principles, and necessary to the existence of an oligarchy, that the ruling body should possess a general, if not an absolute authority over the admission of its members, and over the succession to its dignities, where the vacancies are occasioned by death. In some respects the oligarchy of the Iroquois was wider than those of antiquity. The tribes retained the power of designating successors, independent of the oligarchs; while, for the security of the latter, the number was limited by the fundamental law. It was the province of the ruling body to "raise up" the sachems selected by the tribes, and to invest them with office. In the ancient oligarchies, which were less liberal and much less systematic in their construction, the whole power of making rulers appears to have been appropriated by the rulers themselves.

To perform the ceremony adverted to, of "raising up" sachems, and of confirming the investiture of such chiefs as had been previously raised up by a nation, the Mourning council was instituted. Its name, *Hen-nun-do-nuh'-seh*, signifies, with singular propriety, "a mourning council;" as it embraced the two-fold object of lamenting the deceased with suitable solemnities, and of establishing a successor in the sachem-ship made vacant by his demise.

Upon the death of a sachem, the nation in which the loss had occurred had power to summon a council, and designate the day and place. If the Oneidas, for example, had lost a ruler, they sent out runners at the earliest convenient day, with "belts of invitation" to the sachems of the League, and to the people at large, to assemble around their national council-fire at *Gä-no-a-lo'-häle*. The invitation was circulated in the same manner, and with the same celerity as in con-voking a civil council. These belts or the strings of wampum, sent out on such occasions, conveyed a la-conic message: "the name" of the deceased "calls for a council." It also announced the place and the time.

The name and the appeal fell not in vain upon the ear of the Iroquois. There was a potency in the name itself which none could resist. It penetrated every seclusion of the forest; and reached every *gä-no-sote'* upon the hillside, on the margin of the lakes, or in the deep solitudes of the wood. No warrior, wise man or chief failed to hear, or could withstand the call. A principle within was addressed, which ever responded; respect and veneration for the sachems of the League.

For these councils, and the festivities with which they were concluded, the *Ho-dé'-no-sau-nee* ever re-tained a passionate fondness. No inclemency of sea-son, nor remoteness of residence, nor frailty of age or of sex offered impassable obstructions. To that hardy spirit which led the Iroquois to traverse the

war-paths of the distant south and west, and to leave
their hunting trails upon the Potomac and Ohio, the
distance to a council within their immediate territories
would present inconsiderable hindrances. From the
Mohawk to the Genesee, they forsook their hunting-
grounds, and their encampments, and put themselves
upon the trail for the council-fire. Old men with
gray hairs and tottering steps, young men in the vigor
of youth, warriors inured to the hardships of incessant
strife, children looking out, for the first time, upon
life, and women, with their infants encased in the *gă-
ōs'-hă*, all performed the journey with singular rapidity
and endurance. From every side they bent their
footsteps towards the council; and when the day arrived, a large concourse of warriors, chiefs, wise men
and sachems, from the most remote as well as the subjacent parts of their territory, greeted each other beside the council-fire of the Oneidas.

This council, although entirely of a domestic character, was conducted with many ceremonies. Before
the arrival of the day announced by the belt, the
several nations entered the country of the Oneidas in
separate bands, and encamped at a distance from the
council-house. To advance at once, would have been
a violation of Iroquois usages. Runners were sent on
by the approaching nation to announce its arrival, and
it remained encamped until the Oneidas had signified
their readiness for its reception. On the day appointed,
if the necessary arrangements had been perfected, a
rude reception ceremony opened the proceedings.
The several nations in separate trains, each one preceded by its civil and military dignitaries, drew simul-

taneously towards the council-fire, and were received
and welcomed by the Oneidas in a ceremonious manner. The latter advanced to meet them at a distance
from the village, where a temporary council-fire was
kindled; after which the chief personages of the advancing bands walked around the fire, singing the
songs of mourning designed for the occasion. When
the songs were finished, the pipe of peace was circulated. Speeches were exchanged between the parties,
and the belts of wampum, with which the council had
been called, were returned. The several bands, upon
the completion of these ceremonies, advanced in file, a
funeral procession, and singing the mourning songs, to
the general council-fire at the Indian village, where the
people arrayed themselves in two divisions. The
Mohawks, Onondagas and Senecas, who, as elsewhere
stated, were brother nations to each other, and fathers
to the other three, seated themselves upon one side of
the fire. On the other side were arranged the Oneidas, Cayugas and Tuscaroras, who, in like manner,
were brothers to each other, but children to the three
first. By their peculiar customs, if the deceased sachem
belonged to either of the three elder nations, he was
mourned as a father by the three junior; and it became the duty of the latter to perform the ceremony
of lamentation prescribed by their usages for the deceased, and afterwards that of raising up his successor.
If, on the contrary, the departed ruler belonged to
either of the junior nations, as in the case supposed,
it cast upon the elder nations the duty of lamenting
his death as a child, in the customary form, and of
installing a successor in the vacant sachemship.

These observances were performed with the accustomed gravity and earnestness of the red man; and were, in themselves, neither devoid of interest, nor unadapted to impress the mind. The lament was a tribute to the virtues, and to the memory of the departed sachem, a mourning scene, in which not only the tribe and nation of the deceased, but the League itself participated. Surely, a more delicate testimonial of affection than would have been looked for among our Indian predecessors. The ceremony of raising up a successor, which followed, was a succession of musical chants, with choruses, intermingled with speeches and responses. Upon the whole scene, rendered wild and picturesque by the variety of costumes, there rested a spirit of silence and solemnity which invested it with singular interest.

A prominent part of the ceremonial consisted in the repetition of their ancient laws and usages, and an exposition of the structure and principles of the League, for the instruction of the newly-inducted rulers. In the midst of each division, the chief personages of the elder and junior nations were grouped together. Between the two groups of sachems, the wise-man who conducted the observances walked to and fro, repeating those traditionary lessons, and unfolding those regulations, which had been handed down from the foundation of the Confederacy. Some of them were salutary and instructive, while the most were indicative of wisdom and forethought. Among the injunctions left by *Da-gä-no-we'-dä*, the founder of the League, there was one designed to impress upon their minds the necessity of union and harmony. It was clothed in a figurative dress, as is the custom of the red man when he would produce a vivid impression. He enjoined them to plant a tree with four roots, branching severally to the north, south, east and west. Beneath its shade the sachems of the League must sit down together in perpetual unity, if they would preserve its stability, or secure the advantages it was calculated to bestow. If they did so, the power of the *Ho-de'-no-sau-nee* would be planted as firmly as the oak, and the blasts of adverse fortune would rage against it in vain.

The laws explained at different stages of the ceremonial, were repeated from strings of wampum, into which they "had been talked" at the time of their enactment. In the Indian method of expressing the idea, the string, or the belt can tell, by means of an interpreter, the exact law or transaction of which it was made, at the time, the sole evidence. It operates upon the principle of association, and thus seeks to give fidelity to the memory. These strings and belts were the only visible records of the Iroquois; and were of no use except by the aid of those special personages who could draw forth the secret records locked up in their remembrance.

It is worthy of note, that but little importance was attached to a promise or assurance of a foreign power, unless belts or strings were given to preserve it in recollection. Verbal propositions, or those not confirmed by wampum, were not considered worthy of special preservation.[1] As the laws and usages of the

[1] " It is obvious to all who are the least acquainted with Indian affairs, that they regard no message or invitation, be it of what conse-

Confederacy were intrusted to the guardianship of such strings, one of the Onondaga sachems, *Ho-no-we-nă'-to*, was constituted "Keeper of the Wampum," and was required to be versed in its interpretation.

On these occasions, the wise-man who officiated interpreted strings from time to time, and carried them from one division of sachems to the other. In reply, as many others were subsequently returned with similar forms and explanations. In this manner, with a multitude of forms and ceremonies, consuming the greater part of a day in their repetition, were their sachems raised up. The proceedings were closed with a presentation of the newly-invested rulers to the people, under the names of their respective sachemships, which, from that day forth, they were permitted to assume.

Up to this stage of the Council, neither gaiety nor mirthfulness was exhibited by the old or young. The people were in mourning for the deceased, and rendering the last acts of public respect. When, however, these offices had been performed, and the places left vacant among the rulers had been filled, the reasons for lamentation had disappeared, and with them disappeared the outward signs. The evening was given up to feasting, and to their religious and domestic dances. It was not uncommon to spend several days in these festivities ; devoting the days in succession to athletic games, and the evenings to the feast, and to the social dance.

quence it will, unless attended or confirmed by strings or belts of wampum, which they look upon as we our letters, or rather bonds." Letter of Sir W. Johnson, 1753. Doc. Hist. N. Y., vol. ii. p. 624.

The succession, under these simple regulations, was rendered entirely free from turmoil and strife; and became not only an easy transaction, but an imposing, and, to them, instructive ceremonial. Upon the sachems was bestowed sufficient control over the transmission of the sachemships for their own protection; while the still more important power of naming those to be raised up, and of deposing the unfaithful, which was retained by the tribes, secured the people from oppression and misgovernment.

A wider dissimilarity, than subsists between the institutions of our Indian predecessors and our own, cannot be easily conceived. They are as unlike as the races themselves in their essential characteristics. If, however, a correct impression is desired of the state of society, political and social, in which the Iroquois have existed, and in which they have developed whatever of character they possessed, it must be sought in their customs and institutions; it must be furnished by the practical operation of that stupendous system of inter-relationships by which they were bound together, and from which every act in their social intercourse received a tinge.

The degree of social intercourse between the nations of the League was much greater than would at first be suggested. In the pursuits of the chase and of conquest, and in attendance upon councils, they traversed the whole territory far and near. Their trails penetrated the forest in every direction, and their main thoroughfares were as well beaten as the highways now passing over the same lines. With their habits of travelling over the whole area of the

State, they were doubtless more familiar than ourselves with its hills and plains, rivers and lakes, its wild retreats and forest concealments. Much of their social intercourse, especially between the nations, was around their council-fires. The Councils themselves formed a bond of union, and drew them together instinctively. They furnished the excitements and the recreations of Indian life, as well as relieved the monotony of peace. It was here they recounted their exploits upon the war-path, or listened to the eloquence of favorite chiefs. Here they offered tributes of respect to those deceased sachems who had rendered themselves illustrious by public services; or listened to the laws and regulations of their ancestors, which were explained by their sages in the ceremonial of raising up successors. It was here, also, that they celebrated their athletic games with Olympic zeal; and joined in those national dances, some of which were indescribably beautiful and animated.

Custom required the particular tribe in which sachems had been raised up, to furnish a daily entertainment to the multitude during the continuance of the council. The pursuits of the day were suspended as the shades of evening began to fall, and they all sat down to a common repast, which the matrons of the tribe had prepared. After the business upon which the council convened had been consummated, each day in succession was devoted to the simple but diversified amusements of Indian life, the twilight to the feast, and the evening to the dance. The wild notes of their various tunes, accompanied by the turtle-shell rattle and the drum; the rattles, which entered into the costumes of the warriors, and the noise of the moving throng, all united, sent forth a "sound of revelry" which fell with strange accents in the hours of night upon the solemn stillness of the woods. This sound of pleasure and amusement was continued from day to day, until "pleasure itself became satiety," and amusement had lost its power to charm.

When the spirit of festivity had become exhausted, the fire of the *Hen-nun-do-nuh'-seh* was raked together, and the several nations bent their way homeward through the forest. Silence once more resumed her sway over the deserted scene, as the sounds of merriment subsided, and the lingering hum of the dissolving council died insensibly away. Obscurity next advanced with stealthy mien, and quickly folding the incidents of this sylvan pageant in her dusky mantle, she bore them, with their associations, their teachings, and their remembrances, into the dark realm of Oblivion; from which their recall would be as hopeless as would be the last shout which rang along the valley.

The celebration of their religious festivals was through the instrumentality of councils, and these form the third class. But as they are described in the succeeding pages, no further mention of them will now be made, except to notice them as one of the species into which the councils of the Iroquois are properly divisible. In addition to the religious councils which were held at the period of their festivals, the mourning council was always made an occasion for religious and moral instruction. Many of its exercises were of a strictly religious character, and it would be more proper to designate it as a religious council, than by any other name, but for the circumstance that its object was to raise up rulers, and its ceremonies were entirely distinct from those at the regular festivals.

The influence of the civil, mourning and religious councils upon the people would, of itself, furnish an extensive subject of inquiry. Like all the pursuits of Indian life, they changed but little from age to age, and were alike in their essential characteristics, in their mode of transacting business, in their festivities, and in the spirit by which they were animated. From the frequency of their occurrence, and the deep interest with which they were regarded, it is evident that they exercised a vast influence upon the race. The intercourse and society which they afforded, had, undoubtedly, a power to humanize and soften down the asperities of character which their mode of life was calculated to produce.

Chapter VI

THE Ruling Body of the League, with its
powers, and the tenure of office of its members — the division of the people into tribes,
with the cross-relationships between them — the laws of
succession with their incidents — and the councils of the
Iroquois with their mode of proceeding, spirit and effects, have severally been brought under consideration.

Upon the facts derived from these sources of investigation, the true character of the Iroquois government must be settled. If it is referable to any
determined species, the constituent parts and general features of the League, which have formed the
subjects of the preceding chapters, will determine its
position in the scale of civil organizations established
by political writers.

In their original, well-developed institutions, and
in their government, so systematic in its construction, and so liberal in its administration, there is
much to enforce a tribute of respect to the intelligence of our Indian predecessors. Without such
institutions, and without that animating spirit which
they nourished and diffused, it would be difficult to
account for the production of such men as have

sprung up among the Iroquois. The development of national intellect depends chiefly upon external, reciprocal influences, and is usually proportionate to the vitality and motive which the institutions of a people possess and furnish.

To illustrate, substantially, the nature of their government, it will be necessary to notice the several species which have been instituted among men, the natural order of their origination, the relations in which they mutually stand to each other, and their general characteristics. In no other way can a clear conception be obtained of the character of the Iroquois government, and the relation which it sustains to other political fabrics. No apology, therefore, will be necessary for the digression.

Aristotle, and other Grecian political writers, recognized but three species of government: the monarchical, the aristocratical, and the democratical; the rule of "one," the "few," and the "many." Every other variety was regarded as the wreck, or perversion, of one of the three. If, for example, the first was corrupted, it became a tyranny; if the second degenerated, it was styled an oligarchy; and if the last became tumultuous, it was called an ochlocracy. A polity, or the rule of a large body of select citizens, was a milder form of oligarchy. This classification admits of a qualification to the definition of an aristocracy and oligarchy, hereafter to be noticed.

Modern political writers also recognize three species, as laid down by Montesquieu: the despotic, the monarchical, and the republican. The aristocratic and democratic forms of the Greeks are included in the republican form of modern times : while the monarchical government of the present day — " the rule of a single person by fixed laws " — was entirely unknown to the ancient Greeks. It is further observable that a despotism, as defined by Montesquieu, corresponds precisely with the monarchy of Aristotle.

The order of their origination suggests an important general principle ; that there is a regular progression of political institutions, from the monarchical, which are the earliest in time, on to the democratical, which are the last, the noblest, and the most intellectual. This position can be established by the rise and development of the Grecian institutions, and may be further illustrated by the progressive change in the spirit and nature of other governments.

An unlimited monarchy, or "the rule of a single individual according to his own will," is the form of government natural to a people when in an uncivilized state, or when just emerging from barbarism. In the progress of time, by the growth and expansion of civil liberty, the monarchy becomes liberalized or limited, and a few steps forward introduce universal democracy. Hence it is noticeable in the rise of all races, and in the formation of all states, that the idea of chief and follower, or sovereign and people, is of spontaneous suggestion. This notion may be regarded as inherent to society in its primitive state.

It will be remembered that when the Hellenic tribes came down from Thessaly, and finally settled themselves upon the shores of the Mediterranean, their political relations were those of chief and follower. After they had become subdivided into a

GÄ-KÄ-AH OR SKIRT.

large number of petty states, and migrations and intermixtures had subsided, leaving each principality under its own ruler, and to the formation of its own institutions, the monarchical form of government became fully established. The small territory of Greece was parcelled out between nearly twenty petty kingdoms. During the Heroic ages, which are understood to have commenced with this inundation of the Grecian territory by the Hellenes, and to have terminated with the Trojan war, a period of about two hundred years, the kingly government was the only one among the Greeks.

At the close of the Heroic ages, a new state of affairs became apparent. Around the reigning families in the several kingdoms, there had sprung up a class of Eupatrids, or nobles, who were in possession of most of the landed estates. Having elevated themselves far above the mass of the people, in the social scale, they gradually absorbed political powers which had before been vested in the kings. By the silent but natural growth of this aristocracy, continued encroachments were made upon the prerogatives of royalty, until at last the kings were brought down to a level with their Eupatrids. An aristocracy was thus substituted for monarchy; and nearly all the states of Greece, in their political progress towards democracy, passed out of the monarchical into the aristocratical form of government.

This form, although indicative of more liberality than the former, and adapted to the state of civil society then existing, pressed heavily upon the people; and while it existed, was unfavorable to the elevation of the race. The Demos, or common people, were free, but were excluded from all political privileges; hence, with the increase of their intelligence, would be excited jealousies of the incumbent class. At times, the very existence of the aristocracy depended upon the forcible subjection of the Demos; for when the great and just sentiment of " political equality " began to be coupled with that of " personal liberty," no form of government could rest in permanent security, which limited the one, or denied the other. The Grecian mind was eminently progressive. No power could subdue or enslave that native energy, which had exemplified itself in the hardy enterprises of the Heroic ages. Nothing could repress or lastingly fetter that majestic intellect, out of which, even then, had sprung a system of mythology destined to infuse itself into the literature of all generations, and to quicken the intellects of every clime — a system so remarkable as an exhibition of the unguided devotional nature of man, and so brilliant as a creation of the imagination, that it may be characterized as the greatest production of genius and credulity which ever emanated from the mind of man.

In the progress of events, the aristocracies were successfully invaded by an uprising of men of wealth, or of capacity, from among the common people. These ambitious plebeians demanded a place in the ruling body, and if refused, they became the champions of the people, and engaged in measures for the overthrow of the government. Such difficulties were usually avoided by admitting these new families to a place among the Eupatrids, and to a participation in the administration. In this way the aristocracy of wealth and talent was in a measure placed upon an equality with that of birth; and by the act the government itself was widened, or liberalized.

These inroads upon the aristocracy, which generally resulted in the infusion of the popular element, may be regarded as the introduction or commencement of the oligarchy. The difference between the two species is to be sought in the spirit by which each respectively was actuated, and not in their forms; for the same body of aristocrats usually became oligarchs by a change in the spirit of the government. When an aristocracy became corrupt and odious to the people, and sought only to perpetuate its own power, it became, in the Grecian sense, a faction, an oligarchy. It ceased to be the rule of the " best men " (ἄριστοι), and became the rule of the " few " (ὀλίγοι). This definition admits of a qualification. When an aristocracy became widened or liberalized, by the admission of men of capacity to an equal position, and the government assumed a milder spirit, the aristocracy would, in effect, be changed, but not into a faction. It would be as unlike a rigorous aristocracy as an oligarchical faction, and may be denominated a simple or liberal oligarchy. The government of the Iroquois falls under this precise definition. It cannot be called an aristocracy, because the sachems of the League possessed no landed estates, which, it is well known, are the only true foundation of an aristocracy; neither were their titles or privileges hereditary, in the strict sense, which is another important element of an aristocracy. Their government, however, was the rule of " the few." It was an aristocracy liberalized, until it stood upon the very verge of democracy. It answers to the idea of an oligarchy, which is the last form of government but one, in the progressive series.

The governments of the Grecian states appear to have oscillated for centuries between the rigorous aristocracies, oligarchical factions, and milder oligarchies. These forms were rather transition than permanent conditions of their civil institutions. During the period of their prevalence, the people, who, as before remarked, were personally free, but debarred from political privileges, were gradually improving their condition by the accumulation of wealth, and consolidating their strength by the uprearing of flourishing cities. With the increase of their respectability, and the expansion of their power, the struggle with the incumbent class was continued with greater and still greater success. Principles of government became better understood, and more enlarged views of the rights of man continued to quicken the Grecian mind. Every successive age added to the popular intelligence ; and the people gradually, but constantly, continued to repossess themselves of their original authority. The growth of liberty and free institutions among the Greeks was slow, but irresistible. The struggle of the people for emancipation lasted from generation to generation, from century to century ; until, having emerged from the darkness of barbarism, and worked their way through every species of government ever devised by the genius of man, they achieved at last a triumph ; and their institutions, which had been planted and nourished during this march of ages, finally ripened into universal democracy.

In the history of the States of Greece, there is noticeable in the midst of a wide diversity of events, a great uniformity of progress — with a difference in the period of the development of political changes, a marked tendency to the same results. Every change in their institutions, from the era of absolute monarchy, made them more liberal; but it required upward of seven centuries to liberalize them into a " finished democracy which fully satisfied the Greek notion; a state in which every attribute of sovereignty might be shared, without respect to rank or property, by every freeman." [1] The Greeks began with monarchy, and having passed through all the intermediate species and shades of government in the progressive series, they finally developed their highest capacities, their most brilliant genius, under the bounding pulse of an extreme, even enthusiastic democracy. How truthful the exclamation of Herodotus: " Liberty is a brave thing."

[1] The Trojan War closed 1184 B. C., and the States of Greece soon afterwards passed out of the monarchical form of government. At Athens it was abolished in 1068 B. C. But not until about the year 470 B. C., when Aristides the Just removed the last aristocratical features from the Athenian institutions, could Athens be called a " finished democracy." He broke up the distinctions between the classes which Solon had established, and opened all the dignities of the State to every citizen. Between the Trojan war and this last period, the Athenians had passed through Monarchy, Tyranny, Aristocracy, Faction, Anarchy, Oligarchy, Polity, and limited Democracy. With the legislation of Aristides commenced the rapid elevation of the city of Minerva, and of that noble, unequalled race.

The same tendency of institutions towards democracy, as races elevate themselves in the scale of civilization, can be observed in the progressive improvement of British institutions. No people have been subjected to such tests, civil and religious; and issued from the throes of revolution with more character, more civilization, more majesty of intellect, for achievements in legislation, science and learning, than our parent, Anglo-Saxon race. Their career, with all its vicissitudes, from the union of the Heptarchies under Egbert, down to the final settlement of the government on the expulsion of the second James, is full of instruction — full of great lessons. They have tested monarchy in all its degrees of strength and weakness, of popularity and odium, of oppression and dependence. Their nobles have enjoyed all the privileges, immunities, and powers, which possession of the landed estates, the vassalage of the people, and independence of the crown could secure; while in turn they have been humble and submissive, even servile, under the arbitrary sway of tyrannous kings. The people, before the time of Edward the First, were cyphers in the State. Since then, they have suffered religious bondage, and the oppression of a feudal aristocracy. In the progress of events, however, they have constantly enlarged the quantity of their liberty, and strengthened the guarantees of personal security. But if they finally achieved that personal freedom which the Grecian citizen never lost, they never have secured that " equality of privileges " which was the constant aspiration of the Greek until attained, which was the watchword in the struggle for American freedom, and which now lies at the foundation of our own political edifice.

The British government has been liberalized from age to age, until it may now be said t stand intrenched upon the borders of free institutions.

Returning from this digression, which was designed to illustrate the position, not very recondite, of a progression of institutions, from the monarchical, the earliest form of political society, on to the democratical, the last, and most truly enlightened; we can now take up the government of the Iroquois, and determine the position which it occupies between the two extremes of monarchy on the one hand, and democracy on the other.

The Iroquois had passed out of the earliest form of government, that of chief and follower, which is incident both to the hunter and nomadic states, into the oligarchical form. It is obvious that the hunter life is incompatible with monarchy, except in its miniature form of chief and follower; and the *Ho-dé-no-sau-nee*, in improving upon this last relation, passed over the monarchical, into the rule of "the few." Several tribes first united into one nation. The people mingled by intermarriage, and the power of the chiefs ceased to be several, and became joint. This gave to the nation an aristocratical, or oligarchical form of government, according to the spirit by which it was actuated. By a still higher effort of legislation, several nations were united in a league or confederacy; placing the people upon an equality, and introducing a community of privileges. The national rulers then became in a united body the rulers of the

League. In this manner would be constituted oligarchies within an embracing oligarchy, *imperium in imperio*, presenting the precise government of the Iroquois, and with great probability the exact manner of its origination, growth and final settlement.

The Grecian oligarchies do not furnish an exact type of that of our Indian predecessors. In its construction the latter was more perfect, systematic and liberal than those of antiquity. There was in the Indian fabric more of fixedness, more of dependence upon the people, more of vigor. It would be difficult to find a fairer specimen of the government of *the few*, than the one under consideration. In the happy constitution of its ruling body, and in the effective security of the people from misgovernment it stands unrivalled. In assigning to this government its specific name, it will be sufficient to adopt the etymology of the word oligarchy, *the rule of the few*, rejecting the usual Grecian acceptation of the term, *a degenerated aristocracy*. The substitution of the female line for the male, effecting thereby the disinheritance of the son, the partially elective character of the sachemships, the absence of all landed estates, and the power of deposing lodged with the tribes, are reasons conclusive for regarding the government of the Iroquois as an oligarchy rather than an aristocracy.

The spirit which prevailed in the nations and in the Confederacy was that of freedom. The people appear to have secured to themselves all the liberty which the hunter state rendered desirable. They fully appreciated its value, as is evinced by the liberality of their institutions. The red man was always free from political bondage, and, more worthy still of remembrance, his "free limbs never wore a shackle." His spirit could never be bowed in servitude. In the language of Charlevoix, the Iroquois were "entirely convinced that man was born free, that no power on earth had any right to make any attempts against his liberty, and that nothing could make him amends for its loss." It would be difficult to describe any political society, in which there was less of oppression and discontent, more of individual independence and boundless freedom. The absence of family distinctions, and of all property, together with the irresistible inclination for the chase, rendered the social condition of the people peculiar to itself. It secured to them an exemption from the evils, as well as denied to them the refinements, which flow from the possession of wealth, and the indulgence of the social relations.

At this point the singular trait in the character of the red man suggests itself, that he never felt the "power of gain." The *auri sacra fames* of Virgil, the *studium lucri* of Horace, never penetrated his nature. This great passion of civilized man, in its use and abuse his blessing and his curse, never roused the Indian mind. It was doubtless the great reason of his continuance in the hunter state; for the desire of gain is one of the earliest manifestations of progressive mind, and one of the most powerful passions of which the mind is susceptible. It clears the forest, rears the city, builds the merchantman — in a word, it has civilized our race.

All things considered, the Iroquois oligarchy excites

a belief of its superiority over those of antiquity. Those of Greece were exceedingly unstable, and therefore incline us to regard them as transition states of their institutions; while that of the *Ho-de'-no-sau-nee* was guarded in so many ways for the resistance of political changes, that it would have required a very energetic popular movement for its overthrow. The former retained many elements of aristocracy, while the latter had become so far liberalized as to be almost entirely free. Without the influence of cities, which no people construct who live in the hunter state, and the important consequences which result from the aggregation of society into large communities, the government of the Iroquois would doubtless have retained its oligarchical form through many generations. It would have lasted until the people had abandoned the hunter state; until they had given up the chase for agriculture, the arts of war for those of industry, the hunting-ground and the fishing encampment for the village and the city.

It will not be necessary to extend the inquiry, to exhibit more fully the gradual changes in the government of the Iroquois, by which it was brought upon the verge of free institutions. The creation of the class of chiefs furnishes the clearest evidence of the development of the popular element. The proofs of its extreme liberality have been sufficiently exhibited in the structure of the government itself. Reflections could be multiplied upon its spirit, its influence upon the people, its operative force in the development of talent, and its adaptation to produce its historical results; but it is not deemed necessary to carry forward reflections of this description. An outline of the structure of the League has been drawn, and from its general characteristics its principles can be easily deduced.

Under this simple but beautiful fabric of Indian construction arose the power of the Iroquois, reaching, at its full meridian, over a large portion of our republic. In their Long House, which opened its door upon Niagara, they found shelter in the hour of attack, resources for conquest in the season of ambitious projects, and happiness and contentment in the days of peace. In adaptation to their mode of life, their habits and their wants, no scheme of government could have been devised better calculated for their security against outward attack, their triumph upon the war-path, and their internal tranquillity. It is, perhaps, the only league of nations ever instituted among men, which can point to three centuries of uninterrupted domestic unity and peace.

The institutions which would be expected to exist under such a political system as that of the Iroquois, would necessarily be simple. Their mode of life and limited wants, the absence of property in a comparative sense, and the infrequency of crime dispensed with a vast amount of the legislation and machinery incident to the protection of civilized society. While, therefore, it would be unreasonable to seek those high qualities of mind which result from ages of cultivation, in such a rude state of existence, it would be equally irrational to regard the Indian character as devoid of all those higher characteristics which ennoble the human race. If he has never contributed a page to

science, nor a discovery to art; if he loses in the
progress of generations as much as he gains; still
there are certain qualities of his mind which shine forth
in all the lustre of natural perfection. His simple
integrity, his generosity, his unbounded hospitality,
his love of truth, and, above all, his unshaken fidelity
— a sentiment inborn, and standing out so conspic-
uously in his character, that it has not untruthfully
become its characteristic: all these are adornments of
humanity, which no art of education can instil, nor
refinement of civilization can bestow. If they exist
at all, it is because the gifts of the Deity have never
been perverted.

There was, however, a fatal deficiency in Indian
society, in the non-existence of a progressive spirit.
The same rounds of amusement, of business, of
warfare, of the chase, and of domestic intercourse
continued from generation to generation. There was
neither progress nor invention, nor increase of political
wisdom. Old forms were preserved, old customs
adhered to. Whatever they gained upon one point
they lost upon another, leaving the second generation
but little wiser than the first. The Iroquois, in some
respects, were in advance of their red neighbors.
They had attempted the establishment of their institutions upon a broader basis, and already men of high
capacity had sprung up among them, as their political
system unfolded. If their Indian empire had been
suffered to work out its own results, it is still
problematical whether the vast power they would have
accumulated, and the intellect which would have been
developed by their diversified affairs, would not,

together, have been sufficiently potent to draw the people from the hunter into the agricultural state. The hunter state is the zero of human society, and while the red man was bound by its spell, there was no hope of his elevation.

In a speculative point of view, the institutions of the Iroquois assume an interesting aspect. Would they, at maturity, have emancipated the people from their strange infatuation for a hunter life; as those of the Toltecs and Aztecs had before effected the disenthralment of those races in the latitudes of Mexico? It cannot be denied that there are some grounds for the belief that their institutions would eventually have ripened into civilization. The Iroquois, at all times, have manifested sufficient intellect to promise a high degree of improvement, if it had once become awakened and directed to right pursuits. Centuries, however, might have been requisite to effect the change.

But their institutions have a real, a present value, for what they were, irrespective of what they might have become. The Iroquois were our predecessors in the sovereignty. Our country they once called their country, our rivers and lakes were their rivers and lakes, our hills and intervales were also theirs. Before us they enjoyed the beautiful scenery spread out between the Hudson and Niagara, in its wonderful diversity from the pleasing to the sublime. Before us, were they invigorated by our climate, and were nourished by the bounties of the earth, the forest and the stream. The tie by which we are thus connected carries with it the duty of doing justice to their memory, by preserving their name and deeds, their customs and their institutions, lest they perish from remembrance. We cannot wish to tread ignorantly upon those extinguished council-fires, whose light, in the days of aboriginal dominion, was visible over half the continent.

The political structures of our primitive inhabitants have, in general, proved exceedingly unsubstantial. Isolated nations, by some superiority of institutions, or casual advantage of location, sprang up with an energetic growth, and for a season spread their dominion far and wide. After a brief period of prosperity, they were borne back by adverse fortune into their original obscurity; thus rendering these boundless territories the constant scene of human conflict, and of the rise and fall of Indian sovereignties. It was reserved for the Iroquois to rest themselves upon a more durable foundation, by the establishment of a League. This alliance between their nations they cemented by the imperishable bands of tribal relationship. At the epoch of Saxon occupation, they were rapidly building up an empire, which threatened the absorption or extermination of the whole Indian family east of the Mississippi. Their power had become sufficient to set at defiance all hostile invasions from contiguous nations; and the League itself, while it suffered no loss of numbers by emigrating bands, was endued with a capacity for indefinite expansion. At the periods of their separate discovery, the Aztecs on the south, and the Iroquois in the north were the only Indian races upon the continent, whose institutions promised, at maturity, to ripen into civilization. Such were the condition and prospects of this Indian League, when

Hendrick Hudson, more than two centuries since (1609), sailed up the river which constituted their eastern boundary. This silent voyage of the navigator may be regarded as the opening event in the series, which resulted in reversing the political prospects of the *Ho-de'-no-sau-nee*, and in introducing into their Long House an invader, more relentless in his purposes, and more invincible in arms, than the red men against whose assaults it had been erected.

Their council-fires, so far as they are emblematical of civil jurisdiction, have long since been extinguished, their empire has terminated, and the shades of evening are now gathering thickly over the scattered and feeble remnants of this once powerful League. Race has yielded to race, the inevitable result of the contact of the civilized with the hunter life. Who shall relate with what pangs of regret they yielded up, from river to river and from lake to lake, this fair broad domain of their fathers. The Iroquois will soon be lost as a people, in that night of impenetrable darkness in which so many Indian races have been enshrouded. Already their country has been appropriated, their forests cleared, and their trails obliterated. The residue of this proud and gifted race, who still linger around their native seats, are destined to fade away, until they become eradicated as an Indian stock. We shall ere long look backward to the Iroquois, as a race blotted from existence; but to remember them as a people whose sachems had no cities, whose religion had no temples, and whose government had no record.

BOOK SECOND

SPIRIT OF THE LEAGUE

BOOK II

SPIRIT OF THE LEAGUE

Chapter I

Faith of the Iroquois — Belief in the Great Spirit — The Evil-Minded — He´-No, The Thunderer — Gă´-o, Spirit of the Winds — The Three Sisters — The Invisible Aids — Witches — False Faces — Legendary Literature — Immortality of the Soul — Future Punishments — Moral Sentiments — Burial Customs — Abode of the Great Spirit — Washington — Spirituality of their Faith — Its Influence

THE mind is, by nature, full of religious tendencies. Man, when left to the guidance of his own inward persuasions, searches after the Author of his being, and seeks to comprehend the purposes of his existence, and his final destiny. In every age and condition of society, the best thoughts of the most gifted intellects have been expended upon religious subjects. The conclusions reached by reflective mind, under the inspiration of the works of nature, are propagated from generation to generation, until they grow, by natural enlargement, into a system of fixed Beliefs. Upon them is afterwards engrafted a system of Worship. The two flourish side by side with perpetual vigor. They become interwoven with the civil and social institutions of men, and by nurture and habit acquire such a firm hold upon the affections, that they form a part of the living, thinking, acting mind. Without a

141

knowledge, therefore, of the religious life of a people, their institutions, and their political and domestic transactions would be wholly inexplicable.

Remarkable features are exhibited in the religious system of the Iroquois, when contrasted with other systems of similar origin. Emanating from the mind of man alone, originating in the simplest form of human society, it would naturally be encumbered by the vagaries of fancy, and be upheld by affection rather than logic. But man, shut out from the light of revelation, and left to construct his own theology, will discover some part of the truth, as shadowed forth by the works of nature. This will illuminate his footsteps, in proportion to his appreciation of its excellence, and his faithful adherence to its divine monitions. The faith and worship of the Iroquois are entitled to a favorable consideration, by reason of the principles of belief which they recognized, and the fundamental truths which they inculcated. Established upon some of those luminous principles which lie at the foundation of sound theology, the blemishes in their spiritual edifice are compensated, in some degree, by the purity of its elements.

The Greeks discovered the traces of divinity in every object in nature; in the affections and passions, in the elements of earth and air, in the rivulet, the mountain and the sea. Ascending from these types to their several supposed originals, they grasped at Deity in a multitude of fragments, as proclaimed by the divided works of creation. Failing, with all the acumen and inspiration of their marvellous intellect, to raise their mental vision above Olympus, and to ascend from united nature up to the indivisible and Eternal

One, they perfected and beautified that stupendous production of genius and credulity, the polytheism of the ancient world.

Between the popular belief of the ancients and that of the Iroquois there are some coincidences. This similarity of ideas is observable in a portion of their legends and fables, but more especially in their notions of the spiritual world. Like the ancients, they peopled the invisible world with spiritual existences. In their inferior spiritualities, they fell infinitely below the splendid creations of the ancient mythology; but in their knowledge of the Supreme Being, they rose, in many respects, far above the highest conceptions of the ancient philosophy. It will be at once conceded, that the Supreme Intelligence announced by Anaxagoras, Socrates and Plato, the *Numen Præstantissimæ Mentis* of the ancient philosophical religionists, was in itself a more vague and indefinite conception, than that divine Being worshipped by the entire red race under the appellation of the Great Spirit.

Upon the first great question in theology, the Stoic, the Epicurean, and the other sects of philosophers equally reached the same fundamental conclusion, *esse Deos,* "the Gods exist." This truth, they affirmed, was not only revealed by the works of nature, but it was also innate, and written in the mind of man.[1] But

---

1 Omnibus enim innatum est et in animo quasi insculptum, esse Deos. Cicero De Natura Deorum, Lib. ii. cap. iv. Solus enim vidit, (Epicurus,) primum esse Deos, quod in omnium animis eorum notionem impressisset ipsa natura. Ib. Lib. i. c. xvi. Quid enim potest esse tam apertum tamque perspicuum, quum cælum suspeximus, cælestiaque contemplati sumus, quam esse aliquod numen præstantissimæ mentis, quo hæc segantur? Ib. Lib. ii. c. ii.

in a multitude of Gods, each clothed with separate and distinct offices and powers, and all subject to a gradation in rank, the popular belief reposed. The idea of one Supreme Being was a sublime induction of philosophy, and far above the level of popular intelligence. This great truth, therefore, failed to become even feebly incorporated with the overshadowing mythology of antiquity. With the red race, however, the belief not only prevailed that a Great Spirit existed, but they made the same induction from the works of nature the foundation of their religious system.

There is also a coincidence of belief in relation to the origin of spiritual existences. The ancient mythology taught, that the Gods were born, *nativos esse Deos*, and furnished, at the same time, their genealogy, with all the minuteness of legendary license. The Iroquois, also, believed that the Great Spirit was born; and tradition has handed down the narrative, with embellishments of fancy which Hesiod himself would not have disdained.[1]

Whether the Gods ruled the universe, and were interested in the affairs of men, was a disputed question in the ancient schools. The Epicureans taught that they were unmindful of all human transactions, and spent their existence in ease and pleasure.[2] But the Stoics took the opposite view, and not only affirmed

---

[1] The tradition of the birth of the Good Spirit and the Evil Spirit is much the same among the numerous Indian races within the Republic. It is not peculiar to the Iroquois.

[2] Nihil enim agit : nullis occupationibus est implicatus : nulla opera molitur : sua sapientia et virtute gaudet : habet exploratum, fore se semper tum in maximis, tum in æternis voluptatibus. Hunc Deum rite beatum dixerimus. Cic. De Nat. Deo. Lib. i. cap. xix.

their constant supervision and intervention in human affairs, but also their active administration of the works of nature.[1] This was also the popular belief. The notions of the Iroquois approached nearest to the latter. In error in ascribing to the Great Spirit a finite origin, and with feeble conceptions of his attributes, they yet believed him to be their creator, ruler and preserver; and that in him was the residuum of power.

The creation of the world was also a subject which divided the ancient schools. In a belief in the eternity of matter, they, in general, concurred. Plato and the Stoics, however, taught that the visible universe was fashioned and constructed by the direct agency of God. This opinion, not of the creation of matter, but of the formation of the world, encountered the ridicule of the Epicureans.[2] This is one of those questions with which human wisdom is unable to cope. In their religious system, the Iroquois have but little to do with the creation of the visible universe. According to the tradition, the earth grew miraculously, a self-prepared abode for the Great Spirit. Concerning the universe which existed before the advent of the Great Spirit, they pretend to no knowledge. To the Great Spirit, however, the Iroquois ascribed creative power.

[1] Sunt autem alii philosophi, et hi quidem magni atque nobilis, qui Deorum mente atque ratione omnem mundum administrari et regi censeant : neque vero id solum, sed etiam ab iisdem vitæ hominum consuli et provideri. Id. Lib. i. cap. ii.

[2] Quibus enim oculis animi intueri potuit vester Plato fabricam illam tanti operis, qua construi a Deo atque ædificari mundum facit? Quæ molitio? quæ ferramenta? qui rectes? quæ machinæ? qui ministri tanti muneris fuerunt? Quemadmodum autem obedire et parere voluntati architecti aër, ignis, aqua, terra potuerunt. Id. l. i. c. viii.

He created not only the animal and vegetable world, but also adapted the elements, and the whole visible universe to the wants of man.

That the Indian, without the aid of revelation, should have arrived at a fixed belief in the existence of one Supreme Being, has ever been matter of surprise and admiration. In the existence of the Great Spirit, an invisible but ever-present Deity, the universal red race believed. His personal existence became a first principle, an intuitive belief, which neither the lapse of centuries could efface, nor inventions of man could corrupt. By the diffusion of this great truth, if the Indian did not escape the spell of superstition, which resulted from his imperfect knowledge of the Deity, and his ignorance of natural phenomena; yet he was saved from the deepest of all barbarisms, an idolatrous worship. The Iroquois believed in the constant superintending care of the Great Spirit. He ruled and administered the world, and the affairs of the red race. As Moses taught that Jehovah was the God of Abraham, Isaac and Jacob, and of his chosen people, so the Iroquois regarded the Great Spirit as the God of the Indian alone. They looked up to him as the author of their being, the source of their temporal blessings, and the future dispenser of the felicities of their heavenly home. To him they rendered constant thanks and homage for the changes in the seasons, the fruits of the earth, the preservation of their lives, and for their social privileges and political prosperity; and to him they addressed their prayers for the continuance of his protecting care. Their knowledge of the attributes of the Great Spirit was necessarily limited and imperfect. Of his goodness and beneficence they had a full impression, and some notions, also, of his justice and perfection. But they could not fully conceive of the omnipresence of the Great Spirit, except through the instrumentality of a class of inferior spiritual existences, by whom he was surrounded. His power was evidenced by the creation of man. He was also believed to be self-existent and immortal. The ennobling and exalting views of the Deity which are now held by enlightened and christian nations would not be expected among a people excluded from the light of revelation. In the simple truths of natural religion they were thoroughly indoctrinated, and many of these truths were held in great purity and simplicity. Such is the power of truth over the human mind, and the harmony of all truth, that the Indian, without the power of logic, reached some of the most important conclusions of philosophy, and drew down from heaven some of the highest truths of revelation.

While the religious system of the Iroquois taught the existence of the Great Spirit *Hä-wen-ne'-yu*,[1] it also recognized the personal existence of an Evil Spirit, *Hä-ne-go-ate'-geh*, the Evil-minded. According to the legend of their finite origin, they were brothers, born at the same birth, and destined to an endless existence. To the Evil Spirit, in a limited degree, was ascribed creative power. As the Great Spirit created man, and all useful animals, and products of the earth, so the Evil Spirit created all monsters, poisonous reptiles,

---

[1] This is an original uncompounded word, and in the Seneca dialect. It signifies simply "A Ruler."

and noxious plants. In a word, while the former made everything that was good and subservient, the latter formed everything that was bad and pernicious to man. One delighted in virtue, and in the happiness of his creatures, to which end he exercised over them his unceasing protection. The other was committed to deeds of evil, and was ever watchful to scatter discord among men, and multiply their calamities. Over the Evil-minded the Great Spirit exercised no positive authority, although possessed of the power to overcome him, if disposed to its exertion. Each ruled an independent kingdom, with powers underived. Man's free agency stood between them, with which, in effect, he controlled his own destiny. A life of trust and confidence in the Great Spirit, and of obedience to his commands, afforded a refuge and a shelter to the pious Indian against the machinations of the Evil-minded.

Inferior spiritual beings were also recognized in the theology of the Iroquois. Though not as accurately described and classified as those of the ancient mythology, they yet exhibit with them some singular coincidences ; although these coincidences, real or imaginary, show nothing but the similarity of human ideas in similar conditions of society. They were classified into good and evil, the former being the *assistants* and *subordinates* of the Great Spirit, while the latter were the *emissaries* and *dependents* of the Evil-minded. To some of them was assigned a bodily form, a "local habitation, and a name." To the former class of these spiritual existences, they were wont to render their acknowledg-

ments at their annual festivals for imagined favors,
and to supplicate of the Great Spirit the continuance
of their watchful care. In the creation of these subordinate beings, the Iroquois manifested their knowledge of the necessity of an Omnipresent Ruler; and
at the same time they exhibited their limited com-
prehension of infinite power. Through these instrumentalities, they believed the Great Spirit was enabled,
with ease and convenience, to administer the affairs
of nature, and of man.

To *He'-no* he committed the thunderbolt; at once
the voice of admonition and the instrument of vengeance. He also intrusted to him the formation of
the cloud, and the gift of rain. By *He'-no* was the
earth to be cooled and refreshed, vegetation sustained, the harvest ripened, and the fruits of the
earth matured. The terror of the Thunderer was
held over evil-doers, but especially over witches.
With power to inflict the most instantaneous and
fearful punishment, he was regarded as the avenger
of the deeds of evil. He is represented as having
the form of a man, and as wearing the costume of
a warrior. Upon his head he wore a magical feather,
which rendered him invulnerable against the attacks
of the Evil-minded. On his back he carried a basket filled with fragments of chert rock, which he
launched at evil spirits and witches, whenever he
discovered them, as he rode in the clouds. In the
spring-time when the seeds were committed to the
ground, there was always an invocation of *He'-no*,
that he would water them, and nourish their growth.
At the harvest festival they returned thanks to *He'-no*

for the gift of rain. They also rendered their thanks
to the Great Spirit for the harvest, and supplicated
him to continue to them the watchful care of the
Thunderer. There is a fanciful legend in relation
to *He'-no*, to the effect that he once made his habitation in a cave under Niagara Falls, behind the sheet,
where he dwelt amid the grateful noise and din of
waters. The Great Spirit gave to him three assistants,
who have continued nameless, to enable him to maintain a more vigilant supervision over the important
interests committed to his guardianship. One of
these, the legend declares, was partly of human, and
partly of celestial origin.[1] To bring *He'-no* nearer to

[1] The legend is as follows : A young maiden residing at *Gä'-u-gwa*,
a village above Niagara Falls, at the mouth of Cayuga creek, had been
contracted to an old man of ugly manners and disagreeable person. As
the marriage was hateful to her, and, by the customs of the nation there
was no escape, she resolved upon self-destruction. Launching a bark
canoe into the Niagara, she seated herself within it, and composing her
mind for the frightful descent, directed it down the current. The rapid
waters soon swept them over the falls, and the canoe was seen to fall into
the abyss below, but the maiden had disappeared. Before she reached the
waters underneath, she was caught in a blanket by *He'-no* and his two
assistants, and carried without injury to the home of the Thunderer, behind the fall. Her beauty attracted one of the dependents of *He'-no*, who
willingly joined them in marriage.

For several years before this event, the people at *Gä'-u-gwa* had been
troubled with an annual pestilence, and the source of the scourge had
baffled all conjecture. *He'-no*, at the expiration of a year, revealed to her
the cause, and out of compassion to the people, sent her back to them,
to make known the cause, and the remedy. He told her that a monstrous
serpent dwelt under the village, and made his annual repast upon the
bodies of the dead which were buried by its side. That to insure a
bountiful feast, he went forth once a year, and poisoned the waters of the
Niagara, and also of the Cayuga creek, whereby the pestilence was
created. The people were directed to move to the Buffalo creek. He
also gave her careful directions touching the education of the child of

their affections, the Iroquois always addressed him
under the appellation of Grandfather, and styled
themselves his grandchildren. In every act of his,
however, they recognized the hand of *Hä-wen-ne'-yu.*

Another of the spiritual creations of the Iroquois
is recognized in *Gă'-oh*, the Spirit of the Winds.
He is, also, a mere instrumentality, through whom

which she was to become the mother. With these directions she departed
on her mission.

After the people had removed as directed, the great serpent, disap-
pointed of his food, put his head above the ground to discover the reason, and found that the village was deserted. Having scented their trail,
and discovered its course, he went forth into the lake, and up the Buffalo
creek, in open search of his prey. While in this narrow channel, *He'-no*
discharged upon the monster a terrific thunderbolt which inflicted a
mortal wound. The Senecas yet point to a place in the creek where
the banks are semicircular on either side, as the spot where the serpent,
after he was struck, turning to escape into the deep waters of the lake,
shoved out the banks on either side. Before he succeeded in reaching the
lake, the repeated attacks of the Thunderer took effect, and the monster
was slain.

The huge body of the serpent floated down the stream, and lodged
upon the verge of the cataract, stretching nearly across the river. A
part of the body arched backwards near the northern shore in a semicircle.
The raging waters thus dammed up by the body broke through the rocks
behind ; and thus the whole verge of the fall upon which the body rested
was precipitated with it into the abyss beneath. In this manner, says the
legend, was formed the Horse-Shoe fall.

Before this event there was a passage behind the sheet from one shore
to the other. This passage-way was not only broken up, but the home
of *He'-no* was also destroyed, in the general crash. Since then his habitation has been in the west.

The child of the maiden grew up to boyhood, and was found to possess
the power of darting the lightning at his will. It had been the injunction
of *He'-no* that he should be reared in retirement, and not be allowed to
mingle in the strifes of men. On a certain occasion having been beset by
a playmate with great vehemence, he transfixed him with a thunderbolt.
He'-no immediately translated him to the clouds, and made him the third
assistant Thunderer.

the Great Spirit moves the elements. Having a human form, with the face of an old man, *Gă'-oh* is represented as sitting in solitary confinement, surrounded by a tangle of discordant winds, and ever impatient of restraint. His residence, *Da-yo-dă'-do-go-wä*, the " Great Home of the Winds," is stationary, in a quarter of the heavens toward the west. Surrounded and compressed by the elements, he ever and anon struggles to free himself from their entanglement. When perfectly quiescent, the winds are at rest. A slight motion sends forth the breeze, which is wafted gently over the face of the earth. When he struggles with restlessness and impatience, the strong wind goes forth to move the clouds, ruffle the waters, and shake the foliage of the forest. But when his restlessness mounts up to frenzy, he puts forth his utmost strength to shake off the confining element. These mighty throes of *Gă'-oh* send forth the blasts which sweep the plain, lay low the oak upon the mountain side, and dash the waters against the sky. *Gă'-oh* is represented, however, as a beneficent being, ever mindful of the will of the Great Spirit, and solicitous to fulfil his commands.[1]

Perhaps the most beautiful conception in the mythology of the Iroquois is that in relation to the Three Sisters, the Spirit of Corn, the Spirit of the Bean, and the Spirit of the Squash. These plants were regarded as the special gift of *Hä-wen-ne'-yu*; and

---

1 Æolus naturally suggests himself to the reader, although the analogy is slight.

" Hic vasto rex Æolus antro
Luctantes ventos, tempestatesque sonoras
Imperio premit, ac vinclis et carcere
frænat." Æneid, Lib. i. 52.

they believed that the care of each was intrusted, for the welfare of the Indian, to a separate Spirit. They are supposed to have the forms of beautiful females, to be very fond of each other, and to delight to dwell together. This last belief is illustrated by the natural adaptation of the plants themselves to grow up together in the same field, and perhaps from the same hill. Their apparel was made of the leaves of their respective plants; and in the growing season they were believed to visit the fields, and dwell among them. This triad is known under the name of *De-o-ha'-ko*, which signifies Our Life, or Our Supporters. They are never mentioned separately, except by description, as they have no individual names. There is a legend in relation to corn, that it was originally of easy cultivation, yielded abundantly, and had a grain exceedingly rich with oil. The Evil-minded, being envious of this great gift of *Hä-wen-ne'-yu* to man, went forth into the fields, and spread over it a universal blight. Since then it has been harder to cultivate, yields less abundantly, and has lost its original richness. To this day, when the rustling wind waves the corn leaves with a moaning sound, the pious Indian fancies that he hears the Spirit of Corn, in her compassion for the red man, still bemoaning, with unavailing regrets, her blighted fruitfulness.

Among the inhabitants of the spiritual world, with which the Iroquois surrounded themselves, may be enumerated the Spirits of medicine, of fire, and of water, the Spirit of each of the different species of trees, of each of the species of shrubs bearing fruit, and of the different herbs and plants. Thus there was the Spirit of the oak, of the hemlock, and of the maple, of the whortleberry and of the raspberry, and also of the spearmint, and of tobacco. Most of the objects in nature were thus placed under the watchful care of some protecting Spirit. Some of them were made tangible to the senses, by giving to them a bodily form and specific duties ; as the Spirit of springs, and of each of the several fruit trees. But the most of them were feebly imagined existences. In their worship, the Iroquois were accustomed to return their thanks to these subordinates of *Hä-wen-né'-yu*, under the general name of *Ho-no-che-no'-keh*. This term signifies " the Invisible Aids," and included the whole spiritual world, from *Hé'-no*, the Thunderer, down to the Spirit of the Strawberry. But few of them had specific names, or were mentioned in their worship, except conjointly. The Iroquois appear to have had but a faint conception of the omnipresence of the Great Spirit, as elsewhere observed ; or of any individual power sufficiently potent to administer, un-assisted, the stupendous works of creation, and the complicated affairs of man. In part from this cause, undoubtedly, they believed that the Great Spirit had surrounded himself with subordinate spiritual beings of his own creation, to whom he intrusted the imme-diate supervision of the various works of nature. He thus rendered himself, in a limited sense, omnipresent, and ruled and regulated, with ease and convenience, the works of creation. These Spirits were never objects of worship. The Iroquois regarded them merely as the unseen assistants of *Hä-wen-né'-yu*, and the executors of his will.

Evil spirits were believed to be the creations of *Hä-ne-go-ate'-geh*. Pestilence and disease were supposed to be the work of evil spirits. Witches and enchanters were believed to be possessed with them. There were also the Spirits of poisonous plants and roots. All the agencies of evil were brought into existence by, and held under the dominion of the Evil-minded. To counteract their machinations, the efforts of the Great Spirit and his spiritual host were incessantly put forth. At their religious festivals, the Iroquois invoked *Hä-wen-ne'-yu* to shield them against their secret designs. "Great Spirit, master of all things, visible and invisible; Great Spirit, master of other spirits, whether good or evil; command the good spirits to favor thy children; command the evil spirits to keep at a distance from them." [1]

The Iroquois believed that tobacco was given to them as the means of communication with the spiritual world. By burning tobacco they could send up their petitions with its ascending incense, to the Great Spirit, and render their acknowledgments acceptably for his blessings. Without this instrumentality, the ear of *Hä-wen-ne'-yu* could not be gained. In like manner they returned their thanks at each recurring festival to the Invisible Aids, for their friendly offices, and protecting care. It was also their custom to return thanks to the trees, shrubs and plants, to the springs, rivers and streams, to the fire and wind, and to the sun, moon and stars; in a word, to every object in nature, which ministered to their wants, and thus awakened a feeling of gratitude. But this was done without

[1] La Hontan.

155

the intervention of the incense of tobacco. They addressed the object itself.

A belief in witches is to this day, and always has been, one of the most deeply-seated notions in the minds of the Iroquois. The popular belief on this subject rose to the most extravagant degree of the marvellous and the supernatural. Any person, whether old or young, male or female, might become possessed of an evil spirit, and be transformed into a witch. A person thus possessed could assume, at pleasure, the form of any animal, bird or reptile, and having executed his nefarious purpose, could resume his original form, or, if necessary to escape pursuit, could transmute himself into an inanimate object. They were endued with the power of doing evil, and were wholly bent upon deeds of wickedness. When one became a witch, he ceased to be himself. According to the current belief, he was not only willing to take the life of his nearest friend, but such an one was the preferred object of his vengeance. The means of death employed was an unseen poison. Such was the universal terror of witches, that their lives were forfeited by the laws of the Iroquois. Any one who discovered the act, might not only destroy the witch, but could take to himself the dangerous power of deciding who it was. To this day, it is next to impossible, by any process of reasoning, to divest the mind of a Seneca of his deep-seated belief in witches.[1]

[1] But a year since a woman was shot on the Allegany (Seneca) reservation, on the pretence of witchcraft. Such instances have been frequent among the Senecas within the last fifty years. Not the least singular

FALSEFACES

There is a current belief among the Iroquois, that these demons are banded together in a secret and systematic organization, which has subsisted for ages; that they have periodical meetings, an initiation ceremony, and a novitiate fee. These meetings were held at night, and the fee of the neophyte was the life of his nearest and dearest friend, to be taken with poison, on the eve of his admission.

The tendency of the Iroquois to superstitious beliefs is especially exemplified in their notion of the existence of a race of supernatural beings whom they call Falsefaces. This belief has prevailed among them from the most remote period, and still continues its hold upon the Indian mind. The Falsefaces are believed to be evil spirits or demons without bodies, arms or limbs, simply faces, and those of the most hideous description. It is pretended that when seen they are usually in the most retired places, darting from point to point, and perhaps from tree to tree, by some mysterious power; and possessed of a look so frightful and demoniacal as to paralyze all who behold

Gä-gó-sä, or False Face.

feature of the case is that they sometimes confess the act. There may be some foundation for this strange delusion in the phenomena of nature.

them.   They are supposed also to have power to send plagues and pestilence among men, as well as to devour their bodies when found, for which reasons they were held in the highest terror.   To this day there are large numbers of the Iroquois who believe implicitly in the personal existence of these demons.

Upon this belief was founded a regular secret organization called the Falseface band, members of which can now be found in every Iroquois village both in this State and Canada, where the old modes of life are still preserved.   This society has a species of initiation, and regular forms, ceremonies and dances.   In acquiring or relinquishing a membership their superstitious notions were still further illustrated, for it depended entirely upon the omen of a dream.   If any one dreamed he was a Falseface, it was only necessary to signify his dream to the proper person, and give a feast, to be at once initiated ; and so any one dreaming that he had ceased to be a Falseface, had but to make known his dream and give a similar entertainment to effect his exodus.   In no other way could a membership be acquired or surrendered.   Upon all occasions on which the members appeared in character they wore false faces of the kind represented in the figure, the masks being diversified in color, style and configuration, but all agreeing in their equally hideous appearance.   The members were all males save one, who was a female, and the Mistress of the Band.   She was called *Gä-go-sä Ho-nun-nas-tase-ta*, or the keeper of the Falsefaces ; and not only had charge of the regalia of the band, but was the only organ of communication with the members, for their names continued unknown.

FALSEFACES

The prime motive in the establishment of this organization was to propitiate those demons called Falsefaces, and among other good results to arrest pestilence and disease. In course of time the band itself was believed to have a species of control over diseases, and over the healing art; and they were often invoked for the cure of simple diseases, and to drive away, or exorcise the plague, if it had actually broken out in their midst. As recently as the summer of 1849, when the cholera prevailed through the State, the Falsefaces, in appropriate costume, went from house to house at Tonawanda, through the old school portion of the village, and performed the usual ceremonies prescribed for the expulsion of the pestilence.

When any one was sick with a complaint within the range of their healing powers, and dreamed that he saw a Falseface, this was interpreted to signify that through their instrumentality he was to be cured. Having informed the mistress of the band, and prepared the customary feast, the Falsefaces at once appeared, preceded by their female leader, and marching in Indian file. Each one wore a mask or false face, a tattered blanket over his shoulders, and carried a turtle shell rattle in his hand. On entering the house of the invalid they first stirred the ashes upon the hearth, and then sprinkled the patient over with hot ashes until his head and hair were covered; after which they performed some manipulations over him in turn, and finally led him around with them in the falseface dance (*Gä-go-sä*), with which their ceremonies concluded. When these performances were over, the entertainment prepared for the occasion was distributed to the band, and by them carried away for their private feasting, as they never unmasked themselves before the people. Among the simple complaints which the Falsefaces could cure infallibly, were nose bleed, toothache, swellings, and inflammation of the eyes. The false face shown in the figure was purchased of an Onondaga on Grand river.

The proneness of the Indian mind to superstitious beliefs is chiefly to be ascribed to their legendary literature. The fables which have been handed down from generation to generation, to be rehearsed to the young from year to year, would fill volumes. These fabulous tales, for exuberance of fancy, and extravagance of invention, not only surpass the fireside stories of all other people, but to their diversity and number there is apparently no limit. There were fables of a race of pigmies who dwelt within the earth, but who were endued with such herculean strength as to tear up by its roots the forest oak, and shoot it from their bows; fables of a buffalo of such huge dimensions as to thresh down the forest in his march; fables of ferocious flying-heads, winging themselves through the air; of serpents paralyzing by a look; of a monster mosquito, who thrust his bill through the bodies of his victims, and drew their blood in the twinkling of an eye. There were fables of a race of stone giants who dwelt in the north; of a monster bear, more terrific than the buffalo; of a monster lizard, more destructive than the serpent. There were tales of witches, and supernatural visitations, together with marvellous stories of personal adventure. Super-

added to the fables of this description, were legends
upon a thousand subjects, in which fact was embel-
lished with fiction. These legends entered into the
affairs of private life, and of individuals, and were
explanatory of a multitude of popular beliefs. Mingled up with this mass of fable, were their historical
traditions. This branch of their unwritten literature
is both valuable and interesting. These traditions are
remarkably tenacious of the truth, and between them
all there is a striking harmony of facts. Any one
who takes occasion to compare parts of these traditions with concurrent history, will be surprised at
their accuracy, whether the version be from the Oneida,
the Onondaga, the Seneca, or the Mohawk. The
embellishments gained by their transmission from hand
to hand are usually separable from the substance, and
the latter is entitled to credence. With these fables,
legends and traditions the Indian youth was familiar-
ized from infancy. His mind became stored and
crowded with bewildering fictions. Without books,
and without employment, in the intervals between
the hunt, the council, and the warlike expedition, the
mind naturally fell back upon this unwritten literature
of the wilderness. The rehearsal of these marvellous
tales furnished the chief entertainment at the fireside
in the Indian village, and also at the lodge far hid
in the depths of the forest. The credulity of youth
would know no limits, when the narrator himself
credited the tale he was relating. Growing into manhood under such intellectual influences, the young
warrior would not readily discriminate between that
which was too marvellous for belief and that which

was consistent with truth, but would adopt the whole as equally veritable. That early and constant familiarity with such a mass of uncorrected fancies should beget a permanent tendency of mind to fall into superstitious beliefs, is far less surprising than would be an exemption from all such delusions.

From a vague and indefinable dread, these fables were never related in the summer season, when the imagination was peculiarly susceptible. As soon as the buds had opened on the trees, these stories were hushed, and their historical traditions substituted. But when the leaves began to fall, their rehearsal again furnished the chief amusement of the hours of leisure in Indian society.

The immortality of the soul was another of the fixed beliefs of the Iroquois. This notion has prevailed generally among all the red races, under different forms, and with different degrees of distinctness. " The happy home beyond the setting sun," had cheered the heart, and lighted the expiring eye of the Indian, before the ships of Columbus had borne the cross to this western world. This sublime conclusion is another of those truths, written, as it were, by the Deity, in the mind of man, and one easily to be deciphered from the page of nature by unperverted reason. This truth has always been taught among the Iroquois, as a fundamental article of faith.

In connection with the immortality of the soul, must be placed their belief in future punishments. This is maintained to have been a part of their ancient faith, but with how much truth it is difficult to determine. It is now taught by the unchristianized portion of the Iroquois, as an essential part of their belief.

The worship of the Iroquois, it is believed, has undergone no important change for centuries. It is the same, in all respects, at this day, that it was at the commencement of their intercourse with the whites. But their faith appears to have suffered some enlargement. They seem to have silently adopted such thoughts of the missionaries as could be interwoven harmoniously with their own creed, while at the same time they firmly and constantly excluded all those beliefs which were inconsistent with their own religious system, as a whole. The principal illustration of this position is to be found in their present views of the nature and office of punishment. They believe that the wicked, after death, pass into the dark realm of *Hä-ne-go-ate'-geh*, there to undergo a process of punishment for their evil deeds. Those who are not consumed by the degree of punishment inflicted, are, after this purification, translated to the abode of the Great Spirit, and to eternal felicity. Evil deeds in this life are neutralized by meritorious acts. After the balance is struck between them, if the good predominate, the spirit passes direct to *Hä-wen-ne'-yu-geh*; but if the bad overbalance, it goes at once to *Hä-nis-ha-o-no'-geh*, the dwelling-place of the Evil-minded, where punishments are meted out to it in proportion to the magnitude of its offences. Certain crimes, like those of witchcraft and murder, were punished eternally, but others temporarily. The resemblance between this system of punishment and the purgatory of the Catholic church leads to the inference, that they derived from the Jesuits some of their ideas of the nature and office of punishment, and of its limitations. While, therefore, the Iroquois may have obtained more systematic and enlarged views upon these subjects from without, at the same time, as they affirm, they may always have believed that the wicked were excluded from heaven, and sent to a place of infelicity. Their traditions tend to establish a belief in future punishments, as a tenet of their ancient faith.

There is another practice, now universal among the Iroquois, which appears still more decisively to be of Jesuit origin. It is the confession of sins. Before each of their periodical religious festivals, there is made a general and public confession. Several days before the time designated for the festival, the people assemble by appointment, and each one in turn, who has a confession to make, rising, and taking a string of white wampum in his hand, acknowledges his faults and transgressions, and publicly professes a purpose of amendment. The white wampum is the emblem of purity and sincerity. With it he confirms and records his words. The absolution or forgiveness of sins formed no part of the motive or object in the confession. It had reference to the future conduct exclusively. One who was willing to confess a fault from a sense of religious duty, would, by the act, strengthen his mind against future temptation. This custom has prevailed so long among them, that they have lost its origin. It contains no such analogy to the practices of any Christian community as to compel us to ascribe it to external influences, but yet it has about it so much of the fragrance of Christianity, that it awakens in the mind a doubt of its Indian origin. It is by no means certain, however, but that it is one of their own primitive religious customs, under a modified form.

Reverence for the aged was also one of the precepts of the ancient faith. Among the roving tribes of the wilderness, the old and helpless were frequently abandoned, and in some cases, hurried out of existence, as an act of greater kindness than desertion. But the Iroquois, at the epoch of the formation of the League, resided in permanent villages, which afforded a refuge for the aged. One of the prominent aims of their first lawgiver, *Da-gä-no-we'-dä*, was to bind the people together by the family ties of relationship, and thus create among them an universal spirit of hospitality, and a lasting desire of social intercourse. After the establishment of the Confederacy, certainly, these practices never prevailed among the Iroquois. On the contrary, their religious teachers inculcated the duty of protecting their aged parents, as divinely enjoined. "It is the will of the Great Spirit that you reverence the aged, even though they be as helpless as infants."[1]

The obedience of children, their instruction in virtuous principles, kindness to the orphan, hospitality to all, and a common brotherhood, were among the doctrines held up for acceptance by their religious instructors. These precepts were taught as the will of the Great Spirit, and obedience to their requirements as acceptable in his sight. "If you tie up the clothes of an orphan child, the Great Spirit will notice it, and

---

[1] *Sose-ha'-wä* (Johnson).

reward you for it." "To adopt orphans, and bring them up in virtuous ways, is pleasing to the Great Spirit." "If a stranger wander about your abode, welcome him to your home, be hospitable towards him, speak to him with kind words, and forget not always to mention the Great Spirit." [1]

Respect for the dead was another element of their faith. At various periods of their history, it has manifested itself under different and very singular forms. The burial customs of every people interest the mind. Death is the great catastrophe of humanity. And whether man has reached the highest intellectual elevation, or still sits beside the forest streamlet, in the infancy of his mental growth, this event seizes upon his mind with solemn and absorbing earnestness. With the Iroquois different customs have prevailed, in relation to the mode of burial. At one period they buried in a sitting posture, with the face to the east. Skeletons are still found in this position, in various parts of the State, with a gun barrel resting against the shoulder; thus fixing the period of their sepulture subsequent to the first intercourse of this people with the whites. It is supposed that this custom was abandoned at the persuasion of the missionaries, although there is a tradition ascribing it to a different cause. Another and more extraordinary mode of burial anciently prevailed among them. The body of the deceased was exposed upon a bark scaffolding, erected upon poles, or secured upon the limbs of trees, where it was left to waste to a skeleton. After this had been effected by the process of decomposition in the open air, the bones were re-

[1] Johnson.

moved, either to the former house of the deceased, or to a small bark house by its side, prepared for their reception. In this manner the skeletons of the whole family were preserved from generation to generation, by the filial or parental affection of the living. After the lapse of a number of years, or in a season of public insecurity, or on the eve of abandoning a settlement, it was customary to collect these skeletons from the whole community around, and consign them to a common resting-place. To this custom, which was not confined to the Iroquois, is doubtless to be ascribed the barrows and bone mounds which have been found in such numbers in various parts of the country. On opening these mounds, the skeletons are usually found arranged in horizontal layers, a conical pyramid, those in each layer radiating from a common centre. In other cases they are found placed promiscuously.[1]

The religious system of the Iroquois taught that it was a journey from earth to heaven of many days' duration. Originally, it was supposed to be a year, and the period of mourning for the departed was fixed at that term. At its expiration, it was customary for the relatives of the deceased to hold a feast; the soul of the departed having reached heaven, and a state of felicity, there was no longer any cause for mourning. The spirit of grief was exchanged for that of rejoicing. In modern times the mourning period has been reduced to ten days, and the journey of the spirit is now

[1] There are Senecas now residing at Tonawanda and Cattaraugus, who remember having seen, about sixty years ago, at the latter place, these bark scaffoldings, on which bodies were then exposed. The custom still prevails among the Sioux upon the upper Mississippi, and among some of the tribes in the far west.

believed to be performed in three. The spirit of the
deceased was supposed to hover around the body for a
season, before it took its final departure; and not until after the expiration of a year according to the ancient
belief, and ten days according to the present, did it
become permanently at rest in heaven. A beautiful
custom prevailed in ancient times, of capturing a bird,
and freeing it over the grave on the evening of the
burial, to bear away the spirit to its heavenly rest.
Their notions of the state of the soul when disem-
bodied, are vague and diversified; but they all agree
that, during the journey, it required the same nourish-
ment as while it dwelt in the body. They, therefore,
deposited beside the deceased his bow and arrows,
tobacco and pipe, and necessary food for the journey.
They also painted the face and dressed the body in its
best apparel. A fire was built upon the grave at night,
to enable the spirit to prepare its food. With these
tokens of affliction, and these superstitious concernments for the welfare of the deceased, the children of
the forest performed the burial rites of their departed
kindred.[1] The wail and the lamentation evidenced the
passionate character of their grief.[2] After the mourn-

[1] To this universal custom of the red race, of depositing the valuable
articles of the deceased by his side, as well as utensils and vessels to prepare and contain his food, we are indebted for all the relics we possess of
the earlier epochs of our aboriginal history. Articles are still disentombed from the soil from year to year, some of which reach back to
the era of the Mound Builders.

[2] In ancient times, the practice prevailed of addressing the dead before
burial, under the belief that they could hear, although unable to answer.
The near relatives and friends, or such as were disposed, approached the
body in turn; and after the wail had ceased, they addressed it in a pa-
thetic or laudatory speech. The practice has not even yet fallen entirely

ing period had expired, the name of the deceased was never mentioned, from a sense of delicacy to the tender feelings of his friends.

Unless the rites of burial were performed, it was believed that the spirits of the dead wandered for a time upon the earth, in a state of great unhappiness. Hence their extreme solicitude to procure the bodies of their slain in battle.

Heaven was the abode of the Great Spirit, the final home of the faithful. They believed there was a road down from heaven to every man's door. On this invisible way, the soul ascended in its heavenly flight until it reached its celestial habitation. As

into disuse. The following address of an Iroquois mother over the body of her son was made on a recent occasion. Approaching his inanimate remains to look upon him for the last time, her grief for some moments was uncontrollable. Presently, her wailing ceased, and she thus addressed him : "My son, listen once more to the words of thy mother. Thou wert brought into life with her pains. Thou wert nourished with her life. She has attempted to be faithful in raising thee up. When thou wert young, she loved thee as her life. Thy presence has been a source of great joy to her. Upon thee she depended for support and comfort in her declining days. She had ever expected to gain the end of the path of life before thee. But thou hast outstripped her, and gone before her. Our great and wise Creator has ordered it thus. By his will I am left to taste more of the miseries of this world. Thy friends and relatives have gathered about thy body, to look upon thee for the last time. They mourn, as with one mind, thy departure from among us. We, too, have but a few days more, and our journey shall be ended. We part now, and you are conveyed from our sight. But we shall soon meet again, and shall again look upon each other. Then we shall part no more. Our Maker has called you to his home. Thither will we follow. *Na-ho'.*" After this was over, the wail continued for a few moments, when the body was borne away. The above was furnished to the author by *Hä-sa-no-an'-da* (Ely S. Parker), who heard it delivered. See also a specimen of an address to the dead in La Hontan's Voy. North Am. Lond. ed. 1735, vol. ii. p. 54.

before observed, the spirit was supposed to linger for a time about the body, and perhaps to revisit it. In consequence of this belief, a superstitious custom prevailed of leaving a slight opening in the grave, through which it might reënter its former tenement. To this day, among a portion of the Iroquois, after the body has been deposited in a coffin, holes are bored through it for the same purpose. After taking its final departure, the soul was supposed to ascend higher and higher on its heavenly way, gradually moving to the westward, until it came out upon the plains of heaven.

The inhabitants of this sinless dwelling-place of *Hä-wen-ne'-yu* were believed to possess a body, and the senses, appetites and affections of the earthly life. They carried their knowledge with them, and the memory of former friends. Sex was in effect abolished, but families were reunited, and dwelt together in perpetual harmony. All the powers of the Indian imagination were taxed to picture the glowing beauties of their celestial home. It was fashioned to please the natural senses. A vast plain of illimitable extension, it was spread out with every variety of natural scenery which could please the eye, or gratify the fancy. Forests clothed with ever-living foliage, flowers of every hue in eternal bloom, fruits of every variety in perpetual ripeness, in a word, the meridian charms of nature met the eye in every direction. To form a paradise of unrivalled beauty, the Great Spirit had gathered every object in the natural world which could delight the senses, and having spread them out in vast but harmonious array, and restored their baptismal vestments, he diffused over these congregated beauties of nature the bloom of immortality. In this happy abode, they were destined to enjoy unending felicity. No evil could enter this peaceful home of innocence and purity. No violence could disturb, no passions ruffle the tranquillity of this fortunate realm. In amusement or repose they spent their lives. The festivities in which they had delighted while on the earth were re-celebrated in the presence of the great Author of their being. They enjoyed all the happiness of the earthly life, unencumbered by its ills.

With the Iroquois, heaven was not regarded as a "hunting ground," as it appears to have been by some Indian nations. Subsistence had ceased to be necessary. When the faithful partook of the spontaneous fruits around them, it was for the gratification of the taste, and not for the support of life.

Among the modern beliefs engrafted upon the ancient faith, there is one which is worthy of particular notice. It relates to Washington.[1] According to their present belief, no white man ever reached the Indian heaven. Not having been created by the Great Spirit, no provision was made for him in their scheme of theology. He was excluded both from heaven and from the place of punishment. But an exception was made in favor of Washington. Because of his justice and benevolence to the Indian, he stood preëminent above all other white men. When, by the peace of 1783, the Indians were abandoned by

---

[1] His name among the Iroquois was *Hä-no-dä-gä'-ne-ars,* which signifies "Town Destroyer."

their English allies, and left to make their own terms with the American government, the Iroquois were more exposed to severe measures than the other tribes in their alliance. At this critical moment, Washington interfered in their behalf, as the protector of Indian rights, and the advocate of a policy towards them of the most enlightened justice and humanity. After his death, he was mourned by the Iroquois as a benefactor of their race, and his memory was cherished with reverence and affection. A belief was spread abroad among them, that the Great Spirit had received him into a celestial residence upon the plains of heaven, the only white man whose noble deeds had entitled him to this heavenly favor. Just by the entrance of heaven is a walled enclosure, the ample grounds within which are laid out with avenues and shaded walks. Within is a spacious mansion, constructed in the fashion of a fort. Every object in nature which could please a cultivated taste had been gathered in this blooming Eden, to render it a delightful dwelling-place for the immortal Washington. The faithful Indian, as he enters heaven, passes this enclosure. He sees and recognizes the illustrious inmate, as he walks to and fro in quiet meditation. But no word ever passes his lips. Dressed in his uniform, and in a state of perfect felicity, he is destined to remain through eternity in the solitary enjoyment of the celestial residence prepared for him by the Great Spirit.

Surely the piety and the gratitude of the Iroquois have, jointly, reared a monument to Washington above the skies, which is more expressive in its praise than the proudest recitals on the obelisk, and more imperishable in its duration than the syenite which holds up the record to the gaze of centuries.

The beliefs of our primitive inhabitants, when brought together in a connected form, naturally call forth an expression of surprise. A faith so purely spiritual, so free from the tincture of human passion, and from the grossness of superstition, can scarcely be credited, when examined under the ordinary estimate of the Indian character. It has been the misfortune of the Indian never to be rightly understood, especially in his social relations. Their religious and moral sentiments, such as they were, exercised as decisive an influence upon Indian society, as the precepts of Christianity do over enlightened communities. They furnished springs of action, rules of intercourse, and powers of restraint. And yet, where is the picture of Indian social life which reveals the domestic virtues, the generous friendships, the integrity between man and man, the harmony of intercourse, and the sympathies of the heart, which bloomed and flourished in the depths of the forest? We have met the red man upon the war-path, and not at the fireside. We have dealt with him as his oppressor, and not as his friend. His evil traits, ever present with the mind, form the standard of judgment ; and when his virtues rise up before us, they create surprise, rather than answer expectation, because the standard of estimation is universally unjust.

The mind of the Iroquois was deeply imbued with religious sentiments, the practical results, the actual fruits of which, unseen for the most part, by those who know the Indian only in his intercourse with the whites, reveal themselves in unexpected beauty, when we examine his social relations, and view him in his domestic life. Their influence upon the Iroquois, in their intercourse with other nations, is necessarily secondary. To judge of their religious system from its direct effects, it is necessary to look into Indian society itself. Here its primary influence, at least, must fall. It would be a grateful task to array the virtues, which sprang into existence in the seclusions of the wilderness, to light up the character of the red man. From the harmony which characterized their political relations under the League, down to the domestic quiet of the sylvan home, the picture is much the same. Peace, hospitality, charity, friendship, harmony, integrity, religious enthusiasm, the domestic affections, found a generous growth and cultivation among the Iroquois. Genius, learning, and Christianity change the features of society, and cast over it an artificial garment, but its elements continue the same. It need not awaken surprise that the Indian has rivalled many of the highest virtues of civilized and christianized man; or that in some of the rarest traits in the human character, he has passed quite beyond him.

Whatever excellences the Iroquois character possessed are to be ascribed, in a great measure, to their beliefs, and above all, to their unfailing faith in the Great Spirit. By adhering to that sublime but simple truth, that there was one Supreme Being, who created and preserved them, they not only escaped an idolatrous worship, but they imbibed a more ennobling and spiritual faith than has fallen to the lot of any other unchristianized people.

Chapter II

THE Iroquois had a systematic worship. It consisted in the celebration of periodical festivals, which were held at stated seasons of the year. These observances were suggested by the changes in the seasons, the ripening of the fruits, and the gathering of the harvest. They were performed annually, with the same established ceremonies, which had been handed down from age to age. The worship of the Iroquois, as before remarked, has undergone no change in centuries. It is still the same, in all essential particulars, that it was at the period of their discovery. Some slight additions, ascribable, doubtless, to missionary instructions, will be detected, but they are too inconsiderable to change the form, or disturb the harmony of the whole. Upon an examination of the principal features of the system, it will become apparent that it was chiefly a thanksgiving worship, although the supplication of the Great Spirit for the continuance of his protection entered into it as an essential element.

Six regular festivals, or thanksgivings, were observed by the Iroquois. The first, in the order of time, was the Maple festival. This was a return of thanks to the maple itself, for yielding its sweet waters. Next was the Planting festival, designed, chiefly, as an invocation of the Great Spirit to bless the seed. Third came the Strawberry festival, instituted as a thanksgiving for the first fruits of the earth. The fourth was the Green Corn festival, designed as a thanksgiving acknowledgment for the ripening of the corn, beans and squashes. Next was celebrated the Harvest festival, instituted as a general thanksgiving to " Our Supporters," after the gathering of the harvest. Last in the enumeration is placed the New Year's festival, the great jubilee of the Iroquois, at which the white dog was sacrificed.

The principle involved in the formal worship of the Great Spirit at stated periods, and the fidelity with which the Iroquois, in prosperity and in adversity, adhered to these observances from generation to generation, are of much more importance in forming a judgment of their religious sentiments than the mere ceremonies themselves. In this constant recognition of their dependence upon the divine power, there is much to awaken a feeling of sympathy and a sentiment of respect for a people who, untaught by revelation, had reached such high conclusions. By assembling at periodical seasons to render their thanks to *Hä-wen-ne'-yu* for his gifts, they fully recognized the duty which rested upon them as the recipients of such favors. And, also, by supplicating the continuance of his watchful care, and by invoking his blessing upon their present acts, they manifested the sincerity of their faith, and the fulness

of their trust in the great Author of their being.
But the ceremonies themselves are not without a
peculiar interest. They will convey to the mind a
more distinct impression of the nature and simplicity
of their worship. No attempt will be made to describe these observances with the minuteness of a
picture. An outline of those appropriate to each
festival will sufficiently illustrate their general character and purpose.

The question here presents itself as to the religious
office or priesthood among the Iroquois. Under
the League itself no sacerdotal office was recognized.
Sachems were raised up, and invested with their titles
by a council of all the sachems of the League. Chiefs
were first raised up in the nation to which they belonged, and their title was afterwards confirmed by the
same general council. But no religious dignitaries
were ever raised up by the council of sachems to fill
any priestly station. In each nation, however, there
was a select class appointed by the several tribes to
take the charge of their religious festivals, and the
general supervision of their worship. They were
styled *Ho-nun-de'-ont*, or " Keepers of the Faith," as
the term literally signifies. In the election of this
class, their powers and duties, and the tenure of their
office, there are many circumstances to distinguish
them as a sacerdotal order. To their number
there was no limit, and they were usually about as
numerous as the chiefs. The chiefs themselves were
ex officio keepers of the faith. The office was
elective, and continued as long as the individual was
faithful to his trust. Suitable persons were selected

by the wise men and matrons out of their respective
tribes, and advanced to the office. Their original
names were then taken away, and new ones assigned,
out of a collection of names which belonged to this
class. At the first subsequent council of the nation,
their appointment and names were publicly announced, which in itself completed the investiture.
The number furnished by each tribe was an evidence
of its fidelity to the ancient faith. They were, to
some extent, censors of the people; and their admonitions were received with kindness, as coming
from those commissioned to remonstrate. In some
cases they reported the evil deeds of individuals to
the council, to make of them an example by exposure.
Sometimes they held consultations to deliberate upon
the moral condition of the people. It was the duty
of every individual to accept the office when bestowed; but he could relinquish it at any moment by
laying aside his new name and resuming his old.[68]
It was their duty to designate the times for holding the periodical festivals, to make the necessary
arrangements for their celebration, and to conduct the
ceremonies. Certain ones of their number, by previous appointment, made the opening speech, and the
thanksgiving address at the council, and also delivered
religious discourses whenever they were deemed advisable. All of the members of this class were equal in
authority and privileges. Those animated by the
highest zeal and enthusiasm would naturally assume
the most active charge; but they had no acknowledged head. The distribution of all powers, duties
and offices among a number of equals was the pre-

vailing feature of their civil polity. It was necessary that women as well as men should be appointed keepers of the faith, and about in equal numbers. To the matrons more particularly was intrusted the charge of the feast. The Iroquois never held a mourning or religious council, without preparing an entertainment for all the· people in attendance on the evening of each day. None but those matrons who were keepers of the faith could take any part in its preparation. But their duties were not confined to the supervision of the feast. They had an equal voice in the general management of the festivals, and of all of their religious concernments. During a discourse or address, all the keepers of the faith acted, if necessary, as prompters to the speaker, and through him communicated to the people any injunction or precept which they deemed advisable. For this .reason, one of their names as a class was that of "prompters."

Notwithstanding the systematic organization of the keepers of the faith, and the precise limitation of their duties, there do not seem to be sufficient reasons for calling this class a religious order, or a priesthood, as these terms are usually understood. They were distinguished by no special privileges, except while in the act of discharging their prescribed duties; they wore no costume, or emblem of office, to separate them from the people. In fact they were common warriors, and common women, and, in every sense, of and among the people. The office was one of necessity, and was without reward, like all Indian offices of every name, and also without particular honor to the individual.

O-TÄ-DE-NONE'-NE-O NA WÄ'-TA; OR, THANKS TO THE MAPLE

This was the first festival of the spring. It was usually called the Maple Dance. The primary idea of this ceremonial was to return thanks to the maple itself; but at the same time they rendered their thanks to the Great Spirit for the gift of the maple. It lasted but one day. When the sap began to flow, the keepers of the faith announced the time and place for commemorating the recurrence of this event, and summoned the people to assemble for that purpose. Some days before the time appointed for the festival, the people assembled for the mutual confession of their sins, both as an act of religious duty, and as a preparation for the council. This act preceded all the festivals; but it was more general and thorough at the three last than at the three first, as they were deemed more important, and continued for a greater length of time. This council, *Sa-nun-dät-ha-wä'-ta*, literally " a meeting for repentance," was opened by one of the keepers of the faith, with an address upon the propriety and importance of acknowledging their evil deeds, to strengthen their minds against future temptations. He then took the string of white wampum in his hand, and set the example by a confession of his own faults; after which he handed the string to the one nearest to him, who received it, made his confession in like manner, and passed it to another. In this way the wampum went around from hand to hand; and those who had confessions to make stated wherein they had done wrong, and promised to do better in the future. Old and young, men, women, and even children all united in this public acknowledgment of their faults, and joined in the common resolution of amendment. On some occasions the string of wampum was placed in the centre of the room, and each one advanced in turn to perform the duty, as the inclination seized him. A confession and promise without holding the wampum would be of no avail. It was the wampum which recorded their words, and gave their pledge of sincerity. The object of the confession was future amendment. The Iroquois appear to have had no idea either of the atonement or of the forgiveness of sins. Meritorious acts neutralized evil deeds, but neither the one nor the other, when done, could be recalled, or changed, or obliterated.

The celebration of this festival was not limited to one particular place, but it was observed in all the villages of the several nations of the League, which were too remote to unite around the same council-fire. At the time appointed, the people gathered from the subjacent districts, some to offer religious admonitions, some prepared for the dance, others for the games, and still others for the enjoyment of the feast. It was one of their festive days, awakening the eagerness of expectation in the minds of all. On the morning of the day, the matrons, to whom the duty appertained, commenced the preparation of the customary feast for the people, which was as sumptuous as the season and the means of the hunter life would afford. Towards meridian, the out-door sports and games, which were common to such occasions, were suspended, and the people assembled in council. An opening speech was then delivered, by one of the keepers of the faith. The following, made at the opening of one of these councils among the Senecas, is in the usual form, and will illustrate their general character : —

" Friends and Relatives : — The sun, the ruler of the day, is high in his path, and we must hasten to do our duty. We are assembled to observe an ancient custom. It is an institution handed down to us by our forefathers. 'It was given to them by the Great Spirit. He has ever required of his people to return thanks to him for all blessings received. We have always endeavored to live faithful to this wise command.

" Friends and Relatives, continue to listen : — It is to perform this duty that we are this day gathered. The season when the maple tree yields its sweet waters has again returned. We are all thankful that it is so. We therefore expect all of you to join in our general thanksgiving to the maple. We also expect you to join in a thanksgiving to the Great Spirit, who has wisely made this tree for the good of man. We hope and expect that order and harmony will prevail.

" Friends and Relatives : — We are gratified to see so many here, and we thank you all that you have thought well of this matter. We thank the Great Spirit, that he has been kind to so many of us, in sparing our lives to participate again in the festivities of this season. *Na-ho'.*" [1]

Other speeches often followed, which were in the nature of exhortations to duty. These occasions were seized upon by their moral teachers, to inculcate anew the precepts of their faith, and to offer admonitions for their spiritual guidance. One of the keepers of

[1] It is almost the universal custom among the Iroquois to conclude their speeches, on all occasions, with this exclamation. It signifies simply, "I have done."

the faith, addressing the people at such a time, would inculcate the virtues which became a warrior, and unfold the duties which were incumbent upon them as members of one common brotherhood. The duty of living in harmony and peace, of avoiding evil speaking, of kindness to the orphan, of charity to the needy, and of hospitality to all, would be among the prominent topics brought under consideration. He would remind them that the Great Spirit noticed and rewarded good acts, and that those who hoped for success in the affairs of life, should be ready to do them whenever occasion offered ; that those who had done wrong should not be treated harshly; that enmities were not to be contracted, lest a spirit of revenge should be awakened, which would never sleep ; and finally, that those who pursued the right path would never fall into trouble.

When these speeches and exhortations were concluded, the dance, which was a prominent feature of their religious festivals, was announced. It is proper here to observe, that dancing was regarded by the Iroquois as an appropriate mode of worship. They regarded the dance as a perpetual outward ceremonial of thanksgiving to the Great Spirit. A belief prevailed among them that the custom was of divine origin. " The Great Spirit knew the Indian could not live without some amusement, therefore he originated the idea of dancing, which he gave to them." [1] The dance set apart in a peculiar manner for the worship of the Great Spirit, at their festivals, was one of their

---

[1] *Sose-ha'-wä* (Johnson).

own invention; and the most spirited, graceful and beautiful in their list. It is known as the Great Feather Dance (*O-sto-weh'-go-wä*). It was performed by a select band, in full costume, and was reserved exclusively for religious councils and for great occasions. It lasted about an hour, never failing to arouse a deep spirit of enthusiastic excitement. Before the band came in, one of the keepers of the faith made a brief speech, explanatory of its origin, nature and objects; in which the popular belief was interwoven, that this dance would be enjoyed by the faithful in the future life, in the realm of the Great Spirit, to whose worship it was especially consecrated.

After the conclusion of this dance others followed, in which all participated. Before they were ended, the usual thanksgiving address to the Great Spirit, with the burning of tobacco, was made. In ancient times the Maple festival was terminated with these dances. One of the keepers of the faith made a closing speech, after which the people partook of the feast, and separated for their respective homes.

There is a popular belief among the Iroquois that the early part of the day is dedicated to the Great Spirit, and the after part to the spirits of the dead ; consequently their religious services should properly be concluded at meridian. They still retain the theory, and to this day religious discourses are seldom continued after noon ; but in practice it was found impossible, from the tardiness of the people in assembling, to conclude the ceremonies of the festival before twilight. A further innovation was made many years ago by

GA-KA-AH OR KILT.

devoting the evenings of these festive days to dancing, for the entertainment of guests from other villages or nations, who chanced to be with them. This became, in time, the universal custom, and they now continue the practice for their own amusement. These evening entertainments, however, in strictness, form no part of the festival, although apparently it is one proceeding from the opening of the council until late at night, when the entertainment is ended. A distinction should constantly be held in view, between their proper religious exercises, and their amusements, and also between the ancient mode of celebrating these festivals, and the modern. The regular religious ceremonies at the Maple festival consisted of the opening discourse by one of the keepers of the faith, the exhortations of others, the Feather dance, the thanksgiving address to the Great Spirit, with the incense of tobacco, two or three other dances, the closing speech, and the feast in common.

In ancient times these ceremonies were concluded at meridian, but in modern times at twilight. Formerly all the exercises at these festivals were of a strictly religious character, except certain games which were common to these occasions. But in later times other dances have been added, and also an evening entertainment devoted exclusively to dancing. There were likewise certain games of chance, sports, and athletic games, common to all these festivals, which yet formed no part of their religious ceremonies. They were merely outside diversions for the people. Still the Maple festival, as celebrated at the present day among the descendants of the ancient Iroquois, is

the same, in its essential features, as at the period
of its institution.[1]

A-YENT'-WÄ-TÄ; OR, PLANTING FESTIVAL

This word signifies "the planting season." When
this time arrived another festival was held to celebrate
the event. It continued but one day. In its observances there was nothing to distinguish it very materially
from the Maple festival. A description is therefore
unnecessary, except to point out some peculiarities.
The object of this festival was two-fold: to render
thanks to the Great Spirit for the return of the planting
season, and to invoke his blessing upon the seed which
they had committed to the earth, that it might yield
an abundant harvest.

The Indian had no Sabbath, no sacred writings to
furnish him an inexhaustible fountain of instruction;
but his gratitude was awakened by every returning
manifestation of divine goodness. When nature had
reclothed herself in the vestments of spring, and the
teeming earth invited him to commit the seeds to her
bosom, he recognized in the event the watchful kindness
of the Great Spirit. There is something eminently
spiritual and beautiful in this Indian conception of
the natural periods of worship. Seizing upon the
moment when the most conspicuous evidences of the
protecting care of the Deity were before him, he acknowledged both his existence and his beneficence,

---

[1] The Iroquois have long been in the habit of manufacturing sugar from
the maple. Whether they learned the art from us, or we from them, may
be a difficult question; although the former would seem the more probable, from the want of suitable vessels among them for boiling.

and manifested, at the same time, his gratitude and devotion, by those simple rites which the piety of his heart suggested.

At the time appointed by the keepers of the faith, the people assembled to observe the day. After the speeches were over, the Feather and other dances were performed, as at the Maple festival. In ancient times, the thanksgiving address, or prayer to the Great Spirit, with the burning of tobacco, was confined to the last three, or the principal festivals ; but in later days such a prayer was offered generally at the first three also. As elsewhere observed, when the Iroquois returned thanks to the various objects in nature which ministered to their wants, or when they acknowledged to each other their thankfulness to the Great Spirit, or to the lesser Spirits, they never burned tobacco. In these cases, their thanks were returned to the trees and plants and elements direct, to do which, according to their theology, did not require the use of incense, while, as to the spiritual world, they merely avowed to each other that they returned their thanks. But when they offered a prayer, or called upon the Great Spirit, or his Invisible Aids, they were obliged to use the ascending smoke to put themselves in communication with the spiritual world.

This address occurred at no particular stage in the ceremonies of the day. The keepers of the faith having appointed one of their number to perform this duty, the person designated selected a suitable moment for its delivery. Advancing to the fire prepared for the purpose, he called the attention of the people by an exclamation, which was the known precursor of this address. Having sprinkled a few leaves of Indian tobacco upon the fire, he addressed *Hä-wen-ne'-yu*, as the smoke ascended. The following, delivered at a Planting festival among the Senecas, will illustrate the general character of these prayers or thanksgiving addresses : —

"Great Spirit, who dwellest alone, listen now to the words of thy people here assembled. The smoke of our offering arises. Give kind attention to our words, as they arise to thee in the smoke. We thank thee for this return of the planting season. Give to us a good season, that our crops may be plentiful.

"Continue to listen, for the smoke yet arises. (Throwing on tobacco.) Preserve us from all pestilential diseases. Give strength to us all that we may not fall. Preserve our old men among us, and protect the young. Help us to celebrate with feeling the ceremonies of this season. Guide the minds of thy people, that they may remember thee in all their actions. *Na-ho'*."

There was nothing further to distinguish this festival from the former.

If, after the planting season, a drought should come upon the land, threatening a failure of the harvest, a special council was frequently called, to invoke *Hé'-no*, the Thunderer, to send rain upon the earth. Before the time appointed for this council, the people assembled, as before other festivals, for mutual confession. They feared, as they expressed it, "that some of their number had done some great wrong, for which the Great Spirit was angry with them, and withheld the rain as a merited punishment." After this special council was opened in the usual form, the Thanksgiving dance, and the *Ah-do'-weh*, hereafter to be described, were introduced, which were supposed to be peculiarly acceptable to *He'-no*.   At a proper time, in the progress of these ceremonies, the keeper of the faith, who had been appointed as usual, advanced to the fire, and having laid on the leaves of tobacco, and gained the attention of the people, he made the following invocation of the Thunderer, as the incense ascended : —

" *He'-no*, our Grandfather, listen now to the words of thy grandchildren.   We feel grieved.   Our minds are sorely troubled.   We fear Our Supporters will fail, and bring famine upon us.   We ask our Grandfather that he may come, and give us rain, that the earth may not dry up, and refuse to produce for our support.   Thy grandchildren all send their salutations to their grandfather, *He'-no*."

Then taking another handful of tobacco, and placing it upon the fire, he changed the address to *Hä-wen-ne'-yu* : —

" Great Spirit : listen to the words of thy suffering children.   They come to thee with pure minds.   If they have done wrong, they have confessed, and turned their minds, (at the same time holding up the string of white wampum with which the confession was recorded.)   Be kind to us.   Hear our grievances, and supply our wants.   Direct that *He'-no* may come, and give us rain, that Our Supporters may not fail us, and bring famine to our homes.   *Na-ho'*."

After concluding the dance the assembly was dismissed.

HA-NUN-DÄ'-YO ; OR, BERRY FESTIVAL

In the progress of the seasons, next came the Strawberry, the first fruit of the earth.   The Iroquois seized upon this spontaneous gift of nature for their sustenance, as another suitable occasion for a thanksgiving festival. By such ceremonials they habituated their minds to a recognition of the providential care of *Hä-wen-ne'-yu*; cultivating, at the same time, a grateful spirit for the constant return of his gifts. The observances at this festival were the same as those at the Maple, with a sufficient variation of terms to designate the particular occasion. It was concluded with a feast of strawberries. The berries were prepared with maple sugar, in capacious bark trays, in the form of a jelly; and in this condition the people feasted upon this great luxury of nature.

The ripening of the Whortleberry was often made the occasion of another festival. It was in all respects like the last, the only difference consisting in the fact, that the former was an acknowledgment for the first fruit of plants, and the latter for the first fruit of trees.

AH-DAKE'-WÄ-O; OR, GREEN CORN FESTIVAL

The word from which this takes its name signifies "a feast." It continued four days, the proceedings of each being different in most particulars, but each one terminating with a feast.

When the green corn became fit for use, the season of plenty with the Indian had emphatically arrived. They made it another occasion of general thanksgiving to the Great Spirit, and of feasting and rejoicing among themselves. Corn has ever been the staple article of consumption among the Iroquois. They cultivated this plant, and also the bean and the

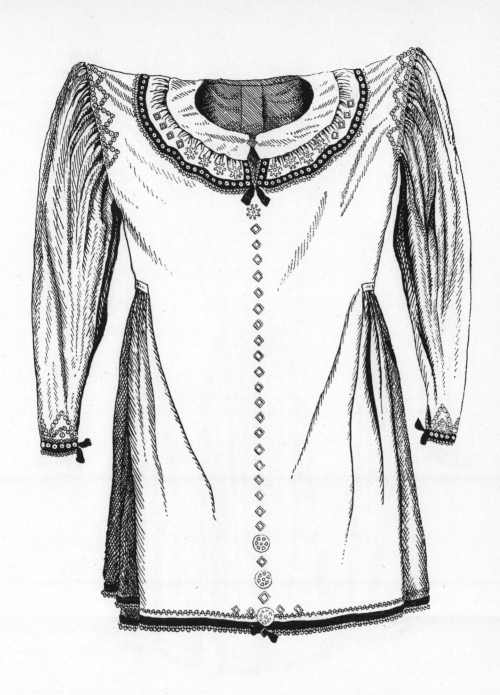

AH·DE·A·DA·WE·SÄ or OVER·DRESS
FRONT

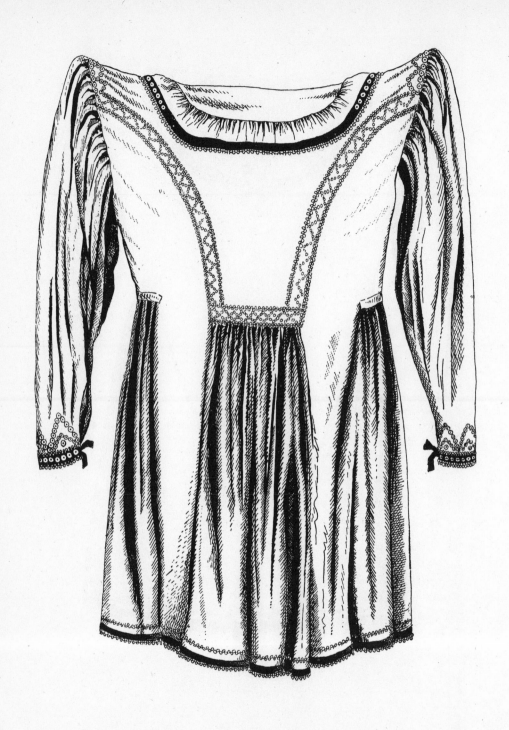

AH-DE-A-DÄ-WE-SÄ or OVER-DRESS

BACK

squash, before the formation of the League. From the most remote period to which tradition reaches, the knowledge of the cultivation and use of these plants has been handed down among them.[1] They raised sufficient quantities of each to supply their utmost wants, preparing them for food in a great variety of ways, and making them at least the basis of their sustenance. In their own mode of expressing the idea, these plants are mentioned together, under the figurative name of "Our Life," or "Our Supporters." It cannot, therefore, be affirmed with correctness, that the Indian subsisted principally by the chase. After the formation of the League, they resided in permanent villages, and within certain well-defined territorial limits. The fruits of the chase then became a secondary, although a necessary means of subsistence.[2]

On the first day of this festival, after the introductory speeches had been made, the Feather dance, the thanksgiving address, with the burning of to-

---

[1] According to the legend, the corn plant sprang from the bosom of the mother of the Great Spirit, after her burial.

[2] The quantities of corn raised by the Iroquois was a constant cause of remark among those who went earliest among them. The first expedition into the Seneca country, of a warlike character, was made by the Marquis De Nonville, as early as 1687, but a few years after the geographical location of the Iroquois nations became known to the French and English. He thus speaks of the quantity of corn: " We remained at the four Seneca villages until the 24th of July. All that time we spent in destroying the corn, which was in such great abundance, that the loss, including old corn which was in *cache* which we burnt, and that which was standing, was computed according to the estimate afterwards made, at four hundred thousand minots of Indian corn" (1,200,000 bushels). Documentary Hist. New York, vol. i. p. 238. This, however, must be regarded as an extravagant estimate.

bacco, and three or four other dances, made up the principal religious exercises. This address was introduced in the midst of one of the dances which succeeded the first. One more specimen of these brief prayers of the Iroquois, as made by the Senecas, will be furnished. Having placed the leaves of tobacco on the fire, as usual, the keeper of the faith thus addressed *Hä-wen-ne'-yu :* ——

"Great Spirit in heaven, listen to our words. We have assembled to perform a sacred duty, as thou hast commanded. This institution has descended to us from our fathers. We salute thee with our thanks, that thou hast preserved so many of us another year, to participate in the ceremonies of this occasion.

"Great Spirit, continue to listen : We thank thee for thy great goodness in causing our mother, the earth, again to bring forth her fruits. We thank thee that thou hast caused Our Supporters to yield abundantly.

"Great Spirit, our words still continue to flow towards thee. (Throwing on tobacco). Preserve us from all danger. Preserve our aged men. Preserve our mothers. Preserve our warriors. Preserve our children. We burn this tobacco; may its smoke arise to thee. May our thanks, ascending with it, be pleasing to thee. Give wisdom to the keepers of the faith, that they may direct these ceremonies with propriety. Strengthen our warriors, that they may celebrate with pleasure the sacred dances of thy appointment.

"Great Spirit; the council here assembled, the aged men and women, the strong warriors, the women and children, unite their voice of thanksgiving to thee. *Na-ho!* " [1]

[1] For a similar address in use among the Ottawas, see La Hontan's North Am., Lond. Ed. 1735, vol. ii. p. 34.

Before partaking of the feast, the people went out to witness some of those games which were often introduced, as an amusement, to accompany the other exercises of these festive days.

The second day commenced with the usual address, after which they had the Thanksgiving dance, *Gä-na'-o-uh*, which was the principal religious exercise of the day. This dance was not necessarily a costume performance, although it was usually given by a select band in full dress. In figure, step, and music, it was precisely like the Feather dance, the chief difference between them being the introduction of short thanksgiving speeches between the songs of the dance. This dance is fully explained elsewhere; but it is proper to say, to make it intelligible here, that the music consisted of a series of thanksgiving songs, performed by select singers, who accompanied themselves with turtle-shell rattles, to mark time. Each song lasted about two minutes, during which the band danced around the room, in column, with great animation. When the song ceased, the dancers walked around the council-house, about the same length of time, to the beat of the rattles. The thanksgiving speeches were made during these intervals between the songs. A person arose, and perhaps thanked the Maple as follows: "We return thanks to the Maple, which yields its sweet waters for the good of man." Again the dance was resumed, and another song danced out, after which another speech was made by some other person, perhaps as follows: "We return thanks to the bushes and trees, which provide us with fruit." The dance was then resumed as before. In this manner the thanksgiving speeches, the songs and the dance were continued, until all the prominent objects in nature had been made the subjects of special notice. There were always set speeches introduced with the Thanksgiving dance, at the Green Corn and Harvest festivals, and they formed a conspicuous part of the worship of the Iroquois. These speeches, or the principal ones, may be collected into one, for the purpose of showing the range of subjects taken; yet it must be borne in mind that each object formed the subject of a separate speech, and was followed by a thanksgiving song, adapted to the case, which the band danced through. It may be proper further to add, that these speeches were consolidated to form the principal part of the annual thanksgiving address to the Great Spirit, made at the burning of the White Dog. The following is their natural order: —

" We return thanks to our mother, the earth, which sustains us. We return thanks to the rivers and streams, which supply us with water. We return thanks to all herbs, which furnish medicines for the cure of our diseases. We return thanks to the corn, and to her sisters, the beans and squashes, which give us life. We return thanks to the bushes and trees, which provide us with fruit. We return thanks to the wind, which, moving the air, has banished diseases. We return thanks to the moon and stars, which have given to us their light when the sun was gone. We return thanks to our grandfather *He'-no*, that he has protected his grandchildren from witches and reptiles, and has given to us his rain. We return thanks to the sun, that he has looked upon the earth with a beneficent eye. Lastly, we return thanks to the Great Spirit, in whom is embodied all goodness, and who directs all things for the good of his children."

After the conclusion of the Thanksgiving dance, two or three other dances followed, and after them the feast, with which the exercises of the day were concluded.

The third morning was set apart for a thanksgiving concert, called the *Ah-do'-weh*, which constituted the chief ceremony of the day. The council was opened by an introductory speech by one of the keepers of the faith, upon its nature, objects, and institution. This novelty in their worship was a succession of short speeches made by different persons, one after another, returning thanks to a great variety of objects, each one following his speech with an appropriate song, the words of which were of his own composing, and often-times the music also. In a chorus to each song all the people joined, thus sending forth a united anthem of praise. They passed through the whole range of natural objects, thanking each one directly, as in the Thanksgiving dance; but they were not in the *Ah-do'-weh* confined either to the natural or to the spirit-ual world. Acts of kindness, personal achievements, political events, in a word, all the affairs of public and private life were open on this occasion to the indul-gence of the grateful affections. Oftentimes one or two hours were consumed, before the people had all expressed their thanks to each other for personal favors, to the works of nature for their constant min-istration to their wants, and to the Great Spirit and

the " Invisible Aids " for their protecting care. Many
of the speeches on these occasions, especially those
which referred to objects in the natural world, were
the same from year to year. But those which grew
out of their private relations would vary with circumstances. This was esteemed one of their highest religious exercises, and it always continued to be one of
their favorite observances. When the *Ah-do'-weh*
was concluded, two or three dances were generally
introduced before the enjoyment of the feast, with
which, as before remarked, each day's proceedings
were terminated.

On the fourth day, the festival was concluded with
the peach-stone game, *Gus-gä'-a*, a game of chance, on
which they bet profusely, and to which they were extravagantly attached. It was not in the nature of a
religious exercise, but a favorite entertainment, with
which to terminate the Green Corn ceremonial. It is
elsewhere described.

It should be held in the memory, that at the period
of the institution of their religious festivals, they were
concluded at meridian; during the middle period of
their history, they were continued until towards twilight; but in modern times, an evening entertainment,
in the way of dancing, always follows each day of the
festival, so long as it continues, although it forms no
part of their religious observances. It may be further
observed, that at the present time, this festival lasts
but three days, the proceedings of the third and fourth
being completed on the former day.

At the close of each day, the people regaled themselves upon a sumptuous feast of succotash. This

was always the entertainment at the green corn season. It was made of corn, beans and squashes, and was always a favorite article of food with the red man. It may be well to state in this connection, that among the Iroquois at the present day, they do not sit down together to a common repast, except at religious councils of unusual interest. The feast, after being prepared at the place of council, is distributed at its close, and carried by the women, in vessels brought for the purpose, to their respective homes, where it is enjoyed by each family at their own fireside. But when the people feasted together after the ancient fashion, as they still do occasionally, they selected the hour of twilight. The huge kettles of soup, or hommony, or succotash, as the case might be, were brought into their midst, smoking from the fire. Before partaking of this evening banquet, they never omitted to say grace, which, with them, was a simple ceremonial, but in perfect harmony with their mode of worship. It was a prolonged exclamation, upon a high key, by the solitary voice of one of the keepers of the faith, followed by a swelling chorus from the multitude, upon a lower note. It was designed as an acknowledgment to each other of their gratitude to the great Giver of the feast.

DA-YO-NUN'-NEO-QUÄ NA DE-O-HA'-KO; OR, HARVEST FESTIVAL

After the gathering of the harvest, the Iroquois held another general thanksgiving for four days. It was the last in the year, as the New Year's observances were not of the same general character. The name given to this festival signifies "Thanksgiving to Our Supporters." It was instituted primarily to return thanks to the corn, beans and squashes, which are always characterized by the Iroquois under this figurative name. Also, to the triad of Spirits, who are so intimately connected in their minds with the plants themselves, that they are nearly inseparable. The resulting object, however, of all these Indian rites, was the praise of *Hä-wen-ne'-yu*. Nature having matured and poured forth her stores for their sustenance, they instituted this ceremonial as a perpetual acknowledgment of their gratitude for each returning harvest.

In the mode of summoning this council, and in the religious ceremonies, and concluding festivities of each day, it so closely resembled the Green Corn worship, that a separate description is rendered unnecessary.

These religious councils were seasons of animation and excitement. The greater activity in social intercourse among the people, generally awakened by these ceremonies and festivities, contributed largely to keep up the spirit of these occasions. In the evening, as soon as the twilight hour was passed, the people gathered for the dance, as this entertainment, since the innovation before referred to, always follows the religious ceremonies of each day. The Iroquois have numerous dances, and to the practice itself they have always been extravagantly addicted. On such occasions the passion was gratified by a free indulgence, and the hours of the night passed by unheeded. With the Iroquois in their festivities, as with more refined communities, neither the admonition of the setting stars,

nor of the fallen dew, "counselled sleep." Not, perhaps, until the faint light of approaching day illumined
the east, did the spirit of enjoyment decline, and the
last murmur of the dispersing council finally subside.

GI'-YE-WÄ-NO-US-QUÄ-GO-WÄ ; OR, NEW YEAR'S JUBILEE

The name given to this festival literally signifies
"The most excellent faith," or "The supreme belief."[1]

Among the ceremonies incident to the worship of
the Iroquois, the most novel were those which ushered
in the new year. In mid-winter, usually about the
first of February, this religious celebration was held.
It continued for seven successive days, revealing, in
its various ceremonials, nearly every feature of their
religious system. The prominent act which characterized this jubilee, and which, perhaps, indicated
what they understood by "The most excellent faith,"
was the burning of the White Dog, on the fifth day
of the festival. This annual sacrifice of the Iroquois
has long been known, attracting at various times considerable attention. But the true principle involved
in it appears not to have been rightly understood. In
the sequel, it will be found to be a very simple and
tangible idea, harmonizing fully with their system of
faith and worship.

Several days before the time appointed for the
jubilee, the people assembled for the confession of
their sins. On this occasion they were more thorough

---

[1] This word will analyze as follows : Gi'-ye-wä, *faith* or *belief*; no-
us'-quä (superlative), *excellent* or *best*; and go'-wä, *great* or *supreme*.

in the work than at any other season, that they
might enter upon the new year with a firm purpose
of amendment. This council not unfrequently lasted
three days, before all the people had performed this
act of religious duty.

The observances of the new year were commenced
on the day appointed, by two of the keepers of the
faith, who visited every house in and about the Indian
village, morning and evening.[95] They were disguised
in bear skins or buffalo robes, which were secured
around their heads with wreaths of corn-husks, and
then gathered in loose folds about the body. Wreaths
of corn-husks were also adjusted around their arms
and ankles. They were robed in this manner, and
painted by the matrons, who, like themselves, were
keepers of the faith, and by them were they commissioned to go forth in this formidable attire, to announce the commencement of the jubilee. Taking
corn-pounders in their hands, they went out in company, on the morning of the day, to perform their
duty. Upon entering a house, they saluted the
inmates in a formal manner, after which, one of them,
striking upon the floor, to restore silence and secure
attention, thus addressed them : —

" Listen, Listen, Listen : — The ceremonies which the
Great Spirit has commanded us to perform, are about to commence. Prepare your houses. Clear away the rubbish.
Drive out all evil animals. We wish nothing to hinder or
obstruct the coming observances. We enjoin upon every one
to obey our requirements. Should any of your friends be taken
sick and die, we command you not to mourn for them, nor
allow any of your friends to mourn. But lay the body aside,

and enjoy the coming ceremonies with us. When they are over, we will mourn with you." [1]

After singing a short thanksgiving song, they passed out.

In the afternoon this visit was repeated in the same manner. After saluting the family as before, one of the keepers of the faith thus addressed them : —

" My Nephews, my Nephews, my Nephews : — We now announce to you that the New Year's ceremonies have commenced, according to our ancient custom. You are, each of you, now required to go forth, and participate in their observance. This is the will of the Great Spirit. Your first duty will be to prepare your wooden blades (*Gä-ger-we-sä*) with which to stir up the ashes upon your neighbors' hearths. Then return to the Great Spirit your individual thanks for the return of this season, and for the enjoyment of this privilege."

Having sung another song, appropriate to the occasion, they departed finally, and when they had in this way made the circuit of the village, the ceremonies of the first day were concluded.

On the first day, however, the White Dog was strangled. They selected a dog, free from phys-

---

[1] This singular injunction exhibits the deep interest taken in the performance of these religious ceremonies. In practice, also, they possessed sufficient self-control to carry out the requirement to the letter. If a person died during this festival, the body was laid aside until it was concluded, and the relatives of the deceased participated both in the religious ceremonies, and in the amusements connected with them, with as much interest and attention as if nothing had happened. Sometimes those festivals were broken up by a bad omen : as if, for instance, a dog should bite one of the keepers of the faith on his visitorial round, they would stop the festival, and appoint a new one.

ical blemish, and of a pure white, if such an one could be found. The white deer, white squirrel, and other chance animals of the albino kind, were regarded as consecrated to the Great Spirit. White was the Iroquois emblem of purity and of faith. In strangling the dog, they were careful neither to shed his blood nor break his bones. The dog was then spotted, in places, over his body and limbs, with red paint, and ornamented with feathers in various ways. Around his neck was hung a string of white wampum, the pledge of their sincerity. In modern times, the dog is ornamented with a profusion of many-colored ribbons, which are adjusted around his body and limbs.[1] The ornaments placed upon the dog were the voluntary offerings of the pious ; and for each gift thus bestowed, the giver was taught to expect a blessing. When the dog had been thus decorated, it was suspended by the neck about eight feet from the ground, on the branching prong of a pole erected for that purpose. Here it hung, night and day, until the morning of the fifth day, when it was taken down to be burned. Oftentimes two dogs were burned, one for each four of the tribes.[57] In this case, the people separated into two divisions, and after going through separate preparatory ceremonies, they united around the same altar for the burning of the dogs, and the offering of the thanksgiving address to the Great Spirit.

On the second day all the people went forth, and

---

[1] The author once (February 6, 1846) counted *nine* different colored ribbons upon a white dog thus hung up during a New Year's celebration among the Senecas at Tonawanda. They were tied around his mouth, neck, legs, body and tail.

visited in turn the houses of their neighbors, either in the morning, at noon, or in the evening. They went in small parties apparelled in their best attire. It was customary, however, for the people to be preceded by the two keepers of the faith who made the recitations the day previous, as a matter of etiquette; the houses not being open to all, until these personages had made their call. At this time was performed the ceremony of stirring the ashes upon the hearth, which appears to have no particular idea attached to it, beyond that of a formal visitation.[95] Putting aside the disguise of the day before, the keepers of the faith assumed the costume of warriors, plumed and painted, in which attire they visited every family three times, in the morning, at noon, and in the evening. Taking in their hands wooden blades or shovels, they entered the lodge and saluted the family. One of them then stirred the ashes, and having taken up a quantity upon the blade of the shovel, and sprinkled them upon the hearth, he thus addressed the inmates, as they were in the act of falling: "I thank the Great Spirit that he has spared your lives again to witness this New Year's celebration." Then repeating the process with another shovel full of ashes, he continued: "I thank the Great Spirit that he has spared my life, again to be an actor in this ceremony. And now I do this to please the Great Spirit." The two then united in a thanksgiving song prepared for the occasion, upon the conclusion of which they took their departure. Other parties of the people then came in successively, and each went through the same performances. In this manner every house was thrice visited on the second day, by the keepers of the faith in the first instance, and afterwards by the whole community.

The proceedings upon the third and fourth days were alike. Small dancing parties were organized, which visited from house to house, and danced at the domestic fireside. Each set selected a different dance, appointed their own leader, and furnished their own music. One party, for instance, took the Feather dance, another the Fish dance, another the Trotting dance, to give variety to the short entertainments which succeeded each other at every house. It was not uncommon, on such occasions, to see a party of juveniles, about a dozen in number, dressed in full costume, feathered and painted, dancing the War dance, from house to house, with all the zeal and enthusiasm which this dance was so eminently calculated to excite. In this manner every house was made a scene of gaiety and amusement, for none was so humble or so retired as to remain unvisited.

Another pastime incident to these days was the formation of a " thieving party," as it was called, a band of mischievous boys, disguised with false faces, paint and rags, to collect materials for a feast. This vagrant company strolled from house to house, accompanied by an old woman carrying a huge basket. If the family received them kindly, and made them presents, they handed the latter to the female carrier, and having given the family a dance in acknowledgment of the present, they retired without committing any depredations. But if no presents were made, or such as were insufficient, they purloined whatever articles they could most adroitly and easily conceal.

If detected, they at once made restitution, but if not, it was considered a fair win. On the return of this party from their rounds, all the articles collected were deposited in a place open to public examination; where any one who had lost an article which he particularly prized, was allowed to redeem it, on paying an equivalent. But no one was permitted to reclaim, as the owner, any article successfully taken by this thieving party on its professional round. Upon the proceeds of this forced collection, a feast was eventually given, together with a dance in some private family.

Guessing dreams was another of the novel practices of the Iroquois, which distinguished these festive days. It is difficult to understand precisely how far the self-delusion under which the dreamer appeared to act was real. A. person with a melancholy and dejected countenance, entering a house, announced that he had a dream, and requested the inmates to guess it. He thus wandered from house to house, until he found a solution which suited him. This was either received as an interpretation of an actual dream, or suggested such a dream as the person was willing to adopt as his own. He at once avowed that his dream had been correctly guessed; and if the dream, as interpreted, prescribed any future conduct, he fulfilled it to the letter at whatever sacrifice. The celebrated Cornplanter, *Gy-ant'-wä-ka*, resigned his chiefship in consequence of a dream.[1] In relation to dreams, the

---

[1] The dream of Cornplanter occurred about the year 1810. His influence with the Senecas had been for some years on the wane, which his friends ascribed to his friendly relations with the whites. During a New

Iroquois had ever been prone to extravagant and supernatural beliefs. They often regarded a dream as a divine monition, and followed its injunctions to the utmost extremity. Their notions upon this subject recall to remembrance the conceit of Homer, that "dreams descend from Jove."

During the first four days the people were without a feast, from the fact that the observances themselves did not require the assembling of the people at the council-house. But entertainments were given in the

Year's celebration at his village on the Allegany, he went from house to house for three days, announcing wherever he went that he had had a dream, and wished to find some one to guess it. On the third day, a Seneca told him that he could relate his dream. Seeing him nearly naked and shivering with cold, he said : "You shall henceforth be called O-no'-no," meaning "cold." This signified that his name, *Gy-ant'-wä-ka*, should pass away from him, and with it his title as a chief. He then explained the interpretation to Cornplanter more fully : "That he had had a sufficient term of service for the good of the nation. That he was grown too old to be of much further use as a warrior or as a counsellor, and that he must therefore appoint a successor. That if he wished to preserve the continued good-will of the Great Spirit, he must remove from his house and sight every article of the workmanship or invention of the white man." Cornplanter, having listened with earnest attention to this interpretation, confessed that it was correctly guessed, and that he was resolved to execute it. His presents, which he had received from Washington, Adams, Jefferson, and others, he collected together, with the exception of his tomahawk, and burned them up. Among the presents thus consumed was a full uniform of an American officer, including an elegant sword and his medal given him by Washington. He then selected an old and intimate friend to be his successor, and sent to him his tomahawk and a belt of wampum, to announce his resolution and his wishes. Although contrary to their customs, the Senecas, out of reverence for his extraordinary dream, at once raised up as a chief the person selected by Cornplanter, and invested him with the name of *Gy-ant'-wä-ka*, which he bore during his life. Cornplanter, after this event, was always known among the Iroquois under the name of *O-no'-no*. This tomahawk, the last relic of Cornplanter, is now in the State Historical Collection at Albany.

evenings at private houses, where the night was devoted to the dance. Another amusement at this particular season was the Snow-snake game, which, like all Indian games, was wont to arouse considerable interest.

On the morning of the fifth day, soon after dawn, the White Dog was burned on an altar of wood erected by the keepers of the faith near the council-house. It is difficult, from outward observation, to draw forth the true intent with which the dog was burned. The obscurity with which the object was veiled has led to various conjectures. Among other things, it has been pronounced a sacrifice for sin. In the religious system of the Iroquois, there is no recognition of the doctrine of atonement for sin, or of the absolution or forgiveness of sins. Upon this whole subject, their system is silent. An act once done was registered beyond the power of change. The greatest advance upon this point of faith was the belief that good deeds cancelled the evil, thus placing heaven, through good works, within the reach of all. The notion that this was an expiation for sin is thus refuted by their system of theology itself. The other idea, that the sins of the people, by some mystic process, were transferred to the dog, and by him thus borne away, on the principle of the scape-goat of the Hebrews, is also without any foundation in truth. The burning of the dog had not the slightest connection with the sins of the people. On the contrary, the simple idea of the sacrifice was, to send up the spirit of the dog as a messenger to the Great Spirit, to announce their continued fidelity to his service, and also to convey to him their united thanks for the blessings of the year. The fidelity of the dog, the companion of the Indian, as a hunter, was emblematical of their fidelity. No messenger so trusty could be found to bear their petitions to the Master of life. The Iroquois believed that the Great Spirit made a covenant with their fathers to the effect, that when they should send up to him the spirit of a dog, of a spotless white, he would receive it as the pledge of their adherence to his worship, and his ears would thus be opened in a special manner to their petitions. To approach *Hä-wen-ne'-yu* in the most acceptable manner, and to gain attention to their thanksgiving acknowledgments and supplications in the way of his own appointing, was the end and object of burning the dog. They hung around his neck a string of white wampum, the pledge of their faith. They believed that the spirit of the dog hovered around the body until it was committed to the flames, when it ascended into the presence of the Great Spirit, itself the acknowledged evidence of their fidelity, and bearing also to him the united thanks and supplications of the people. This sacrifice was the most solemn and impressive manner of drawing near to the Great Spirit known to the Iroquois. They used the spirit of the dog in precisely the same manner that they did the incense of tobacco, as an instrumentality through which to commune with their Maker. This sacrifice was their highest act of piety.

The burning of the dog was attended with many ceremonies. It was first taken down and laid out upon a bench in the council-house, while the fire of the altar was kindling. A speech was then made over it by one of the keepers of the faith, in which he spoke of the antiquity of this institution of their fathers, of its importance and solemnity, and finally enjoined upon them all to direct their thoughts to the Great Spirit, and unite with the keepers of the faith in these observances. He concluded with thanking the Great Spirit, that the lives of so many of them had been spared through another year. A chant or song, appropriate to the occasion, was then sung, the people joining in chorus. By the time this was over, the altar was blazing up on every side ready for the offering. A procession was then formed, the officiating keeper of the faith preceding, followed by four others bearing the dog upon a kind of bark litter, behind which came the people in Indian file. A loud exclamation, in the nature of a war-whoop, announced the starting of the procession. They moved on towards the altar, and having marched around it, the keepers of the faith halted, facing the rising sun. With some immaterial ceremonies, the dog was laid upon the burning altar, and as the flames surrounded the offering, the officiating keeper of the faith, by a species of ejaculation, upon a high key, thrice repeated, invoked the attention of the Great Spirit.

"*Quä, quä, quä :* — (Hail, hail, hail.) Thou who hast created all things, who rulest all things, and who givest laws and commands to thy creatures, listen to our words. We now obey thy commands. That which thou hast made is returning unto thee. It is rising to thee, by which it will appear that our words are true." [1]

[1] Some leaves of tobacco were attached to the wampum around the dog's neck, with the incense of which this invocation was made.

Several thanksgiving songs or chants, in measured verse, were then sung by the keepers of the faith, the people joining in chorus. After this, was made the great thanksgiving address of the Iroquois. The keeper of the faith appointed to deliver it, invoked the attention of *Hä-wen-né'-yu* by the same thrice-repeated exclamation. As the speech progressed, he threw leaves of tobacco into the fire from time to time, that its incense might constantly ascend during the whole address. The following is the address, as delivered among the Senecas:[1] —

" Hail, Hail, Hail : — Listen now, with an open ear, to the words of thy people, as they ascend to thy dwelling, in the smoke of our offering. Behold thy people here assembled. Behold, they have come up to celebrate anew the sacred rites thou hast given them. Look down upon us beneficently. Give us wisdom faithfully to execute thy commands.

" Continue to listen : — The united voice of thy people continues to ascend to thee. Forbid, by thy wisdom, all things which shall tempt thy people to relinquish their ancient faith. Give us power to celebrate at all times, with zeal and fidelity, the sacred ceremonies which thou hast given us.

" Continue to listen : — Give to the keepers of the faith wisdom to execute properly thy commands. Give to our warriors, and our mothers, strength to perform the sacred ceremonies of thy institution. We thank thee that, in thy wisdom, thou hast given to us these commands. We thank thee that thou hast preserved them pure unto this day.

" Continue to listen : — We thank thee that the lives of

[1] Taken down by *Hä-sa-no-an'-dä* (Ely S. Parker), as delivered by his grandfather, *Sose-ha'-wä*, at Tonawanda. This is the ancient address handed down from generation to generation, and unchanged in its essential particulars. *Sose-ha'-wä* has delivered it thus for the past twenty-five years at Tonawanda.

so many of thy children are spared, to participate in the exercises of this occasion. Our minds are gladdened to be made partakers in the execution of thy commands.

"We return thanks to our mother, the earth, which sustains us. We thank thee that thou hast caused her to yield so plentifully of her fruits. Cause that, in the season coming, she may not withhold of her fulness, and leave any to suffer for want.

"We return thanks to the rivers and streams, which run their courses upon the bosom of our mother the earth. We thank thee that thou hast supplied them with life, for our comfort and support. Grant that this blessing may continue.

"We return thanks to all the herbs and plants of the earth. We thank thee that in thy goodness thou hast blest them all, and given them strength to preserve our bodies healthy, and to cure us of the diseases inflicted upon us by evil spirits. We ask thee not to take from us these blessings.

"We return thanks to the Three Sisters. We thank thee that thou hast provided them as the main supporters of our lives. We thank thee for the abundant harvest gathered in during the past season. We ask that Our Supporters may never fail us, and cause our children to suffer from want.

"We return thanks to the bushes and trees which provide us with fruit. We thank thee that thou hast blessed them, and made them to produce for the good of thy creatures. We ask that they may not refuse to yield plentifully for our enjoyment.

"We return thanks to the winds, which, moving, have banished all diseases. We thank thee that thou hast thus ordered. We ask the continuation of this great blessing.

"We return thanks to our grandfather *He'-no*. We thank thee that thou hast so wisely provided for our happiness and comfort, in ordering the rain to descend upon the earth, giving us water, and causing all plants to grow. We thank thee that thou hast given us *He'-no*, our grandfather, to do thy will in the protection of thy people. We ask that this great blessing may be continued to us.

"We return thanks to the moon and stars, which give us light when the sun has gone to his rest. We thank thee that thy wisdom has so kindly provided, that light is never wanting to us. Continue unto us this goodness.

"We return thanks to the sun, that he has looked upon the earth with a beneficent eye. We thank thee that thou hast, in thy unbounded wisdom, commanded the sun to regulate the return of the seasons, to dispense heat and cold, and to watch over the comfort of thy people. Give unto us that wisdom which will guide us in the path of truth. Keep us from all evil ways, that the sun may never hide his face from us for shame and leave us in darkness.

"We return thanks to the *Ho-no-che-no'-keh*.[1] We thank thee that thou hast provided so many agencies for our good and happiness.

"Lastly, we return thanks to thee, our Creator and Ruler. In thee are embodied all things. We believe thou canst do no evil; that thou doest all things for our good and happiness. Should thy people disobey thy commands, deal not harshly with them; but be kind to us, as thou hast been to our fathers in times long gone by. Hearken unto our words as they have

---

[1] The *Ho-no-che-no'-keh* included the whole spiritual world, or subordinate spirits created by *Hä-wen-ne'-yu*. They were believed by the Iroquois to be mere agencies or instrumentalities through whom the Great Spirit administered the government of the world. They were also believed to have been created to minister to the happiness and protection of the Indian upon earth.

It should also be noticed that the leading objects in the natural world which are made the subject of their thanks, are designed to include all lesser objects. Under each head, by a figure of speech, whole classes of objects were included. Thus "the rivers and streams" include all bodies of water, springs, fishes, &c.; "the wind" includes all the birds of the air.

ascended, and may they be pleasing to thee our Creator, the Preserver and Ruler of all things, visible and invisible. *Na-hó'*."

After the delivery of this address, the people, leaving the partly consumed offering, returned to the council-house, where the Feather dance was performed. With this the religious exercises of the day were concluded. Other dances, however, followed, for the entertainment of the people, and the day and evening were given up to this amusement. Last of all came the feast, with which the proceedings of the day were terminated.

On the morning of the sixth day, the people again assembled at the place of council. This day was observed in about the same manner as one of their ordinary religious days, at which the Thanksgiving dance was introduced.

The seventh and last day was commenced with the *Ah-do'-weh*; after which the Peach-stone game was introduced, with the determination of which ended the New Year's jubilee.

Other incidents and circumstances connected with the worship of the Iroquois might be pointed out, and would be necessary to a full explanation of the details of their religious system; but sufficient has been presented to exhibit its framework, and the principles upon which it rested. No attempt has been made to furnish a picture of either of these religious councils, by a minute description of their proceedings. All the detail has necessarily been omitted. To realize these festive and religious ceremonials of our primitive inhabitants, it would be

necessary to have a delineation of the incidents of each
day, step by step, a description of the dances, the
several games, and of the preparation of the feast, and
also an explanation of their modes of social intercourse
and of action, the spirit by which the people were
animated, and the general character of the scene.

These festivals have been observed from generation
to generation, and at the same seasons of the year,
upon the Mohawk, at Oneida, in the valley of
Onondaga, on the shore of the Cayuga, and in the
several villages of the Senecas. Before the voice of
the white man was heard in these peaceful and
secluded retreats of the forest, that of the Indian had
been lifted up to the Great Spirit with thanksgiving
and praise. The origin of these festivals is lost, as
well as the date and order of their institution; but
the Iroquois believe that they have been observed
among them, at least since the formation of the
League. They have no tradition, which professes to
have taken the custody of these dates and events.

To one who has witnessed these observances
from time to time, and learned to comprehend the
principles and motives in which they originated, they
possess a peculiar but almost indefinable interest.
These simple religious rites of a people, sitting, it
must be admitted, near the full meridian of natural
religion, are calculated to fill the mind with serious
impressions. In their earnest and constant efforts
to draw near to the great Author of their being,
to offer thanks for the unnumbered blessings strewn
upon their path, and to supplicate the continuance of
that watchful care without which there was no pres-

ervation, there is a degree of heart-felt piety which the mind cannot resist. We may derive instruction from the faith of any race, if it rises above the grossness of superstition, into the regions of spiritual meditation. The moral nature of man unfolds with thought; and the Indian, in the shades of the forest, as well as Socrates in the groves of Athens, or Moses upon the skirts of Sinai, may contribute some new lessons to the fund of moral instruction.

In this and the preceding chapter, the design has been to expose the structure of the worship of the Iroquois, and to elucidate the beliefs by which it was upheld. By the standard of Christian judgment, it must be confessed that the Faith and Worship of the Iroquois make up a system which, in its approaches to the truth, rises infinitely above the theological schemes of all other races, both ancient and modern, which originated independently of revelation. Having a firm hold upon the great truths of natural religion, they established a ceremonious but simple worship. Unlike the bloody ritual of the Aztecs, its influence upon the mind, and upon the social life of the Indian, was mild, humanizing and gentle. The fruits of their religious sentiments, among themselves, were peace, brotherly kindness, charity, hospitality, integrity, truth and friendship; and towards the Great Spirit, reverence, thankfulness and faith. More wise than the Greeks and Romans in this great particular, they concentrated all divinity into one Supreme Being; more confiding in the people than the priestly class of Egypt, their religious teachers brought down the knowledge of the " Unutterable One " to the minds of all. Eminently pure and spiritual, and internally consistent with each other, the beliefs and the religious ceremonies of the Iroquois are worthy of a respectful consideration. A people in the wilderness, shut out from revelation, with no tablet on which to write the history of passing generations, save the heart of man, yet possessed of the knowledge of one Supreme Being, and striving, with all the ardor of devotion, to commune with him in the language of thankfulness and supplication, is, to say the least, a most extraordinary spectacle ; not less sublime in itself than the spectacle of the persecuted Puritan, on the confines of the same wilderness, worshipping that God in the fulness of light and knowledge, whom the Indian, however limited and imperfect his conceptions, in the Great Spirit most distinctly discerned.

Their limited knowledge of the attributes which pertained to a Being endued with creative power, will not appear so surprising, when it is remembered to be the highest achievement of learning and piety, fully to comprehend the marvellous perfections of the Deity. When the complicated structures of Egypt, Greece and Rome are brought under comparison with the simple and unpretending scheme of theology of the children of the forest, there is found reason to marvel at the superior acuteness and profundity of the Indian intellect. It may be safely averred, that if the sustaining faith and the simple worship of the Iroquois are ever fully explored and carefully elucidated, they will form a more imperishable monument to the Indian than is afforded in the purity of his virtues, or in the mournfulness of his destiny.

GÄ-GEH-TÄ YEN-CHE-NO-HOS-TA-TÀ or KNEE BAND.

YEN-NIS-HO-QUÄ-HOS-TÄ or WRIST BAND.

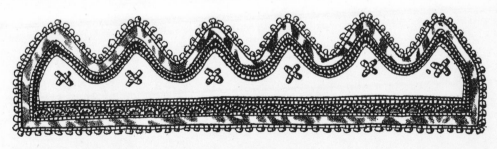

GA-GEH-TA YEN-NIS-HÄ-HOS-TA or ARM BAND.

Chapter III

ABOUT the year eighteen hundred, a new religious teacher arose among the Iroquois, who professed to have received a revelation from the Great Spirit, with a commission to preach to them the doctrines with which he had been intrusted. This revelation was received under circumstances so remarkable, and the precepts which he sought to inculcate contained within themselves such evidences of wisdom and beneficence, that he was universally received among them, not only as a wise and good man, but as one commissioned from *Hä-wen-ne′-yu* to become their religious instructor. The new religion, as it has since been called, not only embodied all the precepts of the ancient faith, and recognized the ancient mode of worship, giving to it anew the sanction of the Great Spirit, but it also comprehended such new doctrines as came in, very aptly, to lengthen out and enlarge the primitive system, without impairing the structure itself. Charges of imposture and deception were at first preferred against him, but disbelief of his divine mission gradually subsided, until, at the time of his death, the whole unchristianized portion of the Iroquois had become firm believers in the new religion, which, to the present day, has continued to be the prevailing faith.

The singular personage who was destined to obtain such a spiritual sway over the descendants of the ancient Iroquois, was *Gä-ne-o-dï'-yo*, or "Handsome Lake," a Seneca sachem of the highest class. He was born at the Indian village of *Gä-no-wau'-ges*, near Avon, about the year 1735, and died at Onondaga in 1815, where he happened to be on one of his pastoral visits. By birth he was a Seneca, of the Turtle tribe, and a half-brother of the celebrated Cornplanter, through a common father. The best part of his life was spent in idleness and dissipation, during which, although a sachem and ruler among the Senecas for many years, and through the most perilous period of their history, he acquired no particular reputation. Reforming late in life, in his future career he showed himself to be possessed of superior talents, and to be animated by a sincere and ardent desire for the welfare of his race. He appears to have adopted the idea of a revelation from Heaven, to give authority and sanction to his projected reformation. At this period, and for a century preceding, the prevailing intemperance of the Iroquois had been the fruitful source of those domestic disorders which, in connection with their political disasters, seemed then to threaten the speedy extinction of the race. A temperance reformation, universal and radical, was the principal and the ultimate object of the mission which he assumed, and the one upon which he chiefly employed his influence and his eloquence, through the residue of his life. Knowing that argument and persuasion were feeble weapons in a contest with this mighty foe, Handsome Lake had the sagacity to address himself to the religious sentiments and the superstitious fears of the people. To secure a more ready reception of his admonitions, he clothed them with the divine sanction; to strengthen their moral principles, he enforced anew the precepts of the ancient faith; and to insure obedience to his teachings, he held over the wicked the terrors of eternal punishment. Travelling from village to village, among the several nations of the League, with the exception of the christianized Oneidas, and continuing his visits from year to year, this self-appointed apostle to the Indians preached the new doctrine with remarkable effect. Numbers, it is said, abandoned their dissolute habits, and became sober and moral men; discord and contention gave place to harmony and order, and vagrancy and sloth to ambition and industry. What peculiar motives induced him, when past the meridian of life, to change the whole tenor of his past career, and embark in this philanthropic enterprise for the social and moral improvement of the Iroquois, it may be difficult to ascertain. The origination of this project has, at times, been ascribed to Cornplanter, as a means to increase his own influence; but this is not only improbable, but is expressly denied. The motives by which Handsome Lake claimed to be actuated were entirely of a religious and benevolent character, and in pursuance of the injunctions of his spiritual guides.

At the time of his supernatural visitation, about the year 1800, Handsome Lake resided at *De-o-no-sä-da'-ga*, the village of Cornplanter, on the Allegany

river, in the State of Pennsylvania. As he explained
the matter to his brethren, having lain ill for a long
period, he had surrendered all hope of recovery, and
resigned himself to death. When in the hourly expectation of departure, three spiritual beings, in the
forms of men, sent by the Great Spirit, appeared before him. Each bore in his hand a shrub, bearing
different kinds of berries, which, having given him to
eat, he was, by their miraculous power, immediately
restored to health. After revealing to him the will
of the Great Spirit, upon a great variety of subjects,
and particularly in relation to the prevailing intemperance, and having commissioned him to promulgate
these doctrines among the Iroquois, they permitted
him to visit, under their guidance, the realm of the
Evil-minded, and to behold with his mortal eyes the
punishments inflicted upon the wicked, that he might
warn his brethren of their impending destiny. Like
Ulysses and Æneas, he was also favored with a glance
at Elysium, and the felicities of the heavenly residence
of the virtuous. With his mind thus stored with divine precepts, and with his zeal enkindled by the dignity of his mission, *Gä-ne-o-dï'-yo* at once commenced
his labors.[1]

After his death, *Sose-ha'-wä* (Johnson) of Tona-

---

[1] The Iroquois are under the impression that Handsome Lake received
a license from Washington to preach. There is no doubt that he applied
to the government during the presidency of Jefferson for some recognition
of his mission ; but the paper which they still call the *license*, now in the
possession of Blacksmith, at Tonawanda, is simply a letter from General
Dearborn, dated in 1802, commending his teachings. *Sose-ha'-wä*
(Johnson) fixes the period of this revelation in June, 1800. This vener-
able man has preached the doctrine upwards of thirty years.

wanda was appointed his successor, the first and only person ever "raised up" by the Iroquois, and invested with the office of supreme Religious Instructor. A sincere believer in the verity of *Gä-ne-o-dï'-yo's* mission, and an eminently pure and virtuous man, *Sose-ha'-wä* has devoted himself with zeal and fidelity to the duties of his office, as the spiritual guide and teacher of the Iroquois. He is a grandson of Handsome Lake, and a nephew of Red Jacket, and was born at the Indian village of *Gä-no-wau'-ges*, near Avon, about the year 1774, and still resides at Tonawanda in the county of Genesee.

At the Mourning and Religious councils of the League, which are still held, at intervals of a few years, among the scattered descendants of the children of the Long House, it has long been customary to set apart portions of two or three days to listen to a discourse from *Sose-ha'-wä* upon the new religion. On these occasions, he explains minutely the circumstances attending the supernatural visitation of Handsome Lake, and delivers the instructions, word for word, which he had been accustomed to give during his own ministration. Handsome Lake professed to repeat the messages which were given to him from time to time by his celestial visitants, with whom he pretended to be in frequent communication, and whom he addressed as his spiritual guardians, thus enforcing his precepts as the direct commands of the Great Spirit.

It is singular that the credulity, not only of the people, but of their most intelligent chiefs should have been sufficiently great to give credence to these supernatural pretensions; but yet it is in itself no greater than that indicated by their belief in witchcraft, or in the omens of dreams. The influence of the new religion has been extremely salutary and preservative, without the restraints of which, the fears of *Gä-ne-o-dï'-yo* might have been realized ere this, in the rapid decline, if not extinction of the race. Their downward tendencies were arrested, and their constant diminution of numbers was changed to a gradual increase. Its beneficent effects upon the people doubtless contributed more to its final establishment than any other cause.

At their councils and religious festivals, it was customary for the chiefs and keepers of the faith to express their confidence in the new religion, and to exhort others to strengthen their belief. The late Abraham La Fort, *De-ät-ga-dose*, an educated Onondaga sachem, thus expressed himself upon this subject at a Mourning council of the Iroquois, held at Tonawanda as late as October, 1847 : —

"Let us observe the operations of nature. The year is divided into seasons, and every season has its fruits. The birds of the air, though clothed in the same dress of feathers, are divided into many classes; and one class is never seen to associate or intermingle with any but its own kind. So with the beasts of the field and woods; each and every class and species have their own separate rules by which they seem to be governed, and by which their actions are regulated. These distinctions of classes and colors the Great Spirit has seen fit to make. But the rule does not stop here; it is universal. It embraces man also. The human race was created and divided into different classes, which were placed separate from each other, having different customs, manners, laws, and religions. To the Indian, it seems that no more religion had originally been given than was to be found in the operations of nature, which taught him that there was a Supreme Being, all powerful and all wise ; and on this account, as well as on account of his great goodness, they learned to love and reverence him. But in these latter times, when the restless and ambitious spirit of the white-skinned race had crossed the boundary line, and made inroads upon the manners, customs and primitive religion of the Indian, the Great Spirit determined to, and through his servant *Gä-ne-o-dï'-yo* did reveal his will to the Indian. The substance of that will was no more than to confirm their ancient belief that they were entitled to a different religion, a religion adapted to their customs, manners, and ways of thinking." [1]

As the discourse delivered by *Sose-ha'-wä*, from time to time, contains a very full exposition of their ancient beliefs, and mode of worship, together with the recent views introduced by Handsome Lake, mingled up in one collection, presenting, probably, a better idea of their ethical and religious system than could be conveyed in any other manner, it is given entire, and will explain itself. [2]

[1] Furnished to the author by *Hä-sa-no-an'-dä* (Ely S. Parker), from notes taken at the time.

[2] The subjoined translation was prepared by *Hä-sa-no-an'-dä* (Ely S. Parker), from copious notes taken by him at the time of its last delivery in October, 1848, at a general Mourning council of the Iroquois, held at Tonawanda. It is proper to add, that he has listened to its delivery on several occasions, and is perfectly familiar with the subject. With some slight alterations, the language is his own. This discourse, as it is given, was made on the forenoons of the 4th, 5th, and 6th days of October, 1848.

" The Mohawks, the Onondagas, the Senecas, and our children (the Oneidas, Cayugas and Tuscaroras) have assembled here to-day to listen to the repetition of the will of the Great Spirit, as communicated to us from heaven through his servant, *Gä-ne-o-dï'-yo.*

" Chiefs, warriors, women and children: — We give you a cordial welcome. The sun has advanced far in his path, and I am warned that my time to instruct you is limited to the meridian sun. I must therefore hasten to perform my duty. Turn your minds to the Great Spirit, and listen with strict attention. Think seriously upon what I am about to speak. Reflect upon it well, that it may benefit you and your children. I thank the Great Spirit that he has spared the lives of so many of you to be present on this occasion. I return thanks to him that my life is yet spared. The Great Spirit looked down from heaven upon the sufferings and the wanderings of his red children. He saw that they had greatly decreased and degenerated. He saw the ravages of the fire-water among them. He therefore raised up for them a sacred instructor, who having lived and travelled among them for sixteen years, was called from his labors to enjoy eternal felicity with the Great Spirit in heaven. Be patient while I speak. I cannot at all times arrange and prepare my thoughts with the same precision. But I will relate what my memory bears.

" It was in the month of *O-nike'-ya* (June), that Handsome Lake was yet sick. He had been ill four years. He was accustomed to tell us that he had resigned himself to the will of the Great Spirit. ' I nightly returned my thanks to the Great Spirit,' said he, ' as my eyes were gladdened at evening by the sight of the stars of heaven. I viewed the ornamented heavens at evening, through the opening in the roof of my lodge,[124] with grateful feelings to my Creator. I had no assurance that I should at the next evening contemplate his works. For this reason my acknowledgments to him were more fervent and sincere. When night was gone, and the sun again shed his light upon the earth, I saw, and acknowledged in the return of day his continued goodness to me, and to all mankind. At length I began to have an inward conviction that my end was near. I resolved once more to exchange friendly words with my people, and I sent my daughter to summon my brothers *Gy-ant'-wä-ka* (Cornplanter), and *Ta-wan'-ne-ars* (Blacksnake).' She hastened to do his bidding, but before she returned, he had fallen into insensibility and apparent death. *Ta-wan'-ne-ars*, upon returning to the lodge, hastened to his brother's couch, and discovered that portions of his body were yet warm. This happened at early day, before the morning dew had dried. When the sun had advanced half-way to the meridian, his heart began to beat, and he opened his eyes. *Ta-wan'-ne-ars* asked him if he was in his right mind ; but he answered not. At meridian he again opened his eyes, and the same question was repeated. He then answered and said, ' A man spoke from without, and asked that some one might come forth. I looked, and saw some men standing without. I arose, and as I attempted to step over the threshold of my door, I stumbled, and should have fallen had they not caught me. They were three holy men who looked alike, and were dressed alike. The paint they wore seemed but one day old. Each held in his hand a shrub bearing different kinds of fruit. One of them addressing me said, " We have come to comfort and relieve you. Take of these berries and eat ; they will restore you to health. We have been witnesses of your lengthened illness. We have seen with what resignation you have given yourself up to the Great Spirit. We have heard your daily return of thanks. He has heard them all. His ear has ever been open to hear. You were thankful for the return of night, when you could contemplate the beauties of heaven. You were accustomed to look upon the moon, as she coursed in her nightly paths. When there were no hopes to you that you would again behold these things, you willingly resigned yourself to the mind of the Great Spirit. This was right. Since the Great Spirit made the earth and put man upon it, we have been his constant servants to guard and protect his works. There are four of us. Some other time you will be permitted to see the other. The Great Spirit is pleased to know your patient resignation to his will. As a reward for your devotion, he has cured your sickness. Tell your people to assemble to-morrow, and at noon go in and speak to them." ' After they had further revealed their intentions concerning him they departed.

" At the time appointed Handsome Lake appeared at the council, and thus addressed the people upon the revelations which had been made to him : 'I have a message to deliver to you. The servants of the Great Spirit have told me that I should yet live upon the earth to become an instructor to my people.

Since the creation of man, the Great Spirit has often raised up men to teach his children what they should do to please him; but they have been unfaithful to their trust. I hope I shall profit by their example. Your Creator has seen that you have transgressed greatly against his laws. He made man pure and good. He did not intend that he should sin. You commit a great sin in taking the fire-water. The Great Spirit says that you must abandon this enticing habit. Your ancestors have brought great misery and suffering upon you. They first took the fire-water of the white man, and entailed upon you its consequences. None of them have gone to heaven. The fire-water does not belong to you. It was made for the white man beyond the great waters. For the white man it is a medicine; but they too have violated the will of their Maker. The Great Spirit says that drunkenness is a great crime, and he forbids you to indulge in this evil habit. His command is to the old and young. The abandonment of its use will relieve much of your sufferings, and greatly increase the comfort and happiness of your children. The Great Spirit is grieved that so much crime and wickedness should defile the earth. There are many evils which he never intended should exist among his red children. The Great Spirit has, for many wise reasons, withheld from man the number of his days; but he has not left him without a guide, for he has pointed out to him the path in which he may safely tread the journey of life.

"'When the Great Spirit made man, he also made woman. He instituted marriage, and enjoined upon them to love each other, and be faithful. It is pleasing to him to see men and women obey his will. Your Creator abhors a deceiver and a hypocrite. By obeying his commands you will die an easy and a happy death. When the Great Spirit instituted marriage, he ordained to bless those who were faithful with children. Some women are unfruitful, and others become so by misfortune. Such have great opportunities to do much good. There are many orphans, and many poor children whom they can adopt as their own. If you tie up the clothes of an orphan child, the Great Spirit will notice it, and reward you for it. Should an orphan ever cross your path be kind to him, and treat him with tenderness, for this is right. Parents must constantly teach their children morality, and a reverence for their Creator. Parents must also guard their children against improper marriages. They, having much experience, should select a suitable match for their child. When the parents of both parties have agreed, then bring the young pair together, and let them know what good their parents have designed for them. If at any time they so far disagree that they cannot possibly live contented and happy with each other, they may separate in mutual good feeling; and in this there is no wrong. When a child is born to a husband and wife, they must give great thanks to the Great Spirit, for it is his gift, and an evidence of his kindness. Let parents instruct their children in their duty to the Great Spirit, to their parents, and to their fellow-men. Children should obey their parents and guardians, and submit to them in all things. Disobedient children occasion great pain and misery. They wound

their parents' feelings, and often drive them to desper-
ation, causing them great distress, and final admission
into the place of Evil Spirits. The marriage obligations should generate good to all who have assumed
them. Let the married be faithful to each other, that
when they die it may be in peace. Children should
never permit their parents to suffer in their old age.
Be kind to them, and support them. The Great
Spirit requires all children to love, revere and obey
their parents. To do this is highly pleasing to
him. The happiness of parents is greatly increased
by the affection and the attentions of their children.
To abandon a wife or children is a great wrong, and
produces many evils. It is wrong for a father or
mother-in-law to vex a son or daughter-in-law; but
they should use them as if they were their own
children. It often happens that parents hold angry
disputes over their infant child. This is also a great
sin. The infant hears and comprehends the angry
words of its parents. It feels bad and lonely. It
can see for itself no happiness in prospect. It concludes to return to its Maker. It wants a happy
home, and dies. The parents then weep because
their child has left them. You must put this evil
practice from among you, if you would live happy.

"' The Great Spirit, when he made the earth, never
intended that it should be made merchandise; but he
willed that all his creatures should enjoy it equally.
Your chiefs have violated and betrayed your trust
by selling lands. Nothing is now left of our once
large possessions, save a few small reservations.
Chiefs and aged men — you, as men, have no lands

to sell. You occupy and possess a tract in trust for your children. You should hold that trust sacred, lest your children are driven from their homes by your unsafe conduct. Whoever sells lands offends the Great Spirit, and must expect a great punishment after death.' "

Sose-ha'-wä here suspended the narration of the discourse of Handsome Lake, and thus addressed the council : —

" Chiefs, keepers of the faith, warriors, women and children : — You all know that our religion teaches, that the early day is dedicated to the Great Spirit, and that the late day is granted to the spirits of the dead. It is now meridian, and I must close. Preserve in your minds that which has been said. Accept my thanks for your kind and patient attention. It is meet that I should also return my thanks to the Great Spirit, that he has assisted me thus far, in my feeble frame, to instruct you. We ask you all to come up again to-morrow, at early day, to hear what further may be said. I have done."

The next morning, after the council had been opened in the usual manner, *Sose-ha'-wä* thus continued : —

" Relatives, uncover now your heads and listen : — The day has thus far advanced, and again we are gathered around the council-fire. I see around me the several nations of the Long House ; this gives me great joy. I see also seated around me my counsellors (keepers of the faith), who have been regularly appointed, as is the custom of our religion. Greetings have been exchanged with each other. Thanks have been returned to *Gä-ni-o-di'-yo.* Thanks also have been returned to our Creator, by the council now assembled. At this moment the Great Spirit is looking upon this assembly. He hears our words, he knows our thoughts, and is always pleased to see us gathered together for good. The sun is now high, and soon it will reach the middle heavens. I must therefore make haste. Listen attentively, and consider well what you shall hear. I return thanks to our Creator, that he has spared your lives through the dangers of darkness. I salute and return my thanks to the four Celestial beings, who have communicated what I am about to say to you. I return thanks to my grandfather (Handsome Lake), from whom you first heard what I am about to speak. We all feel his loss. We miss him at our councils. I now occupy his place before you; but I am conscious that I have not the power which he possessed.

"Counsellors, warriors, mothers and children:— Listen to good instruction. Consider it well. Lay it up in your minds, and forget it not. Our Creator, when he made us, designed that we should live by hunting. It sometimes happens that a man goes out for the hunt, leaving his wife with her friends. After a long absence he returns, and finds that his wife has taken another husband. The Great Spirit says that this is a great sin, and must be put from among us.

"The four Messengers further said, that it was wrong for a mother to punish a child with a rod. It is not right to punish much, and our Creator never intended that children should be punished with a whip, or be used with any violence. In punishing a refractory child, water only is necessary, and it is sufficient. Plunge them under. This is not wrong. Whenever a child promises to do better, the punishment must cease. It is wrong to continue it after promises of amendment are made. Thus they said.

" It is right and proper always to look upon the dead. Let your face be brought near to theirs, and then address them. Let the dead know that their absence is regretted by their friends, and that they grieve for their death. Let the dead know, too, how their surviving friends intend to live. Let them know whether they will so conduct themselves, that they will meet them again in the future world. The dead will hear and remember. Thus they said.

" Continue to listen while I proceed to relate what further they said : — Our Creator made the earth. Upon it he placed man, and gave him certain rules of conduct. It pleased him also to give them many kinds of amusements. He also ordered that the earth should produce all that is good for man. So long as the earth remains, it will not cease to yield. Upon the surface of the ground berries of various kinds are produced. It is the will of the Great Spirit, that when they ripen, we should return our thanks to him, and have a public rejoicing for the continuance of these blessings. He made everything which we live upon, and requires us to be thankful at all times for the continuance of his favors. When Our Life (corn, &c.) has again ap-

peared, it is the will of the Great Ruler that we assemble for a general thanksgiving. It is his will
also that the children be brought and made to participate in the Feather dance. Your feast must consist of the new production. It is proper at these
times, should any present not have their names published, or if any changes have been made, to announce
them then. The festival must continue four days.
Thus they said. Upon the first day must be performed the Feather dance. This ceremony must
take place in the early day, and cease at the middle
day. In the same manner, upon the second day, is
to be performed the Thanksgiving dance. On the
third, the Thanksgiving concert, *Ah-do'-weh*, is to
be introduced. The fourth day is set apart for
the Peach-stone game. All these ceremonies, instituted by our Creator, must be commenced at the
early day, and cease at the middle day. At all these
times, we are required to return thanks to our Grandfather *Hé-no* and his assistants. To them is assigned
the duty of watching over the earth, and all it
produces for our good. The great Feather and
Thanksgiving dances are the appropriate ceremonies
of thanksgiving to the Ruler and Maker of all things.
The Thanksgiving concert belongs appropriately to
our Grandfathers. In it, we return thanks to them.
During the performance of this ceremony, we are
required also to give them the smoke of tobacco.
Again, we must at this time return thanks to our
mother the earth, for she is our relative. We must
also return thanks to Our Life and its Sisters. All
these things are required to be done by the light of

the sun. It must not be protracted until the sun has hid his face, and darkness surrounds all things.

"Continue to listen : — We have a change of seasons. We have a season of cold. This is the hunting season. It is also one in which the people can amuse themselves. Upon the fifth day of the new moon *Nis-go-wuk'-na* (about Feb. 1st), we are required to commence the annual jubilee of thanksgiving to our Creator. At this festival all can give evidence of their devotion to the will of the Great Spirit, by participating in all its ceremonies.

"Continue to listen : — The four Messengers of the Great Spirit have always watched over us, and have ever seen what was transpiring among men. At one time, Handsome Lake was translated by them to the regions above. He looked down upon the earth and saw a great assembly. Out of it came a man. His garments were torn, tattered and filthy. His whole appearance indicated great misery and poverty. They asked him how this spectacle appeared to him. He replied that it was hard to look upon. They then told him that the man he saw was a drunkard. That he had taken the fire-water, and it had reduced him to poverty. Again he looked, and saw a woman seated upon the ground. She was constantly engaged in gathering up and secreting about her person her worldly effects. They said, the woman you see is inhospitable. She is too selfish to spare anything, and will never leave her worldly goods. She can never pass from earth to heaven. Tell this to your people. Again he looked, and saw a man carrying in each hand large pieces of meat. He went about the assembly giving to each a piece. This man, they said, is blessed, for he is hospitable and kind. He looked again, and saw streams of blood. They said, Thus will the earth be, if the fire-water is not put from among you. Brother will kill brother, and friend friend. Again they told him to look towards the east. He obeyed, and as far as his vision reached, he saw the increasing smoke of numberless distilleries arising, and shutting out the light of the sun. It was a horrible spectacle to witness. They told him that here was manufactured the fire-water. Again he looked, and saw a costly house, made and furnished by the pale-faces. It was a house of confinement, where were fetters, ropes and whips. They said that those who persisted in the use of the fire-water would fall into this. Our Creator commands us to put this destructive vice far from us. Again he looked, and saw various assemblages. Some of them were unwilling to listen to instruction. They were riotous, and took great pride in drinking the strong waters. He observed another group who were half inclined to hear, but the temptations to vice which surrounded them allured them back, and they also revelled in the fumes of the fire-water. He saw another assemblage which had met to hear instructions. This they said was pleasing to the Great Spirit. He loves those who will listen and obey. It has grieved him that his children are now divided by separate interests, and are pursuing so many paths. It pleases him to see his people live together in harmony and quiet. The fire-water creates many dissensions and divisions among us. They said that the use of it would cause many to die unnatural deaths; many will be exposed to cold, and freeze; many will be burned, and others will be drowned while under the influence of the fire-water.

"Friends and Relatives: — All these things have often happened. How many of our people have been frozen to death; how many have been burned to death; how many have been drowned while under the influence of the strong waters. The punishments of those who use the fire-water commence while they are yet on the earth. Many are now thrown into houses of confinement by the pale faces. I repeat to you, the Ruler of us all requires us to unite and put this evil from among us. Some say that the use of the fire-water is not wrong, and that it is food. Let those who do not believe it wrong, make this experiment. Let all who use the fire-water assemble and organize into a council; and those who do not, into another near them. A great difference will then be discovered. The council of drunkards will end in a riot and tumult, while the other will have harmony and quiet. It is hard to think of the great prevalence of this evil among us. Reform, and put it from among you. Many resolve to use the fire-water until near death, when they will repent. If they do this, nothing can save them from destruction, for them medicine can have no power. Thus they said.

"All men were made equal by the Great Spirit; but he has given to them a variety of gifts. To some a pretty face, to others an ugly one; to some a comely form, to others a deformed figure. Some are fortunate in collecting around them worldly goods. But you are all entitled to the same privileges, and therefore must put pride from among you. You are not your own makers, nor the builders of your own fortunes. All things are the gift of the Great Spirit, and to him must be returned thanks for their bestowal. He alone must be acknowledged as the giver. It has pleased him to make differences among men; but it is wrong for one man to exalt himself above another. Love each other, for you are all brothers and sisters of the same great family. The Great Spirit enjoins upon all, to observe hospitality and kindness, especially to the needy and the helpless; for this is pleasing to him. If a stranger wanders about your abode, speak to him with kind words; be hospitable towards him, welcome him to your home, and forget not always to mention the Great Spirit. In the morning, give thanks to the Great Spirit for the return of day, and the light of the sun; at night renew your thanks to him, that his ruling power has preserved you from harm during the day, and that night has again come, in which you may rest your wearied bodies.

"The four Messengers said further to Handsome Lake:—Tell your people, and particularly the keepers of the faith, to be strong-minded, and adhere to the true faith. We fear the Evil-minded will go among them with temptations. He may introduce the *fiddle*. He may bring *cards*, and leave them among you. The use of these are great sins. Let the people be on their guard, and the keepers of the faith be watchful and vigilant, that none of these evils may find their way among the people. Let the keepers of the faith preserve the law of moral conduct in all its purity. When meetings are to be held for instruction, and the people are preparing to go, the Evil-minded is then busy. He goes from one to another, whispering many temptations, by which to keep them away. He will even follow persons into the door of the council, and induce some, at that time, to bend their steps away. Many resist until they have entered, and then leave it. This habit, once indulged, obtains a fast hold, and the evil propensity increases with age. This is a great sin, and should be at once abandoned. Thus they said.

"Speak evil of no one. If you can say no good of a person, then be silent. Let not your tongues betray you into evil. Let all be mindful of this; for these are the words of our Creator. Let all strive to cultivate friendship with those who surround them. This is pleasing to the Great Spirit.

"Counsellors, warriors, women and children:— I shall now rest. I thank you all for your kind and patient attention. I thank the Great Spirit, that he has spared the lives of so many of us to witness this day. I request you all to come up again to-morrow at early day. Let us all hope, that, until we meet again, the Creator and Ruler of us all may be kind to us, and preserve our lives. *Na-ho'*."

The council, on the following day, was opened with a few short speeches, from some of the chiefs or keepers of the faith, returning thanks for the privileges of the occasion, as usual at councils; after which *Sose-ha'-wä*, resuming his discourse, spoke as follows:—

"Friends and Relatives, uncover now your heads:— Continue to listen to my rehearsal of the sayings communicated to Handsome Lake by the four Messengers of the Great Spirit. We have met again around the council-fire. We have followed the ancient custom, and greeted each other. This is right, and highly pleasing to our Maker. He now looks down upon this assembly. He sees us all. He is informed of the cause of our gathering, and it is pleasing to him. Life is uncertain. While we live let us love each other. Let us sympathize always with the suffering and needy. Let us also always rejoice with those who are glad. This is now the third day, and my time for speaking to you is drawing to a close. It will be a long time before we meet again. Many moons and seasons will have passed, before the sacred council-brand shall be again uncovered. Be watchful, therefore, and remember faithfully what you may now hear.

" In discoursing yesterday upon the duties of the keepers of the faith, I omitted some things important. The Great Spirit created this office. He designed that its duties should never end. There are some who are selected and set apart by our Maker, to perform the duties of this office. It is therefore their duty to be faithful, and to be always watching. These duties they must ever perform during their lives. The faithful, when they leave this earth, will have a pleasant path to travel in. The same office exists in heaven, the home of our Creator. They will take the same place when they arrive there. There are dreadful penalties awaiting those keepers of the faith who resign their office without a cause. Thus they said.

" It was the original intention of our Maker, that all our feasts of thanksgiving should be seasoned with the flesh of wild animals. But we are surrounded by the pale-faces, and in a short time the woods will be

all removed. Then there will be no more game for
the Indian to use in his feasts. The four Messengers
said, in consequence of this, that we might use the
flesh of domestic animals. This will not be wrong.
The pale-faces are pressing you upon every side. You
must therefore live as they do. How far you can do
so without sin, I will now tell you. You may grow
cattle, and build yourselves warm and comfortable
dwelling-houses. This is not sin; and it is all that
you can safely adopt of the customs of the pale-faces.
You cannot live as they do. Thus they said.

"Continue to listen: — It has pleased our Creator
to set apart as our Life, the Three Sisters. For this
special favor, let us ever be thankful. When you have
gathered in your harvest, let the people assemble, and
hold a general thanksgiving for so great a good. In
this way you will show your obedience to the will and
pleasure of your Creator. Thus they said.

"Many of you may be ignorant of the Spirit of
Medicine. It watches over all constantly, and assists
the needy whenever necessity requires. The Great
Spirit designed that some men should possess the gift
of skill in medicine. But he is pained to see a medicine man making exorbitant charges for attending the
sick. Our Creator made for us tobacco. This plant
must always be used in administering medicines.
When a sick person recovers his health, he must
return his thanks to the Great Spirit by means of
tobacco; for it is by his goodness that he is made well.
He blesses the medicine; and the medicine man must
receive as his reward whatever the gratitude of the restored may tender. This is right and proper. There

are many who are unfortunate, and cannot pay for attendance. It is sufficient for such to return thanks to the medicine man upon recovery. The remembrance that he has saved the life of a relative, will be a sufficient reward.

" Listen further to what the Great Spirit has been pleased to communicate to us: — He has made us, as a race, separate and distinct from the pale-face. It is a great sin to intermarry, and intermingle the blood of the two races. Let none be guilty of this transgression.

"At one time the four Messengers said to Handsome Lake, Lest the people should disbelieve you, and not repent and forsake their evil ways, we will now disclose to you the House of Torment, the dwelling-place of the Evil-minded. Handsome Lake was particular in describing to us all that he witnessed ; and the course which departed spirits were accustomed to take on leaving the earth. There was a road which led upwards. At a certain point it branched ; one branch led straight forward to the Home of the Great Spirit, and the other turned aside to the House of Torment. At the place where the roads separated were stationed two keepers, one representing the Good, and the other the Evil Spirit. When a person reached the fork, if wicked, by a motion from the Evil keeper, he turned instinctively upon the road which led to the abode of the Evil-minded. But if virtuous and good, the other keeper directed him upon the straight road. The latter was not much travelled ; while the former was so frequently trodden, that no grass could grow in the pathway. It sometimes happened that the keepers

had great difficulty in deciding which path the person
should take, when the good and bad actions of the
individual were nearly balanced. Those sent to the
House of Torment sometimes remain one day (which
is there one of our years). Some for a longer period.
After they have atoned for their sins, they pass to
heaven. But when they have committed either of the
great sins (witchcraft, murder, and infanticide), they
never pass to heaven, but are tormented forever.
Having conducted Handsome Lake to this place, he
saw a large and dark-colored mansion covered with
soot, and beside it stood a lesser one. One of the
four then held out his rod, and the top of the house
moved up, until they could look down upon all that
was within. He saw many rooms. The first object
which met his eye, was a haggard-looking man; his
sunken eyes cast upon the ground, and his form
half consumed by the torments he had undergone.
This man was a drunkard. The Evil-minded then
appeared, and called him by name. As the man
obeyed his call, he dipped from a caldron a quantity
of red-hot liquid, and commanded him to drink it, as
it was an article he loved. The man did as he was
directed, and immediately from his mouth issued a
stream of blaze. He cried in vain for help. The
Tormentor then requested him to sing and make himself merry, as was his wont while on earth, after drinking the fire-water. Let drunkards take warning from
this. Others were then summoned. There came
before him two persons, who appeared to be husband
and wife. He told them to exercise the privilege they
were so fond of while on the earth. They immediately

commenced a quarrel of words. They raged at each other with such violence, that their tongues and eyes ran out so far they could neither see nor speak. This, said they, is the punishment of quarrelsome and disputing husbands and wives. Let such also take warning, and live together in peace and harmony. Next he called up a woman who had been a witch. First he plunged her into a caldron of boiling liquid. In her cries of distress, she begged the Evil-minded to give her some cooler place. He then immersed her in one containing liquid at the point of freezing. Her cries then were, that she was too cold. This woman, said the four Messengers, shall always be tormented in this manner. He proceeded to mention the punishment which awaits all those who cruelly ill-treat their wives. The Evil-minded next called up a man who had been accustomed to beat his wife. Having led him up to a red-hot statue of a female, he directed him to do that which he was fond of while he was upon the earth. He obeyed, and struck the figure. The sparks flew in every direction, and by the contact his arm was consumed. Such is the punishment, they said, awaiting those who ill-treat their wives. From this take seasonable warning. He looked again and saw a woman, whose arms and hands were nothing but bones. She had sold fire-water to the Indians, and the flesh was eaten from her hands and arms. This, they said, would be the fate of rum-sellers. Again he looked, and in one apartment he saw and recognized *Ho-ne-yä'-wus* (Farmer's Brother), his former friend. He was engaged in removing a heap of sand, grain by grain; and although he labored continually, yet the heap of sand was not diminished. This, they said, was the punishment of those who sold land. Adjacent to the house of torment was a field of corn filled with weeds. He saw women in the act of cutting them down; but as fast as this was done, they grew up again. This, they said, was the punishment of lazy women. It would be proper and right, had we time, to tell more of this place of torment. But my time is limited, and I must pass to other things.

"The Creator made men dependent upon each other. He made them sociable beings; therefore, when your neighbor visits you, set food before him. If it be your next door neighbor, you must give him to eat. He will partake and thank you.

Again they said: — You must not steal. Should you want for anything necessary, you have only to tell your wants, and they will be supplied. This is right. Let none ever steal anything. Children are often tempted to take things home which do not belong to them. Let parents instruct their children in this rule.

Many of our people live to a very old age. Your Creator says that your deportment towards them must be that of reverence and affection. They have seen and felt much of the misery and pain of earth. Be always kind to them when old and helpless. Wash their hands and face, and nurse them with care. This is the will of the Great Spirit.

"It has been the custom among us to mourn for the dead one year. This custom is wrong. As it causes the death of many children, it must be abandoned. Ten days mourn for the dead, and not longer. When one dies, it is right and proper to make an address over the body, telling how much you loved the deceased. Great respect for the dead must be observed among us.

"At another time the four Messengers said to Handsome Lake, they would now show him the 'Destroyer of Villages' (Washington [1]), of whom you have so frequently heard. Upon the road leading to heaven he could see a light, far away in the distance, moving to and fro. Its brightness far exceeded the brilliancy of the noonday sun. They told him the journey was as follows: First, they came to a cold spring, which was a resting-place. From this point they proceeded into pleasant fairy grounds, which spread away in every direction. Soon they reached heaven. The light was dazzling. Berries of every description grew in vast abundance. Their size and quality were such that a single berry was more than sufficient to appease the appetite. A sweet fragrance perfumed the air. Fruits of every kind met the eye. The inmates of this celestial abode spent their time in amusement and repose. No evil could enter there. None in heaven ever transgress again. Families were reunited, and dwelt together in harmony. They possessed a bodily form, the senses, and the remembrances of the earthly life. But no white man ever entered heaven. Thus they said. He looked, and

---

[1] Washington was named by the Iroquois *Ha-no-dä-gä'-ne-ars*, which signifies the Destroyer of Villages. The Presidents have ever since been called by this name. They named the Governors of all the provinces with which they had intercourse, and afterwards continued the names to their successors.

saw an inclosure upon a plain, just without the entrance of heaven. Within it was a fort. Here he saw the 'Destroyer of Villages,' walking to and fro within the inclosure. His countenance indicated a great and a good man. They said to Handsome Lake : The man you see is the only pale-face who ever left the earth. He was kind to you, when on the settlement of the great difficulty between the Americans and the Great Crown (*Go-wek'-go-wä*), you were abandoned to the mercy of your enemies. The Crown told the great American, that as for his allies, the Indians, he might kill them if he liked. The great American judged that this would be cruel and unjust. He believed they were made by the Great Spirit, and were entitled to the enjoyment of life. He was kind to you, and extended over you his protection. For this reason, he has been allowed to leave the earth. But he is never permitted to go into the presence of the Great Spirit. Although alone, he is perfectly happy. All faithful Indians pass by him as they go to heaven. They see him, and recognize him, but pass on in silence. No word ever passes his lips.

" Friends and Relatives : — It was by the influence of this great man, that we were spared as a people, and yet live. Had he not granted us his protection, where would we have been ? Perished, all perished.

" The four Messengers further said to Handsome Lake, they were fearful that, unless the people repented and obeyed his commands, the patience and forbearance of their Creator would be exhausted; that he would grow angry with them, and cause their increase to cease.

"Our Creator made light and darkness. He made the sun to heat, and shine over the world. He made the moon, also, to shine by night, and to cool the world, if the sun made it too hot by day. The keeper of the clouds, by direction of the Great Spirit, will then cease to act. The keeper of the springs and running brooks will cease to rule them for the good of man. The sun will cease to fulfil its office. Total darkness will then cover the earth. A great smoke will rise, and spread over the face of the earth. Then will come out of it all monsters, and poisonous animals created by the Evil-minded; and they, with the wicked upon the earth, will perish together.

"But before this dreadful time shall come, the Great Spirit will take home to himself all the good and faithful. They will lay themselves down to sleep, and from this sleep of death, they will rise, and go home to their Creator. Thus they said.

"I have now done. I close thus, that you may remember and understand the fate which awaits the earth, and the unfaithful and unbelieving. Our Creator looks down upon us. The four Beings from above see us. They witness with pleasure this assemblage, and rejoice at the object for which it is gathered. It is now forty-eight years since we first began to listen to the renewed will of our Creator. I have been unable, during the time allotted to me, to rehearse all the sayings of *Gä-ne-o-dï'-yo*. I regret very much that you cannot hear them all.

"Counsellors, Warriors, Women and Children: — I have done. I thank you all for your attendance, and for your kind and patient attention. May the

Great Spirit, who rules all things, watch over and protect you from every harm and danger, while you travel the journey of life. May the Great Spirit bless you all, and bestow upon you life, health, peace and prosperity ; and may you, in turn, appreciate his great goodness. *Na-ho'*."

Chapter IV

SUFFICIENT has been said in the preceding
pages to convey an impression of the uses of
the Dance among the Iroquois. It remains
to notice the several dances themselves, to point out
some of the characteristics of each, and also to exhibit
more fully the spirit of this amusement, and its power
over the minds of the people.

With the Iroquois, as with the red race at large,
dancing was not only regarded as a thanksgiving
ceremonial, in itself acceptable to the Great Spirit,
but they were taught to consider it a divine art, designed by *Hä-wen-ne'-yu* for their pleasure, as well
as for his worship. It was cherished as one of the
most suitable modes of social intercourse between
the sexes, but more especially as the great instrumentality for arousing patriotic excitement, and for
keeping alive the spirit of the nation. The popular
enthusiasm broke forth in this form, and was nourished and stimulated by this powerful agency. These
dances sprang, as it were, a living reflection from the
Indian mind. With their wild music of songs and
rattles, their diversities of step and attitude, their
graces of motion, and their spirit-stirring associations,

they contain within themselves both a picture and a realization of Indian life. The first stir of feeling of which the Indian youth was conscious was enkindled by the dance; the first impulse of patriotism, the earliest dreams of ambition were awakened by their inspiring influences. In their patriotic, religious and social dances, into which classes they are properly divisible, resided the soul of Indian life. It was more in the nature of a spell upon the people than of a rational guiding spirit. It bound them down to trivial things, but it bound them together; it stimulated them to deeds of frenzy, but it fed the flame of patriotism.

The Iroquois had thirty-two distinct dances, out of which number twenty-six were claimed to be wholly of their own invention. Twenty-one of these are still in use among the present Iroquois. To each a separate history and object attached, as well as a different degree of popular favor. Some were costume dances, and were performed by a small and select band; some were designed exclusively for females, others for warriors alone; but the greater part of them were open to all of both sexes who desired to participate. Many of these dances, without doubt, have been handed down among the Iroquois for centuries, transmitted from generation to generation, until their origin is lost even to tradition. Others spread throughout the whole Indian family, and were known and used from Maine to Oregon. Indian amusements, as well as arts, were eminently diffusive, as Indian life was much the same from ocean to ocean. They are better described by their effects than by a minute examination of the mode, manner and circumstances of each in detail. It is to their influence, as a means of action, that they owe their chief importance. And it is to the zeal and enthusiasm with which they were cherished and performed, that attention should principally be directed. Their overpowering influence in arousing the Indian spirit, and in excluding all thoughts of a different life, and their resulting effect upon the formation of Indian character cannot be too highly estimated.

The tenacity with which the Iroquois have always adhered to these dances furnishes the highest evidence of their hold upon the affections of the people. From the earliest days of the Jesuit missions, the most unremitted efforts of the missionaries have been put forth for their suppression. Christian parties were organized at an early day in each nation, of such as were willing to abandon the dance and their religious festivals, and lead a different life. These parties, down to the present time, have always been largely in the minority, except among the unexpatriated Oneidas, who are now entirely denationalized, and, perhaps, the Tuscaroras, who are partially so; but the body of the Senecas, Onondagas and Cayugas, upon their several reservations, still cling to their ancient customs, and glory in the dance as ardently as did their forefathers. When it loses its attractions, they will cease to be Indians.[1]

[1] A Mourning council of the Iroquois was held at Tonawanda, in October, 1846, to raise up sachems. There were about six hundred Iroquois in attendance, representing all of the Six Nations. On the second day the Great Feather Dance was performed by a select band of Onondaga and Seneca dancers. The author then first had occasion to realize

The Feather dance and the War dance were the two great performances of the Iroquois. One had a religious, and the other a patriotic character. Both were costume dances. They were performed by a select band, ranging from fifteen to twenty-five, who were distinguished for their powers of endurance, activity and spirit. Besides these, there were four other costume dances. In the residue, the performers, who were the people at large, appeared in their ordinary apparel, and sometimes participated to the number of two or three hundred at one time. The Iroquois costume may be called strictly an apparel for the dance. This was the chief occasion on which the warrior was desirous to appear in his best attire. Before describing these dances, it will be proper to notice the various articles of apparel which made up the full-dress costume of the Iroquois.

One of the most prominent articles of apparel was the Kilt, *Gä-kä'-ah* (see plate, I. 184), which was secured around the waist by a belt, and descended to the knee. In ancient times this was made of deerskin. It was fringed and embroidered with porcupine quill-work. Some of these kilts would excite admiration by the exactness of their finish and adjustment, and the neatness of the material. In modern times various fabrics have been substituted for the deer-skin, although the latter is still used.

the magical influence which these dances have upon the Indian. It was impossible even for the spectator to resist the general enthusiasm. It was remarked to *Da-ät'-ga-dose* (Abraham La Fort), an educated Onondaga sachem, that they would be Indians forever, if they held to these dances. He replied, that he knew it, and for that reason he would be the last to give them up.

COSTUME

The porcupine (*Gä-ha'-dä*) is covered with a species of quill perfectly round, without down or feather, and terminating in a sharp point. The small quills are from one to four inches in length, and are white with the exception of the tip ends or about one-fifth of the quills, which are of a dark brown color, and give to the animal its dark appearance. After being picked and seasoned they are colored red, blue and yellow by artificial dyes, and then used in connection with the white ones. For heavy border work the quills are moistened and flattened down, and in that form are used, as will be seen in the plate (I. 44); but for vine or figure work, a thread is stitched through the deer-skin and around the quill, and drawn down so as to compress it. This process is repeated at intervals, the quill being bent between the stitches. No patterns are used to work from, the eye and the taste being the principal guides. In combining colors much taste is displayed.

Upon the head-dress, *Gus-to'-weh* (see plate, I. 254), the most conspicuous part of the costume, much attention was bestowed. The frame consisted of a band of splint, adjusted around the head, with in some instances a cross-band arching over the top, from side to side. A cap of net-work, or other construction, was then made to enclose the frame. Around the splint, in later times, a silver band was fastened, which completed the lower part. From the top a cluster of white feathers depended. Besides this, a single feather of the largest size was set in the crown of the head-dress, inclining backwards from the head. It was secured in a small tube, which was

253

fastened to the cross-splint, and in such a manner as to allow the feather to revolve in the tube. This feather, which was usually the plume of the eagle, is the characteristic of the Iroquois head-dress.

Gus-to'-weh, or Head Dress.

Next was the Leggin, *Gise'-hă* (see plate, I. 256), which was fastened above the knee, and descended upon the moccason. It was also made originally of deer-skin, and ornamented with quill-work upon the bottom and side, the embroidered edge being worn in front. In later times, red broadcloth, embroidered with bead-work, as represented in the plate, has been substituted for deer-skin in most cases. Much ingenuity and taste were displayed in the designs, and in the execution of the work upon this article of apparel. The warrior might well be proud of this part of his costume.

GOS-TO-WEH OR HEAD DRESS.

GA-DE-US-HA OR NECK LACE

The Moccason, *Ah-tä-quä-o'-weh* (see plate, I. 35), was also made of deer-skin. In the modern moccason, represented in the plate, the front part is worked with porcupine quills after the ancient fashion, while the part which falls down upon the sides is embroidered with bead-work according to the present taste.

Not the least important article was the belt, *Gä-geh'-tä* (see plate, I. 101), which was prized as highly as any part of the costume. The one represented in the plate is of Indian manufacture. These belts were braided by hand, the beads being interwoven in the process of braiding.   Belts of deer-skin were also worn. These belts were worn over the left shoulder and around the waist.

Arm Bands, Knee Bands, and Wrist Bands, made of various articles and ornamented in divers ways,

Knee Rattle of Deers' Hoofs.

were likewise a part of the costume. Sometimes they were made of deer-skin, sometimes of white dog-skin, and in later times of red and blue velvet, embroidered with bead-work, as represented in the plate (I. 216).

In addition to the knee-bands, Knee Rattles of deers' hoofs, as shown in the figure, and in modern

times, of strips of metal, or of bells, made a necessary part of the costume. Personal ornaments of
various kinds, together with the war-club, the tomahawk, and the scalping-knife, completed the attire.

The war-club used in the dance, was usually a light
article, of which the following is a representation : —

Gä-je^l-wä, or War-Club.

The various articles of apparel which now make up
the costume of the Iroquois, are precisely the same
that they were at the epoch of the discovery. No
change has been made in the articles themselves, although there have been changes in the materials of
which they were made. The deer-skin, in later days,
has been laid aside for the broadcloth, and the porcupine quill for the bead. By making a resubstitution
of material, the original costume would be recovered
in full.

In preparing for the dance, all the articles above
described were not necessarily used by each individual.
Those strictly needful were the head-dress, the belt
and kilt, to which each wearer added such ornaments
and rattles as he was disposed. Usually they were
nude down to the waist, and also below the knees, to
give greater freedom to their limbs. A great diversity
could be seen in their costumes when brought together
in the dance, in consequence of the different fabrics of

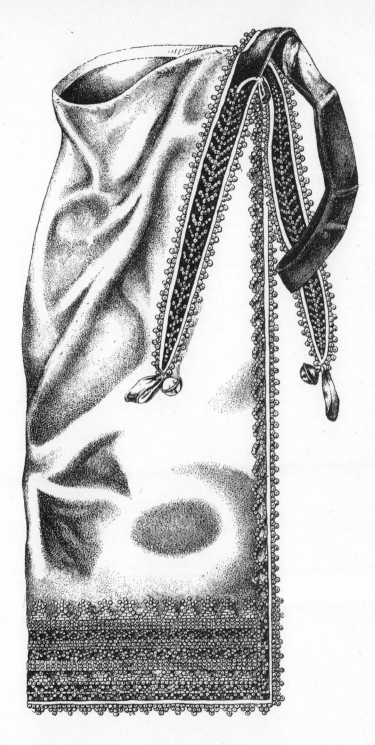

GISE-HA or MALE LEGGIN.

which they were composed, and the variety in their personal ornaments, notwithstanding every article of apparel was of the same pattern. Specimens of full Iroquois costumes, both male and female, are given in the engravings which are introduced as frontispieces.[14] These, and the several plates which are given to illustrate the male costume in detail, will save the necessity of any further description.

Gä-no-jo'-o, or Indian Drum.
1 foot.

The two dances mentioned before this digression were the highest in the popular favor. One was of original invention, the other imported; one was of a strictly religious character, and the other of a patriotic; but both were equally effective to arouse the enthusiasm of the people. All things considered, however, the last of the two, the War dance, *Wä-sä'-seh*, was the favorite. It was the mode of enlistment for a perilous expedition, the dance which preceded the departure of the band, and with which they celebrated their return. It was the dance at the ceremony of raising up sachems, at the adoption of a captive, at the entertainment of a guest, the first dance taught to the young. It was not of Iroquois origin, but was adopted from the Sioux, as its name imports, reaching back through them to a remote antiquity.[1] The characteristic feature of this dance is to be found in the speeches which were made by those surrounding the band of dancers between each tune, or at each break in the dance. From this source the people derived as much entertainment as they did excitement from the performance itself. It was the only dance in which speeches and replies were appropriate, or ever introduced; and in this particular it was a novelty, leading oftentimes to the highest amusement. By these speeches, which both relieved the performers and diverted the people, the dance was lengthened out to two and even three hours, before the spirits of the company were expended.

The War dance was usually performed in the evening. It was only brought out on prominent occasions, or at domestic councils of unusual interest. Fifteen made a full company, but oftentimes twenty-five and even thirty participated. After the business of the day was disposed of, and the dusk of evening had crept in,

---

[1] The name of the Sioux in the Seneca dialect is *Wä-sä'-seh-o-no.* By contraction and usage, the word *Wä-sä'-seh* is now used for the Sioux dance, the name by which the War dance has always been known among the Iroquois. This dance has been ascribed by some to the Shawnees, and called *Sa-wä-no'-o-no,* or the Shawnee dance, this being the Seneca name of the Shawnees. One of the Iroquois names of this dance is *Ne-ja';* but *Wä-sä'-seh* is the customary name.

preparations began for the dance. The people gathered within the council-house, usually in increased numbers, because of this expected entertainment, and arranging themselves in favorable positions, they quietly awaited the approach of the dancers. The arrangements were made, including the selection of the number, the appointment of the leader, and of the singers of the war-songs, by the keepers of the faith. In an adjacent lodge, the band assembled to array themselves in their costumes, and to paint and decorate their persons for the occasion. The war-whoop ever and anon broke in upon the stillness of the evening, indicating to the listening and expectant throng within the council-house, that their preparations were progressing to a completion. A keeper of the faith, in the mean time, occupied the attention of the people with a brief speech upon the nature and objects of this dance. Presently, a nearer war-whoop ringing through the air, announced that the band were approaching. Preceded by their leader, and marching in file to the beat of the drum, they drew near to the council-house. As they came up, the crowd gave way, the leader crossed the threshold, followed quickly by his feathered band, and immediately opened the dance. In an instant they grouped themselves within a circular area, standing thick together, the singers commenced the war-song, the drums beat time, and the dancers made the floor resound with their stirring feet. After a moment the song ceased, and with it the dance; the band walking around a common centre to the beat of the drum at half time. Another song soon commenced, the drums quickened their time, and the dance was resumed. In the middle of the song there was a change in the music, accompanied with a slight cessation of the dance, after which it became more animated than before, until the song ended, and the band again walked to the beat of the drum. Each tune or war-song lasted about two minutes, and the interval between them was about as long. These songs were usually recited by four singers, using two drums of the kind represented in the figure, to mark time, and as an accompaniment. The drums beat time about twice in a second, the voices of the singers keeping pace, thus making a rapid and strongly accented species of music.[1]

It would be difficult, if not impossible, to describe the step, except generally. With the whites, the dancing is entirely upon the toe of the foot, with rapid changes of position, and but slight changes of attitude. But with the Iroquois, it was chiefly upon the heel, with slow changes of position, and rapid changes of attitude. The heel is raised and brought down with great quickness and force, by muscular strength, to keep time with the beat of the drum, to make a re-sounding noise by the concussion, and at the same time to shake the knee-rattles, which contributed materially to the "pomp and circumstance" of the dance. In the War dance, the attitudes were those of

---

[1] These war songs are in a dead language, or, at all events, the Iroquois are unable to interpret them. They are in regular verses, or measured sentences, and were learned by them with the dance originally. Charlevoix has furnished a translation of some of these songs as follows : "I am brave and intrepid. I do not fear death, nor any kind of torture. Those who fear them are cowards. They are less than women. Life is nothing to those who have courage. May my enemies be confounded with despair and rage." These songs were sung by captives at the torture ; and doubtless those used in the War dance are of the same general character.

the violent passions, and consequently were not graceful. At the same instant of time, in a group of dancers, one might be seen in the attitude of attack, another of defence; one in the act of drawing the bow, another of striking with the war-club; some in the act of throwing the tomahawk, some of listening, or of watching an opportunity, and others of striking the foe. These violent motions of the body, while they, perhaps, increased the spirit and animation of the dance, led to disagreeable distortions of the countenance, as well as to uncouth attitudes. But, at the same time, the striking costumes of the dancers, their erect forms at certain stages of the figure, their suppleness and activity, the wild music, the rattle of the dance, together with the excitable and excited throng around them, made up a scene of no common interest.

In this dance, the war-whoop and the response always preceded each song. It was given by the leader, and answered by the band. A description of this terrific outbreak of human voices is scarcely possible. It was a prolonged sound upon a high note, with a decadence near the end, followed by an abrupt and explosive conclusion, in which the voice was raised again to the original pitch. The whole band responded in a united scream upon the same key with which the leader concluded, and at the same instant.[1]

[1]

Solo.

Ah . . . . . . ah.

An attempt is here made to represent this wild cry. It is given by the Indian with wide-open mouth. His voice slides down the descending notes, when he pauses an instant to take a new inspiration, all which is to be expended in the sudden and far-reaching yell with which

In this celebrated dance, therefore, which has doubtless been used for centuries, and been performed
throughout the whole area of the American republic,
we find this simple succession of acts: the war-whoop
and responses, the simultaneous commencement of the
war-song and the dance, the slight cessation at the
middle of the tune, with a change in the music, the re-
newal of the dance with redoubled animation, and the
final conclusion of the war-song in perhaps less than
two minutes from its commencement; and lastly, the
walk at the beat of the drum around a central point
for about two minutes, until the war-whoop again
sounded, and another war-song was introduced. This
round was continued until the spirit of the dancers
began to flag, and the desires of the people had been
reasonably gratified. Without any speeches between
the tunes to relieve the band, it usually lasted about
an hour; but with speeches, it often continued for
three hours with unabated animation.

Any one present was at liberty to make a speech
at any stage of the dance. His desire was manifested
by a rap. At the sound the dance ceased, or, if
finished, and the band were walking, they were required to stop, and all present, as well as the music,
to be silent. The only condition affixed to the right
of making a speech, was that of bestowing a present
at its close upon the dancers, or upon the one to
whom it was addressed. After the speech was concluded, and the present delivered, the war-whoop and
responses were again sounded, the drums beat, the

the piece concludes. On this last note the whole band join in chorus, using
the syllables "ah um," connected in one, or something like it.

song and the dance commenced, and were ended
as before. Then followed another speech, and still
others, alternating with the songs, or suspending
the dance at the moment of its highest animation,
at the pleasure of the speaker. In this manner the
War dance was continued until the spirit of enjoyment
began to subside, when the final war-whoop put an end
to the dance, and the band retired.

These speeches were often pleasantries between
individuals, or strictures upon each other's foibles,
or earnest exhortations, or perchance patriotic ebul-
litions of feeling, according to the fancy of the
person and of the moment. Some of them were
received with rounds of applause, some with jeers,
and others with seriousness and deference. They
usually lasted but two or three minutes. The Indian
has a keen appreciation of wit, and is fond of both
jest and repartee, as well as of ridicule.

To convey a fuller impression of the character of
these speeches, and of the nature of the dance itself,
a few specimens will be introduced. These speeches
are short and rather unmeaning, when separated
from the occasion, and the connection in which they
were called forth. Those most interesting would
require an explanation of collateral circumstances to
be understood, and they are therefore excluded.
Those to be given are not particularly interesting;
but they explain themselves, and will answer the purpose for which they are introduced as fully as if they
sparkled with wit.

After the band came in and opened the War dance,
several songs were performed before any one was

disposed to interrupt them. All eyes were turned upon the several costumes of the band, upon the spirit and activity of individuals in the dance, and the animation and enthusiasm of the party. Round after round followed, until the spirit of the company was fully aroused, when it began to expend itself in speeches and witticisms. The first rap was made by *To-no-aï-o* a humorous old chief. Silence being restored, he spoke as follows: " Friends and Relatives — I am occasionally fond of a drink of the strong waters. I do not know how it is with *Tä-yä-dä-o-wuh'-kuh*, (the guest to whom the War dance was given),[9] but presume it is something the same with him, and therefore I send him a sixpence to buy a drink with on his way home." Gives the money. Again the drum sounded, the war-whoop and responses were given, and the music and the dance were resumed. At the end of the tune another rap restored silence. *Hä-sque'-sa-o*, another chief, and one somewhat noted for his fondness for the fire-water, spoke as follows: " Friends and Relatives — I am much pleased with the dance, and hope it will continue to be well sustained. I return my thanks to the war-dancers for the spirit with which they perform their duty. I wish them all prosperity and long life. If any one should look at me, they will find that I keep my eye fixed upon the dancers, and furthermore, that I have a good eye, so much so, that one would think I wore glasses. I take from my pocket a shilling for the dancers." Gives the money. The dance was then resumed. At the end of the song, the speech of *Hä-sque-sa-o* called out a reply from *Sä-de-wä'-na*, as follows: "Friends and Relatives — We have just heard some one on the other side of the house announce, that he had an eye so bright that one would think he wore spectacles. But as he has a pair of red eyes, we must, I suppose, conclude that he uses red spectacles." Gives tobacco to the dancers. This hit at *Hä-sque'-sa-o's* infirmity was received with applause. Again the dance goes on as usual. Among the dancers were men of all sizes, figures and heights. There was one warrior, especially, of such herculean proportions that he might be called a giant. He furnished a theme for the next speech, which was made by *Hä-sa-no-an'-da*, the dance having ceased, as follows: "Friends and Relatives — I admire the ease and grace with which *Hä-ho'-yäs* manages his wonderful proportions. He has every reason to be proud of his size and dignity. I propose to give him a present of two plugs of tobacco, supposing that it will be sufficient for *one quid*." Gives the tobacco. *Hä-ho'-yäs* received the tobacco with seeming pleasure, and the people the jest with considerable merriment. At the conclusion of the next song, he thus replied: "Friends and Relatives —- I return my thanks to *Hä-sa-no-an'-da* for his present. I assure him that my intellectual capacities correspond very justly with my physical dimensions. I hope my brother will publish my fame from the rising to the setting sun." Again the war-whoop sounded, the music opened, and the dance was renewed.

Other speeches were made from time to time, some of which called forth applause, and in due time a reply adapted to the case. After a number had thus spoken, *Sä-de-wä'-na* rapped again. When the music and the dancers were still, he thus said : " Friends and Relatives — I have made another strike. I desire to make a present to the women who have assisted in preparing the feast. But as I cannot give presents to all, I wish to see the one who has to-day eaten the most beef, and is considered the most greedy. I request her to come forward and receive the present." One of them, *Gi-an'-ok*, advanced and received the money, good-naturedly, which the people applauded. After a few more courses of the dance, a speech was made by *O-no'-sä*, of a more serious cast, as follows : " Friends and Relatives — We have reason to glory in the achievements of our ancestors. I behold with sadness the present declining state of our noble race. Once the warlike yell and the painted band were the terror of the white man. Then our fathers were strong, and their power was felt and acknowledged far and wide over the American continent. But we have been reduced and broken by the cunning and rapacity of the white-skinned race. We are now compelled to crave, as a blessing, that we may be allowed to live upon our own lands, to cultivate our own fields, to drink from our own springs, and to mingle our bones with those of our fathers. Many winters ago, our wise ancestors predicted that a great monster, with white eyes, would come from the east, and, as he advanced, would consume the land. This monster is the white race, and the prediction is near its fulfilment. They advised their children, when they became weak, to plant a tree with four roots, branching to the north, the south, the east, and the west; and then collecting under its shade, to dwell together in unity and harmony. This tree, I propose, shall be this very spot. Here we will gather, here live, and here die." Gives tobacco to the dancers. The dance was then resumed as before, and continued until a rap announced another speech from *To-no-aï-o*, the first speaker, who, after silence was restored, addressed the dancers: "In my view of the dance you do not do it as well as it can be done; although you doubtless have done as well as you know how. When I was a young man, I was the greatest dancer of my time. I did not know any one who could surpass me in the War dance. Furthermore, I was considered the best singer of the war-songs. I hope, however, you will continue to do the best you can, even though you fail to perform this dance as well as it can be done. I have another piece of the leaf which I will turn over to the singers. I wish them to swallow the juice, as it will make their voices clear, and help their singing." Gives the tobacco. Again the dance was resumed. After the next tune, this speech called out a reply from *Jä-ese'*, as follows: "Friends and Relatives — We have just heard a speaker, on the other side of the house, boasting of what he had done in his younger days. I do not like to hear such high speaking of one's self. I should like to see *To-no-aï-o* come out and show the people what he can do, or what he used to do in his younger days." Gives money to the dancers. Again the war-whoop sounded, the responses followed, and the music and the dance made the house resound. In this manner was this famous dance conducted by our primitive inhabitants around their domestic council-fires.

These illustrations will suffice to exhibit the general character of these speeches, as well as of the dance itself. In the numerous addresses and witticisms which the War dance called forth, the Iroquois took the highest delight. They served the double purpose of relieving the dancers themselves, who would soon have been exhausted by continuous exertion, and of entertaining the people in the interval. This was the secret of its great popularity as a dance, and of its universal adoption. To this day, a well-conducted War dance is the highest entertainment known among the Iroquois.

Gus-dä'-wa-sä, or Rattle.

Second in the public estimation, but first intrinsically, stood the great Feather dance, *O-sto-weh'-go-wä*, sometimes called the Religious dance, because it was specially consecrated to the worship of the Great Spirit. The invention, or at least the introduction of this dance, is ascribed to the first *To-do-dä'-ho*, at the period of the formation of the League. In its Iroquois origin, they all concur. It was performed by a select band, ranging from fifteen to thirty, in full costume, and was chiefly used at their religious festivals, although it was one of the prominent dances on all great occasions in Indian life. This dance was the most splendid, graceful and remarkable in the whole collection, requiring greater powers of endurance, suppleness and flexibility of person, and gracefulness of deportment, than either of the others. The *saltandi ars*, or dancing art, found in the Feather dance its highest achievement, at least in the Indian family; and it may be questioned whether a corresponding figure can be found among those which are used in refined communities, which will compare with it in those particulars which make up a spirited and graceful dance.

The music was furnished by two singers, seated in the centre of the room, each having a turtle-shell rattle of the kind represented in the figure.[1] It consisted of a series of songs or measured verses, which required about two minutes each for their recitation. They were all religious songs, some of them in praise of the Great Spirit, some in praise of various objects in nature which ministered to their wants, others in the nature of thanksgivings to *Ha-wen-ne'-yu*, or supplications of his continued protection. The rattles were used to mark time, and as an accompaniment to the songs. In using them, they were struck upon the seat as often as twice or thrice in a second, the song and the step of the dancers keeping time, notwithstanding the rapidity of the beat.

The band arrayed themselves in their costumes in

---

[1] To make this rattle they remove the animal from the shell, and after drying it, they place within it a handful of flint-corn, and then sew up the skin which is left attached to the shell. The neck of the turtle is then stretched over a wooden handle.

an adjacent lodge, came into the council-house, and
opened in all respects as in the case last described.
Instead of grouping, however, within the area of a
circle, they ranged themselves in file, and danced
slowly around the council-house in an elliptical line.
When the music ceased, the dance also was suspended,
and the party walked in column to the beat of the
rattles. After an interval of about two minutes, the
rattles quickened their time, the singers commenced
another song, and the warriors, at the same instant,
the dance. The leader, standing at the head of the
column, opened, followed by those behind. As they
advanced slowly around the room, in the dance, they
gestured with their arms, and placed their bodies in a
great variety of positions, but, unlike the practice in
the War dance, always keeping their forms erect.
None of the attitudes in this dance were those of the
violent passions, but rather of the mild and gentle
feelings. Consequently, there were no distortions
either of the countenance or the body; but all their
movements and positions were extremely graceful,
dignified and imposing. The step has the same
general peculiarities as that in the dance last described,
but yet is quite distinct from it. Each foot in succession is raised from two to eight inches from the floor,
and the heel is then brought down with great force as
frequently as the beat of the rattles. Frequently one
heel is brought down twice or three times before it
alternates with the other. This will convey an impression of the surprising activity of this dance, in
which every muscle of the body appears to be strung
to its highest degree of tension. The concussion of

the foot upon the floor served the double purpose of shaking the rattles and bells, which form a part of the costume, and of adding to the noise and animation of the dance.

The dancers were usually nude down to the waist, with the exception of ornaments upon their arms and necks, as represented in the engraving, thus exposing their well-formed chests, finely rounded arms, and their smooth, evenly colored skins, of a clear and brilliant copper color. This exposure of the person, not in any sense displeasing, contributed materially to the beauty of the costume, and gave a striking expression to the figure of the dancer. Such was the physical exertion put forth in this dance, that before it closed, the vapor of perspiration steamed up, like smoke, from their uncovered backs. No better evidence than this need be given, that it was a dance full of earnestness and enthusiasm. One of their aims was to test each other's powers of endurance. It not unfrequently happened that a part of the original number yielded from exhaustion before the dance was ended. Nothing but practice superadded to flexibility of person and great muscular strength would enable even an Indian to perform this dance. When the popular applause was gained by one of the band for spirited or graceful dancing, he was called out to stand at the head of the column, and lead the party : in this way several changes of leaders occurred before the final conclusion of the figure.

In this dance the women participated, if they were disposed. They wore, however, their ordinary apparel, and entered by themselves at the foot of the column. The female step is entirely unlike the one described. They moved sideways in this figure, simply raising themselves alternately upon each foot from heel to toe, and then bringing down the heel upon the floor, at each beat of the rattle, keeping pace with the slowly advancing column. With the females dancing was a quiet and not ungraceful amusement.

As a scene, its whole effect was much increased by the arrangement of the dancers into column. In this long array of costumes, the peculiar features of each were brought more distinctly into view, and by keeping the elliptical area around which they moved, entirely free from the pressing throng of Indian spectators, a better opportunity was afforded to all to witness the performance. To one who has never seen this dance, it would be extremely difficult to convey any notion of its surprising activity, and its inspiring influence upon the spectators. Requiring an almost continuous exertion, it is truly a marvellous performance.

The Thanksgiving dance, *Gä-na'-o-uh*, was likewise a costume dance, and given by a select band. It resembles the one last described so closely, both in step and plan, that it is not necessary to describe it.

One of the most simple figures among the Iroquois, was called the Trotting dance, *Gä-dä'-shote*. It was usually the opening dance at councils, and at private entertainments, when no costume figures were introduced. A person appointed to act as leader, followed by a few others, took the floor and began. Others joined in as the column passed around the room.

The music was entirely vocal, and furnished by those who danced. It consisted of about twenty different songs, each lasting something less than two minutes. In this dance the tune was the mere repetition of one exclamation by those at the head of the column, followed by a response, in chorus, from the residue. Three specimens are given in illustration. The leader, in concert with those nearest him, sang the following syllables: *Yä-hä'-we-yä-hä'*, to which all the others responded, *Hä-hä'*. This would be repeated and responded to, for about two minutes, the pronunciation of the syllables being subjected to a musical variation each time. When the tune ended, the band walked for about the same length of time. The next song might consist of the syllables *Gä-no'-oh-he-yo'*, with the response *Wä-hä'-ah-he-yo'*. This would be continued, and the key varied, in the same manner as the last. After this was ended, and the dancers had refreshed themselves by walking, perhaps the next song would consist of the following syllables: *Yu-wä'-na-he-yo'*, and the response *Wä-hä'-ah-ha'*.

As to the step it was very simple, being nearly a trot, or alternate step on each foot. In dancing, those engaged stood close to each other, and advanced slowly around the council-house. The women participated, but they were by themselves at the foot of the column. As this dance was extremely simple, it was not uncommon to see two and even three hundred engaged in it at one time, moving around in three or four concentric lines.

Another figure, in very general use, was called the Fish dance, *Ga-so-wä'-o-no*. It was of foreign origin. The music consisted of singing, accompanied with the drum, and the squash-shell rattle; the two singers seating themselves in the centre of the room facing each other, and using the drum and rattle to mark time, and increase the volume of the music. The step was merely an elevation from heel to toe, twice repeated upon each foot alternately; bringing down the heel each alternate time with considerable force, to mark time and make the floor resound.

The dance was commenced by the leader, who took the floor, followed by others, and walked to the beat of the drum. When the song commenced, each alternate dancer faced round, thus bringing the column into sets of two each, face to face, those who turned dancing backwards, but the whole band moving around the room, as in other cases. Each song or tune lasted about three minutes. At the end of the first minute there was a break in the music, and the sets turned, thus reversing their positions; at the end of the second there was another change in the music, in the midst of which the sets turned again, which brought them back to their original positions. Through the third and last subdivision of the time, the dance was continued with increased animation. At the close of it, those who had been dancing backwards faced around, and the whole column walked about two minutes, to the beat of the drum. Another tune was then commenced and finished in the same manner.

The peculiarity of this dance was the opportunity which it afforded the Indian maiden to select whomever she preferred as a partner. In this particular the custom of refined communities was reversed. The warrior never solicited the maiden to dance with him; that privilege was accorded to her alone. In the midst of

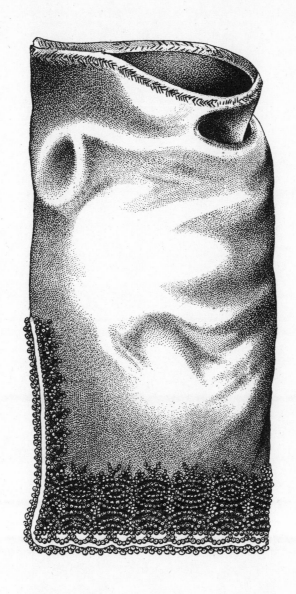

GISE-HĂ or FEMALE LEGGIN.

the dance, the females present themselves in pairs between any set they may select, thus giving to each a partner. This rule prevails in all Indian dances ; so that the Indian maiden at her own convenience " gracefully presents her personage to the one she designs to favor, and thus quietly engages herself in the dance." In none of the changes of position in this dance do the partners join hands. This figure usually continues less than an hour. Sometimes, as a mark of respect to a guest, or distinguished chief, two women presented themselves before him, as partners in the dance.

The Passing dance, *Ga-no'-ga-yo*, was also in high favor. It is similar to the last, the column being divided into sets of two each, the women engaging in whichever set they please. At a certain stage of the song, the woman passed her partner, and took the next, her place being supplied from behind. They danced around the room, facing each other in pairs, the men moving backwards. The music and the step were about the same as in the dance last described.

An occasional and very singular figure was called the Dance for the Dead. It was known as the *O-ke'-wä*. It was danced by the women alone. The music was entirely vocal, a select band of singers being stationed in the centre of the room. To the songs for the dead, which they sang, the dancers joined in chorus. It was plaintive and mournful music. This dance was usually separate from all councils, and the only dance of the occasion. It commenced at dusk or soon after, and continued until towards morning, when the shades of the dead, who were believed to be present and participate in the dance, were supposed to disappear. This dance was had whenever a family, which had lost a member, called for it, which was usually about a year after the event. In the spring and fall, it was often given for all the dead indiscriminately, who were believed then to revisit the earth and join in the dance.

One of their performances was called the Buffalo dance, *Da-ge'-yă-go-o-an'-no.* It was designed for males alone. The music consisted of singing, accom-

Gus-dă'-wa-să, or Squash-shell Rattles.

panied with the drum and the rattle. Its principal feature was the attempt to imitate the actions of the buffalo. According to tradition, this dance originated in a warlike expedition of the Iroquois against the Cherokees. When they had proceeded as far as the Kentucky salt lick, they heard, for the first time, the buffaloes, "singing their favorite songs" (bellowing and grumbling). From this bellowing the music, and from their actions the plan of the dance, were made.

In connection with the dances of the Iroquois, may be mentioned their concerts, which occupy a conspicuous place in their amusements. But one will be noticed of the four, which make up the number of kinds. It was called the *O-ee-dose'*. It was given in the night, in a dark room, and no women were allowed to be present. Those engaged in the concert were seated on benches around the room, in a continuous row, each one holding in his hand a rattle, of the kind represented in the figure. These rattles were made to give each one a different note, by means of different-sized shells, and holes bored in them to emit the sound. Among twenty of them, rattled together at such a concert, no two would give the same sound. Corn was placed inside the shell. When the parties were ready, one of their number sang a song, to which they all beat time with their rattles, and at certain intervals all joined in the song in chorus. Another then commenced a song, which was continued and finished in the same manner. After each one in turn had sung his song, which, with the accompaniments and the choruses, made a not unpleasant entertainment, the concert was ended.[1]

The other three are the Medicine concert, *Gä-no-dä'-yo-suh;* the Female concert, *O-e-un'-do-tä;* and the Thanksgiving concert, *Ah'-do-weh*, before described.

[1] The Indian appears to have had a good perception of time, and to have measured it, in his music and dances, with considerable exactness; but in tune he was sadly deficient. He knew nothing of the natural intervals of tones and semi-tones. There runs always through his music one predominant and constantly recurring sound, from which the others vary by all kinds of irregular intervals and fractions of intervals. The tunes of the Iroquois, if the name may be given to their rude minstrelsy, were both numerous and varied, and capable, also, of inspiring enthusiasm or sadness. In their occasional songs, as in the *Ah-do'-weh*, the music, as well as the words, was often *impromptu*. The Indian voice, especially that of the female, is musical, and highly capable of cultivation.

It will not be necessary to describe the remaining dances. Sufficient, at least, has been presented, to give a general idea of the Dance among the Iroquois. A few of them have been given in detail, as they seemed calculated to furnish a glimpse of Indian society. These amusements of our primitive inhabitants are not, in themselves, devoid of interest, although they indicate a tendency of mind unbefitting rational men. A hunter by nature and by inclination, averse to cities, and impatient of labor, the chase, the war-path, and the council-fire, with the dance, furnished the three great employments of his life. Who shall tell how much the hopes, the friendships, the happiness, and even the virtues of the Indian, were bound up in indissoluble connection with the Dance? With it the Iroquois kindled the flame of patriotism which glowed in his breast, while vindicating the prowess of his race upon the hills of New England, on the prairies of the Mississippi, or in the trackless forests of the South. With it he celebrated his victories, and in the days of peace cultivated his social affections. And with it, also, at stated seasons of the year, he offered up his praise and homage to the Great Spirit, the ever present Author of his being.[1]

[1] SCHEDULE OF IROQUOIS DANCES.

Those marked thus *, are of foreign origin; thus †, are now obsolete; and thus ‡, are costume dances.

1	O-sto-weh'-go-wä, ‡	Great Feather Dance.	For both sexes.
2	Gä-na'-o-uh, ‡	Great Thanksgiving Dance.	"
3	Da-yun'-da-nes-hunt-hä,	Dance with Joined Hands.	"
4	Gä-dä'-shote, *	Trotting Dance.	"
5	O-to-wa'-ga-kä, * †	North Dance.	"

6	Je-hä′-yä,	Antique Dance.	For both sexes.
7	Gä′-no-jit′-ga-o,	Taking the Kettle out.	"
8	Ga-so-wä′-o-no,*	Fish Dance.	"
9	Os-ko-dä′-tä,	Shaking the Bush.	"
10	Ga-no′-ga-yo,‡	Rattle Dance.	"
11	So-wek-o-an′-no,*	Duck Dance.	"
12	Jă-ko′-wä-o-an′-no,	Pigeon Dance.	"
13	Guk-să′-gä-ne-a,†	Grinding Dishes.	"
14	Gä-so′-ă,†	Knee Rattle Dance.	"
15	O-ke′-wä,	Dance for the Dead.	For Females.
16	O-as-ka-ne′-a,	Shuffle Dance.	"
17	Da-swä-da-ne′-a,	Tumbling Dance.	"
18	Gä-ne-ä′-seh-o,†	Turtle Dance.	"
19	Un-dä-da-o-at′-hä,†	Initiation Dance for Girls.	"
20	Un-to-we′-sus,	Shuffle Dance.	"
21	Da-yo-dä′-sun-dä-e′-go,	Dark Dance.	"
22	Wä-sä′-seh,* ‡	Sioux, or War Dance.	For Males.
23	Da-ge′-yä-go-o-an′-no,	Buffalo Dance.	"
24	Ne-ä′-gwi-o-an′-no,*	Bear Dance.	"
25	Wä-a-no′-a,†	Striking the Stick.	"
26	Ne-ho-sä-den′-da,†	Squat Dance.	"
27	Gä-na-un′-dä-do,† ‡	Scalp Dance.	"
28	Un-de-a-ne-suk′-tä,† ‡	Track Finding Dance.	"
29	Eh-nes′-hen-do,†	Arm Shaking Dance.	"
30	Gä-go′-sä,	False Face Dance.	"
31	Gä-je′-sa,	" " "	"
32	Un-da-de-a-dus′-shun-ne-at′-hä,†	Preparation Dance.	"

Chapter V

National Games — Betting — Ball Game — Game of Javelins — Game of Deer Buttons — Snow Snake Game — Snow Boat Game — Archery — Peach-Stone Game — Enthusiasm for Games

I N their national games is to be found another fruitful source of amusement in Indian life. These games were not only played at their religious festivals, at which they often formed a conspicuous part of the entertainment, but special days were frequently set apart for their celebration. They entered into these diversions with the highest zeal and emulation, and took unwearied pains to perfect themselves in the art of playing each successfully. There were but six principal games among the Iroquois, and these are divisible into athletic games, and games of chance.

Challenges were often sent from one village to another, and were even exchanged between nations, to a contest of some of these games. In such cases the chosen players of each community or nation were called out to contend for the prize of victory. An intense degree of excitement was aroused, when the champions were the most skilful players of rival villages, or adjacent nations.[1] The people enlisted

[1] Tradition relates that the war which ended in the expulsion of the Eries, about the year 1654, from the western part of New York, originated in a breach of faith or treachery on the part of the Eries, in a Ball game to which they had challenged the Senecas.

upon their respective sides, with a degree of enthusiasm, which would have done credit, both to the spectators and the contestants, at the far-famed Elian games. For miles, and even hundreds of miles, they flocked together at the time appointed to witness the contest.

Unlike the prizes of the Olympic games, no chaplets awaited the victors. They were strifes between nation and nation, village and village, or tribes and tribes; in a word parties against parties, and not champion against champion. The prize contended for was that of victory; and it belonged, not to the triumphant players, but to the party which sent them forth to the contest.

When these games were not played by one community against another, upon a formal challenge, the people arranged themselves on two sides, according to their tribal divisions. By an organic provision of the Iroquois, as elsewhere stated, the Wolf, Bear, Beaver and Turtle tribes were brothers to each other, as tribes, and cousins to the other four. In playing their games they always went together, and formed one party or side. In the same manner the Deer, Snipe, Heron and Hawk tribes were brothers to each other, as tribes, and cousins to the four first named. These formed a second, or opposite party. Thus in all Indian games, with the exceptions first mentioned, the people divided themselves into two sections, four of the tribes always contending against the other four.[57] Father and son, husband and wife, were thus arrayed in opposite ranks.

Betting upon the result was common among the

Iroquois. As this practice was never reprobated by their religious teachers, but, on the contrary, rather encouraged, it frequently led to the most reckless indulgence. It often happened that the Indian gambled away every valuable article which he possessed; his tomahawk, his medal, his ornaments, and even his blanket. The excitement and eagerness with which he watched the shifting tide of the game, was more uncontrollable than the delirious agitation of the pale-face at the race-course, or even at the gaming-table. Their excitable temperament and emulous spirits peculiarly adapted them for the enjoyment of their national games.

These bets were made in a systematic manner, and the articles then deposited with the managers of the game. A bet offered by a person upon one side, in the nature of some valuable article, was matched by a similar article, or one of equal value, by some one upon the other. Personal ornaments made the usual gaming currency. Other bets were offered and taken in the same manner, until hundreds of articles were sometimes collected. These were laid aside by the managers, until the game was decided, when each article lost by the event was handed over to the winning individual, together with his own, which he had risked against it.

With the Iroquois, the Ball game, *O-tä-dä-jish'-quä-äge*, was the favorite among their amusements of this description. This game reaches back to a remote antiquity, was universal among the red races, and was played with a degree of zeal and enthusiasm which would scarcely be credited. It was played with a small deer-skin ball, by a select band, usually from six to eight on a side, each set representing its own party. The game was divided into several contests, in which each set of players strove to carry the ball through their own gate. They went out into an open plain or field, and erected gates, about eighty rods apart, on its

Gä-ne-ä, or Ball Bat.
5 feet.

opposite sides. Each gate was simply two poles, some ten feet high, set in the ground about three rods asunder. One of these gates belonged to each party; and the contest between the players was, which set would first carry the ball through its own a given number of times. Either five or seven made the game, as the parties agreed. If five, for example, was the number, the party which first carried, or drove the ball through its own gate this number of times, won the victory. Thus, after eight separate contests, the parties might stand equal, each having won four; in which case the party which succeeded on the ninth contest would carry the game. The players commenced in the centre of the field, midway between the gates. If one of them became fatigued or disabled during the progress of the game, he was allowed to leave the ranks, and his party could supply his place with a fresh player, but the original numbers were not at any time allowed to be increased. Regular managers were appointed on each side to see that the rules of the game were strictly and fairly observed. One rule forbade the players to touch the ball with the hand or foot.

In preparing for this game, the players denuded themselves entirely, with the exception of the waist-cloth [1] (see plate, I. 51). They also underwent, frequently, a course of diet and training, as in a preparation for a foot-race.

When the day designated had arrived, the people gathered from the whole surrounding country, to witness the contest. About meridian they assembled at the appointed place, and having separated themselves into two companies, one might be seen upon each side of the line, between the gates, arranged in scattered groups, awaiting the commencement of the game. The players, when ready, stationed themselves in two parallel rows, facing each other, midway on this line, each one holding a ball bat, of the kind

---

[1] The *Gä'-kä*, or waist-cloth, was a strip of deer-skin or broadcloth, about a quarter wide and two yards long, ornamented at the ends with bead or quill work. It was passed between the limbs, and secured by a deer-skin belt, passing around the waist, the embroidered ends falling over the belt, before and behind, in the fashion of an apron.

represented in the figure, and with which alone the
ball was to be driven. As soon as all the preliminaries were adjusted, the ball was dropped between
the two files of players, and taken between the bats
of the two who stood in the middle of each file,
opposite to each other. After a brief struggle between them, in which each player endeavored, with
his bat, to get possession of the ball, and give it the
first impulse towards his own gate, it was thrown out,
and then commenced the pursuit. The flying ball,
when overtaken, was immediately surrounded by a
group of players, each one striving to extricate it,
and, at the same time, direct it towards his party
gate. In this way the ball was frequently imprisoned
in different parts of the field, and an animated
controversy maintained for its possession. When
freed, it was knocked upon the ground, or through
the air; but the moment a chance presented, it was
taken up upon the deer-skin network of the ball bat,
by a player in full career, and carried in a race towards
the gate. To guard against this contingency, by
which one contest of the game might be determined
in a moment, some of the players detached themselves from the group contending around the ball,
and took a position from which to intercept a runner
upon a diagonal line, if it should chance that one of
the adverse party got possession of the ball. These
races often formed the most exciting part of the
game, both from the fleetness of the runners, and
the consequences which depended upon the result.
When the line of the runner was crossed, by an adversary coming in before him upon a diagonal line,

and he found it impossible, by artifice or stratagem, to elude him, he turned about, and threw the ball over the heads of both of them, towards his gate; or, perchance, towards a player of his own party, if there were adverse players between him and the gate. When the flight of the ball was arrested in any part of the field, a spirited and even fierce contest was maintained around it; the players handled their bats with such dexterity, and managed their persons with such art and adroitness, that frequently several minutes elapsed before the ball flew out. Occasionally in the heat of the controversy, but entirely by accident, a player was struck with such violence that the blood trickled down his limbs. In such a case, if disabled, he dropped his bat and left the field, while a fresh player from his own party supplied his place. In this manner was the game contested: oftentimes with so much ardor and skill that the ball was recovered by one party at the very edge of the adverse gate; and finally, after many shifts in the tide of success, carried in triumph through its own. When one contest in the game was thus decided, the prevailing party sent up a united shout of rejoicing.

After a short respite for the refreshment of the players, the second trial was commenced, and continued like the first. Sometimes it was decided in a few moments, but more frequently it lasted an hour, and sometimes much longer, to such a system had the playing of this game been reduced by skill and practice. If every trial was ardently contested, and the parties continued nearly equal in the number decided, it often lengthened out the game, until the approaching twilight made it necessary to take another day for its conclusion.

On the final decision of the game, the exclamations of triumph, as would be expected, knew no bounds. Caps, tomahawks and blankets were thrown up into the air, and for a few moments the notes of victory resounded from every side. It was doubtless a considerate provision, that the prevailing party were upon a side of the field opposite to, and at a distance from, the vanquished, otherwise such a din of exultation might have proved too exciting for Indian patience.

In ancient times they used a solid ball of knot. The ball bat, also, was made without network, having a solid and curving head. At a subsequent day, they substituted the deer-skin ball and the network ball bat in present use. These substitutions were made so many years ago that they have lost the date.

Gä-geh'-dä, or Javelin.

The game of Javelins, *Gä-na'-gä-o*, was very simple, depending upon the dexterity with which the javelin was thrown at a ring, as it rolled upon the ground. They frequently made it a considerable game, by enlisting skilful players to prepare for the contest, and by betting upon the result. The people divided by tribes, the four brothers playing against their four cousin tribes, as in the last case, unless the game was played on a challenge between neighboring communities.

The javelin was five or six feet in length, by three-fourths of an inch in diameter, and was usually made of hickory or maple. It was finished with care, sharpened at one end, and striped as shown in the figure. The ring was about eight inches in diameter, made either into a hoop or solid like a wheel, by winding with splints. Sometimes the javelin was thrown horizontally, by placing the forefinger against its foot, and supporting it with the thumb and second finger; in other cases it was held in the centre, and thrown with the hand raised above the shoulder.

On either side, from fifteen to thirty players were arranged, each having from three to six javelins, the number of both depending upon the interest in the game, and the time they wished to devote to the contest. The javelins themselves were the forfeit, and the game was gained by the party which won them.

Among the preliminaries to be settled by the managers, was the line on which the ring was to be rolled, the distance of the two bands of players from each other, and the space between each and the line itself. When these points were adjusted, and the parties stationed, the ring was rolled by one party on the line, in front of the other. As it passed the javelins were thrown. If the ring was struck by one of them, the players of the adverse party were required, each in turn, to stand in the place of the person who struck it, and throw their javelins in succession at the ring, which was set up as a target, on the spot where it was hit. Those of the javelins which hit the target when thus thrown were saved; if any missed they were passed to the other party, and by them were again thrown at the ring from the same point. Those which hit were won, finally, and laid out of the play, while the residue were restored to their original owners. After this first contest was decided, the ring was rolled back, and the other party, in turn, threw their javelins. If it was struck, the party which rolled it was required, in the same manner, to hazard their javelins, by throwing them at the target. Such as missed were delivered to the other party, and those which hit the target when thrown by them, were won also, and laid out of the play. In this manner the game was continued, until one of the parties had lost their javelins, which, of itself, determined the contest.

There was another game of javelins, *Gä-ga-dä-yan'-duk*, played by shooting them through the air. In this game, the javelin used was made of sumac, because of its lightness, and was of the same length and size as in the former. This game was divided into contests, as the Ball game, and was won by the party which first made the number agreed upon. The game was usually from fifteen to twenty, and the number of players on a side ranged from five to ten. When the parties were ready, the one which had the first throw selected the object upon which the javelin was to be thrown, to give it an upward flight, and also its distance from the standing point. If, for example, it was a log, at the distance of a rod, the player placed his forefinger against the foot of the javelin, and, supporting it with his thumb and second finger, he threw it in such a manner, that it would strike the upper side of the log, and thus be thrown up into the air, and forward, until its force was spent. In this manner all the players, in turn, threw their javelins. The one which was thrown the greatest distance won a point. If another, upon the same side, was in advance of all upon the opposite side, it counted another, and so on for every one which led all those upon the opposite side. In the next contest, the second party chose the object over which to throw the javelin, and the distance. The game was thus continued, until the number of points were gained which' were agreed upon for the game.

Gus-ga-e-sa'-tä, or Deer-buttons.

This was strictly a fireside game, although it was sometimes introduced as an amusement at the season of religious councils, the people dividing into tribes, as usual, and betting upon the result. Eight buttons, about an inch in diameter, were made of elk-horn, and having been rounded and polished, were slightly burned upon one side to blacken them. When it was made a public game, it was played by two at a time, with a change of players, as elsewhere described in the Peach-stone game. At the fireside, it was played by two or more, and all the players continued in their seats until it was determined. A certain number of beans, fifty perhaps, were made the capital, and the game continued until one of the players had won them all. Two persons spread a blanket, and seated themselves upon it. One of them shook the deer-buttons in his hands, and then threw them down. If six turned up of the same color, it counted two, if seven, it counted four, and if all, it counted twenty, the winner taking as many beans from the general stock as he made points by the throw. He also continued to throw as long as he continued to win. When less than six came up, either black or white, it counted nothing, and the throw was passed to the other player. In this manner the game was continued until the beans were taken up between the two players. After that the one paid to the other out of his own winnings, the game ending as soon as the capital in the hands of either player was exhausted. If four played, each had a partner, or played independently, as they were disposed; but when more than two played, each one was to pay to the winner the amount won. Thus, if four were playing independently, and after the beans were distributed among them, in the progress of the game, one of them should turn the buttons up all black, or all white, the other three would be obliged to pay him twenty each; but if the beans were still in bank, he took up but twenty. The deer-buttons were of the same size. In the figure they are represented at different angles.

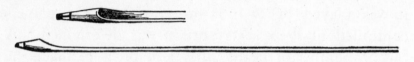

Ga-wä'-sa, or Snow-Snake.

Among the amusements of the winter season, in Indian life, was the game with Snow snakes. It was primarily designed as a diversion for the young; but it was occasionally made a public game between the tribes like the other, and aroused a great degree of spirit, and the usual amount of betting. The snake was thrown with the hand by placing the forefinger against its foot, and supporting it with the thumb and remaining fingers. It was thus made to run upon the snow crust with the speed of an arrow, and to a much greater distance, sometimes running sixty or eighty rods. The success of the player depended upon his dexterity and muscular strength.

The snakes were made of hickory, and with the most perfect precision and finish. They were from five to seven feet in length, about a fourth of an inch in thickness, and gradually diminishing from about an inch in width at the head, to about half an inch at the foot. The head was round, turned up slightly, and pointed with lead to increase the momentum of the snake.

This game, like that of ball, was divided into a number of separate contests; and was determined when either party had gained the number of points agreed upon, which was generally from seven to ten. The players were limited and select, usually not more than six. A station was determined upon, with the line, or general direction in which the snake was to be thrown. After they had all been thrown by the players on both sides, the next question was to determine the count. The snake which ran the greatest distance was a point for the side to which it belonged. Other points might be won on the same side, if a second or third snake was found to be ahead of all the snakes upon the adverse side. One count was made for each snake which outstripped all upon the adverse side. These contests were repeated until one of the parties had made the requisite number of points to determine the game.

Top view

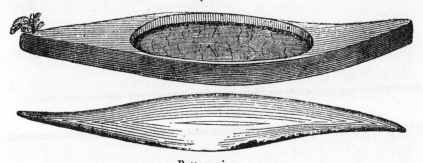

Bottom view

Da-ya-no-tä-yen-dä-quä, or Snow Boat.

With the snow boat was played one of the winter games of the Iroquois, in which the strife was to discover which boat would run the farthest in an iced trench or path. The boat was about fifteen inches in length, and made of beech, or other hard wood, something in the fashion of a canoe. It was solid, with the exception of an oblong cavity in the centre, over which arched a hickory bow, designed to suspend bells or other rattles upon. In the stern of this little vessel a white feather was inserted for a flag, by which to follow it in its descent. On the bottom the boat was rounded, but with a slight wind lengthwise, as shown in the figure, to give it a true direction.

A side hill with an open plain below was the kind of place selected to try the speed of the boats. Trenches in a straight line down the hill, and about a foot wide, were made by treading down the snow; after which water was poured into them that it might freeze and line the trenches throughout their whole extent with ice. These trenches to the number of a dozen, side by side, if as many individuals intended to play, were finished with the greatest care and exactness, not only down the hill side, but to a considerable distance across the plain below. At the same time the boats themselves were dipped in water that they might also be coated with ice.

The people divided by tribes in playing this, as in all other Iroquois games; the Wolf, Bear, Beaver, and Turtle tribes playing against the Deer, Snipe, Heron, and Hawk. At the time appointed the people assembled at the base of the hill and divided off by tribes, and then commenced betting upon the result, a custom universally practised on such occasions. The game was played by select players who were stationed at the top of the hill, each with two or three boats, and standing at the head of his own trench. When all was in readiness the boats were started off together at the appointed moment, and their rapid descent was watched with eager interest by the people below. It is not necessary to describe the scene. If the game was twenty it would be continued until one side had made that number of points. A count of one was made for every boat which led all upon the adverse side, so that if there were six players on a side it was possible for that number to be made at one trial. On the contrary, if all the boats but one upon one side were in advance of all on the adverse side but one, and the latter was in advance of all, this head boat would win and count one. The principles of the game are precisely the same as in the Snow Snake game. All of these Indian games were played with great zeal and enthusiasm. To us they appear to be puerile amusements for men in the prime of manhood; but yet they were adapted to the ways and habits of a people living without arts, and without the intellectual employments which pertain to civilized life. Such games mark the infancy of the human mind, but they often beget a generous emulation and a ready skill which lead to future improvement and elevation.

In archery the Indian has scarcely been excelled. With a quick eye and a powerful muscle, he could send the arrow as unerringly as the archers of Robin Hood. It cannot be called, in strictness, a game, but trials of skill were common in ancient times; successful archery raising the individual into high repute.

The Indian bow was usually from three and a half to four feet in length, with such a difficult spring that an inexperienced person could scarcely bend it sufficiently to set the string. To draw the string back, when set, an arm's length, could only be done by practice, superadded to the most powerful muscular strength. An arrow thus sent would strike its object with fearful velocity. The arrow was about three feet in length, and feathered at the small end

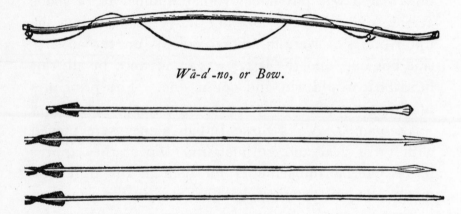

Wä-ä'-no, or Bow.

Gä'-no, or Arrow.

with a twist to make it revolve in its flight. It gave to its motion horizontality and precision, doubtless suggesting, at a later day, the idea of the twist in the rifle barrel, by which the ball is made to revolve in the same manner. The English and Scottish archers feathered their arrows, but without this peculiarity. Three feathers were also used by them, which were set parallel with the arrow and with each other. But they were set upon one side of the arrow at its three quarters, and in such a way that the three parallel feathers formed obtuse angles with each other. The Indian

used but two feathers, which passed around the opposite sides of the arrow in a twist, as shown in the
figure. For this purpose the feather was stripped off
from the quill and tied to the arrow with sinew.
Originally, the Indian arrow was pointed with a flint
or chert-head, which would enable it to penetrate
deeply any object at which it was directed. With
such an arrow, it was an easy matter to bring down
the deer, the wild fowl, or the warrior himself. Skeletons have been disentombed, having the skull penetrated with an arrow-head of this description, with
the flint-head itself still in the fracture, or entirely
within the skull. In Oregon and on the upper Mississippi, the Indian arrow is still pointed with flint.
Thus it was with the Iroquois, until the bow was
laid aside for the rifle. Arrow-heads of this description are still found scattered over the whole surface
of the State. With Indian youth, the bow and the
arrow is still a favorite source of amusement.

Gä'-no, or Arrow.
3 feet.

In ancient times arrows were pointed with horn or
bone as well as with flint, and made even more dangerous missiles in the former cases. The above is a
representation of an arrow of this description, which,
with several others, was purchased of an Oneida on
Grand river. It is about three feet in length and
pointed with deer's horn.

The sheaf is an Indian invention of great antiquity, and universal among Indian races. It was

sometimes made of the skin of a small animal, like the wolf, which was taken off entire, dressed with the hair on, and hung upon the back, the arrows being placed within it. But the choicer articles were made of dressed unhaired deer-skin, and embroidered with porcupine quills as represented in the figure. It was made of two strips of deer-skin about two feet in length and of unequal width : one of these was narrow for the back side ; the other about three times its width so as to make a convex front, thus forming a species of sac in which the arrows were deposited. The ordinary sheaf, as used by the Iroquois in ancient times, would hold from fifteen to twenty-five arrows ;

Gä-däs-hă, or Sheaf.
2 feet.

but those used by the western Indians were generally large enough for forty or fifty. It was worn on the back inclining from the left shoulder down towards the belt on the right side of the body, crossing the back diagonally. There are deer-string fastenings at each end, the lower ones being attached to the waist-belt, and the upper ones passing around the neck and under the left arm. To draw forth an arrow and place it in the bow, it was necessary to raise the right hand to the left shoulder when it came at once in contact with the feathered end, which projected from the sheaf ; so that it was but the work of a second to set an arrow in its place.

FOOT-RACES

Foot-races furnished another pastime for the Iroquois. They were often made a part of the entertainment with which civil and mourning councils were concluded. In this athletic game the Indian excelled. The exigencies, both of war and peace, rendered it necessary for the Iroquois to have among them practiced and trained runners. A spirit of emulation often sprang up among them, which resulted in regular contests for the palm of victory. In these races, the four tribes put forward their best runners against those of the other four, and left the question of superiority to be determined by the event of the contest. Before the time appointed for the races, they prepared themselves for the occasion by a process of training. It is not necessary to describe them. They dressed in the same manner for the race as for the game of ball. Leaping, wrestling and the other gymnastic exercises appear to have furnished no part of the public amusements of our primitive inhabitants.

An ancient and favorite game of the Iroquois, *Gus-kä'-eh*, was played with a bowl and peachstones. It was always a betting game, in which the people divided by tribes. By established custom, it was introduced as the concluding exercise on the last day of the Green Corn and the Harvest festivals, and also of the New Year's jubilee. Its introduction among them is ascribed to the first *To-do-dä'-ho*, who flourished at the formation of the League. A popular belief prevailed, that this game would be enjoyed by them in the future life, in the realm of the Great Spirit; which is, perhaps, but an extravagant way of expressing their admiration for the game.

A dish, about a foot in diameter at the base, was carved out of a knot, or made of earthen. Six peach-stones were then ground, or cut down into an oval form, reducing them in the process about half in size, after which the heart of the pit was removed, and the stones themselves were burned upon one side, to blacken

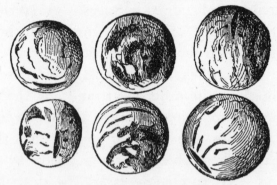

Gus-kä'-eh, or Peach Stones.

Ga-jih, or Bowl.

them. The above representation will exhibit both the bowl and the peach-stones; the latter being drawn in different positions to show the degree of their convexity.

It was a very simple game, depending, in part, upon the dexterity of the player, but more upon his good fortune. The peach-stones were shaken in the bowl by the player, the count depending upon the number which came up of one color, after they had ceased rolling in the dish. It was played in the public council-house by a succession of players, two at a time, under the supervision of managers appointed to represent the two parties, and to conduct the contest. Its length depended somewhat upon the number of beans which made the bank, usually one hundred, the victory being gained by the side which finally won them all.

A platform was erected a few feet from the floor and spread with blankets. When the betting was ended, and the articles had been delivered into the custody of the managers, they seated themselves upon the platform in the midst of the throng of spectators, and two persons sat down to the game between the two divisions into which they arranged themselves. The beans, in the first instance, were placed together in a bank. Five of them were given to each player, with which they commenced. Each player, by the rules of the game, was allowed to keep his seat until he had lost this outfit, after which he surrendered it to another player on his own side selected by the managers of his own party. And this was the case, notwithstanding any number he might have won of his adversary. Those which he won were delivered to his party managers. The six peach-stones were placed in the bowl and shaken by the player; if five of them came up of one color, either white or black, it counted one, and his adversary paid to him the forfeit, which was one bean; the bean simply representing a unit in counting the game. On the next throw, which the player having won, retained, if less than five came up of the same color, it counted nothing, and he passed the bowl to his adversary. The second player then shook the bowl; upon which, if they all came up of one color, either white or black, it counted five. To pay this forfeit required the whole outfit of the first player, after which, having nothing to pay with, he vacated his seat, and was succeeded by another of his own side, who received from the bank the same number of beans which the first had. The other player followed his throw as long as he continued to win; after which he repassed the bowl to his adversary. If a player chanced to win five, and his opponent had but one left, this was all he could gain. In this manner the game continued, with varying fortune, until the beans were divided between the two sides in proportion to their success. After this the game continued in the same manner as before, the outfit of each new player being advanced by the managers of his own party; but as the beans or counters were now out of sight, none but the managers knew the state of the game with accuracy. In playing it there were but two winning throws, one of which counted one and the other five. When one of the parties had lost all their beans, the game was done.

There were some other peculiarities and variations in this game which would be necessary to a full understanding of it, but sufficient has been given to illustrate its general character. As they began to play this game about meridian, it often happened that it was necessary to take another day for its conclusion. It was made a long game by its constitution, as it was carefully guarded against the extreme fickleness of most games of chance. It so happens that games of this description do not depend for their interest upon the striking combinations involved in their construction. This is dependent very much upon practice, habit, and association. Oftentimes the most simple game in its contrivance is the most attractive and absorbing to the practiced player. This game, as simple as it may appear, was productive of a great degree of excitement, and when finally decided, the exultation of the victors broke forth in vehement rejoicings. Having intently watched, for hours, the ever-changing tide of the game, when the long suspense was over, and the tension of the mind was ended, its rebound, under the impulse of victory, exhibited itself in extravagant exclamations.

A brief description of the plan of these games will no more exhibit their hidden sources of entertainment, than a volume descriptive of chess would reveal the fascinations of the game itself. These games all depend, for their interest, upon circumstances. The Olympic, Pythian and other games of the Greeks, and the Apollinarian, Circensian and other games of the Romans, consisted chiefly, as is well known, of running, leaping, wrestling, riding, and chariot-racing. Aside from the last, they were not, intrinsically, much superior to the games of the Iroquois. But in the hands of the Greeks, especially, they were made the most extraordinary entertainments of the ancient world. Among the Iroquois, in the celebration of their national games, as far as they went, is to be found the same species of enthusiasm and emulation which characterized the celebration of the games of antiquity. Although the national games, like the popular songs of one people, may be incapable of exciting the enthusiasm or awakening the patriotic spirit of another; yet they are not, for this reason, devoid of interest. If it be asked what interest for us can attach to these games of the Iroquois, one answer at least may be given;—they show that the American wilderness, which we have been taught to pronounce a savage solitude until the white man entered its borders, had long been vocal in its deepest seclusions, with the gladness of happy human hearts.

Chapter VI

NOTWITHSTANDING the simplicity of Indian life, and its barrenness of those higher social enjoyments which pertain to refined communities, Indian society was bound together by permanent institutions, governed by fixed laws, and impelled and guided by well-established usages and customs. The diversified powers, motives, and restraints embraced within them, exercised an important influence upon their social life, and therefore they present fruitful and interesting subjects of investigation. To form a judgment of the Indian character, which is founded upon a knowledge of his motives and principles of action, he must be seen in his social relations. But it is not deemed advisable to consider these topics minutely.

The Iroquois resided in permanent villages. Not knowing the use of wells, they fixed their residences upon the banks of rivers and lakes, or in the vicinity of copious springs. About the period of the formation of the League, when they were exposed to the inroads of hostile nations, and the warfare of migratory bands, their villages were compact and stockaded. Having run a trench several feet deep, around five or ten acres of land, and thrown up the ground upon the inside, they set a continuous row of stakes or palisades in this bank of earth, fixing them at such an angle that they inclined over the trench. Sometimes a village was surrounded by a double, or even triple row of palisades. Within this enclosure they constructed their bark-houses, and secured their stores. Around it was the village field, consisting, oftentimes, of several hundred acres of cultivated land, which was subdivided into planting lots; those belonging to different families being bounded by uncultivated ridges. *Nun-da-wä'-o*, at the head of Canandaigua lake, the oldest village of the Senecas, was stockaded; so also were *Skä-hase'-gă-o* on the site of Lima, and two or three other of their oldest towns.

But at the commencement of the seventeenth century, which may be called the middle period of the history of the Iroquois, when their power had become consolidated, and most of the adjacent nations had been brought under subjection, the necessity of stockading their villages in a measure ceased, and with it the practice. At the period of the discovery of the inland Iroquois, about the year 1640,[1] few, if any, of the villages of the Senecas, Cayugas, or Onondagas were surrounded with palisades; but the Oneidas and Mohawks continued to stockade their villages for many years afterwards, in consequence of the inroads of the French. At this period, also, their villages were compactly built.

The modern village was a cluster of houses, planted

---

[1] The Franciscan Le Caron passed through the country of the Iroquois in 1616. (Bancroft's Hist. U. S., iii. 120.) But little, however, was known of them prior to 1640.

like the trees of the forest, at irregular intervals, and over a large area. No attempt was made at a street, or at an arrangement of their houses in a row; two houses seldom fronting the same line. They were merely grouped together sufficiently near for a neighborhood.

As their villages, at an early day, were reckoned by the number of houses, it is important to remark the difference between the *Gä-no'-sote*, or Bark-house of the middle and the modern period, to arrive at an estimate of the number of inhabitants. When the village was scattered over a large area, the houses were single, and usually designed for one family; but when compact, as in ancient times, they were very long, and subdivided, so as to accommodate a number of families. The long house was generally from fifty to a hundred and thirty feet in length, by about sixteen in width, with partitions at intervals of about ten or twelve feet, or two lengths of the body. Each apartment was, in fact, a separate house, having a fire in the centre, and accommodating two families, one upon each side of the fire. Thus a house one hundred and twenty feet long would contain ten fires and twenty families.[124] A Mr. Greenhalgh, in 1677, visited the Seneca village of *Dä-yo-de-hok'-to*, signifying " a bended creek," situated upon a bend of the Honeoye outlet, west of Mendon, in the county of Monroe. Under the name of " Tiotohatton," he thus speaks of it : — " Tiotohatton lies on the brink or edge of a hill; has not much cleared ground; is near the river Tiotohatton, which signifies bending. It lies to the westward of Canagorah," probably *Nun-da-wä'-o*, " about thirty miles, containing about one hundred and twenty houses, being the largest of all the houses we saw, (the ordinary being from fifty to sixty feet long), with from twelve to thirteen fires in one house. They have good store of corn, growing about a mile to the northward of the town." [1] The Marquis De Nonville, in 1687, captured this, with three other villages of the Senecas, at the time of his invasion of the Seneca territory. In the *Acté*, executed at this village, by which the French took formal possession of the territories of the Seneca-Iroquois, on behalf of France, it is written " Totiakton," and is called " the largest of the Seneca villages." [2] It is not improbable that the largest villages of the Iroquois contained three thousand inhabitants.

The *Gä-no'-sote*, or Bark-house (see plate, I. 3), was a simple structure. When single, it was about twenty feet by fifteen upon the ground, and from fifteen to twenty feet high. The frame consisted of upright poles firmly set in the ground, usually five upon the sides, and four at the ends, including those at the corners. Upon the forks of these poles, about ten feet from the ground, cross-poles

[1] Documentary Hist. New York, i. 13. He further states that Canagorah contained one hundred and fifty houses; Onondaga, one hundred and forty; Oneida village, one hundred; ib. 12–13.

[2] Doc. Hist. N.Y., i. 242. The three other villages taken by De Nonville were Gannagaro, as it is called in the acté, or *Gä-o-să-g'ä-o*, signifying " in the Basswood country," situated a short distance southeast of Victor in the county of Ontario, Gannondata and Gannongarae, one of which was doubtless *Gä-nun-dă'-gwa*, " place selected for a settlement," upon the site of the present village of Canandaigua. De Nonville estimated the population of the four villages at fifteen thousand, and the Indian corn destroyed by his troops at four hundred thousand minots. (Doc. Hist., i. 239.) Doubtless, both of these estimates were exaggerations.

were secured horizontally, to which the rafters, also poles, but more numerous and slender, were adjusted. The rafters were strengthened with transverse poles, and the whole were usually so arranged as to form an arching roof. After the frame was thus completed, it was sided up, and shingled with red elm or ash bark, the rough side out. The bark was flattened and dried, and then cut in the form of boards. To hold these bark boards firmly in their places, another set of poles, corresponding with those in the frame, were placed on the outside; and by means of splints and bark rope fastenings, the boards were secured horizontally between them. It usually required four lengths of boards, and four courses from the ground to the rafters to cover a side, as they were lapped at the ends, as well as clapboarded; and also in the same proportion for the ends. In like manner, the roof was covered with bark boards, smaller in size, with the rough side out, and the grain running up and down; the boards being stitched through and through with fastenings, and thus held between the frames of poles, as on the sides. In the centre of the roof was an opening for the smoke, the fire being upon the ground in the centre of the house, and the smoke ascending without the guidance of a chimney. At the two ends of the house were doors, either of bark hung upon hinges of wood, or of deer or bear skins suspended before the opening; and however long the house, or whatever the number of fires, these were the only entrances. Over one of these doors was cut the tribal device of the head of the family. Within, upon the two sides, were arranged wide seats, also of bark boards, about two feet from the ground, well supported underneath, and reaching the entire length of the house. Upon these they spread their mats of skins, and also their blankets, using them as seats by day and couches at night. Similar berths were constructed on each side, about five feet above these, and secured to the frame of the house, thus furnishing accommodations for the family. Upon cross-poles, near the roof, was hung, in bunches, braided together by the husks, their winter supply of corn. Charred and dried corn, and beans were generally stored in bark barrels, and laid away in corners. Their implements for the chase, domestic utensils, weapons, articles of apparel, and miscellaneous notions,[1] were stowed away, and hung up, whenever an unoccupied place was discovered. A house of this description would accommodate a family of eight, with the limited wants of the Indian, and afford shelter for their necessary stores, making a not uncomfortable residence. After they had learned the use of the axe, they began to substitute houses of hewn logs, but they constructed them after the ancient model. Many of the houses of their modern villages in the valley of the Genesee were of this description.

There was another species of house occasionally constructed, either for temporary use or for a small family. It was triangular at the base, the frame consisting of three poles on a side, gathered at the top, but with space sufficient between them for a chimney opening. They were sided up in the same manner as the rectangular *Gä-no'-sote*. During the hunt, bark-

[1] For some account of their fabrics, implements and utensils, see Book iii. ch. i.

houses of this description were often erected as a shelter.

The Iroquois were accustomed to bury their surplus corn, and also their charred green corn, in caches, in which the former would preserve uninjured through the year, and the latter for a much longer period. They excavated a pit, made a bark bottom and sides, and having deposited their corn within it, a bark roof, water tight, was constructed over it, and the whole covered up with earth. Pits of charred corn are still found near their ancient settlements. Cured venison and other meats were buried in the same manner, except that the bark repository was lined with deer-skins.

In this connection, the marriage customs of the Iroquois naturally suggest themselves. They exhibit novel, if not distinctive features. Marriage was not founded upon the affections, which constitute the only legitimate basis of this relation in civilized society, but was regulated exclusively as a matter of physical necessity. It was not even a contract between the parties to be married, but substantially between their mothers, acting oftentimes under the suggestions of the matrons and wise-men of the tribes to which the parties respectively belonged. In a general sense, therefore, the subject of marriage was under the supervision of the older members of each tribe ; but practically, it was under maternal control. With the improvement and elevation of the race, changes were gradually introduced in relation to the marriageable age, and the disparity of age between the sexes. In ancient times, the young warrior was always united to a woman several years his senior, on the supposition that he needed a companion experienced in the affairs of life. The period was also deferred on his part until twenty-five, that he might first become inured to the hardships of the war-path and of the chase, before his freedom was curtailed and his responsibilities were increased by the cares of a family, light as these cares seem to have been under their social system. Thus, it often happened that the young warrior at twenty-five was married to a woman of forty, and oftentimes a widow ; while the widower at sixty was joined to the maiden at twenty. But these were their primitive customs ; the ages of the parties afterwards drew nearer to an equality, and the marriageable age was, in time reduced to twenty, and even below it.

When the mother considered her son of a suitable age for marriage, she looked about her for a maiden, who, from report or acquaintance, she judged would accord with him in disposition and temperament. A negotiation between the mothers ensued, and a conclusion was speedily reached. Sometimes the near relatives and the elderly persons of the tribes to which each belonged were consulted ; but their opinions were of no avail, independently of the wishes of the mothers themselves. Not the least singular feature of the transaction was the entire ignorance in which the parties remained of the pending negotiation ; the first intimation they received being the announcement of their marriage, without, perhaps, ever having known or seen each other. Remonstrance or objection on their part was never attempted ; they received each other as the gift of their parents. As obedience to them in all their requirements was inculcated as a paramount duty, and disobedience was followed by disownment, the operative force of custom, in addition to these motives, was sufficient to secure acquiescence. The Indian father never troubled himself concerning the marriage of his children. To interfere would have been an invasion of female immunities ; and these, whatever they were, were as sacredly regarded by him, as he was inflexible in enforcing respect for his own.

When the fact of marriage had been communicated to the parties, a simple ceremonial completed the transaction. On the day following the announcement, the maiden was conducted by her mother, accompanied by a few female friends, to the home of her intended husband. She carried in her hand a few cakes of unleavened corn bread, which she presented on entering the house, to her mother-in-law, as an earnest of her usefulness and of her skill in the domestic arts. After receiving it, the mother of the young warrior returned a present of venison, or other fruit of the chase, to the mother of the bride, as an earnest of his ability to provide for his household. This exchange of presents ratified and concluded the contract, which bound the new pair together in the marriage relation. Thus simple was the formation of the nuptial bond among our primitive inhabitants.

From the very nature of the marriage institution among the Iroquois, it follows that the passion of love was entirely unknown among them. Affection after marriage would naturally spring up between the parties from association, from habit, and from mutual dependence; but of that marvellous passion which originates in a higher development of the powers of the human heart, and is founded upon a cultivation of the affections between the sexes, they were entirely ignorant. In their temperaments, they were below this passion in its simplest forms. Attachments between individuals, or the cultivation of each other's affections before marriage, was entirely unknown; so also were promises of marriage. The fact that individuals were united in this relation, without their knowledge or consent, and perhaps without even a previous acquaintance, illustrates and confirms this position. This invasion of the romances of the novelist, and of the conceits of the poet, upon the attachments which sprang up in the bosom of Indian society, may, perhaps, divest the mind of some pleasing impressions; but these are entirely inconsistent with the marriage institution as it existed among them, and with the facts of their social history.

Intercourse between the sexes was restrained by circumstances and by inclination. Indian habits and modes of life divided the people socially into two great classes, male and female. The male sought the conversation and society of the male, and they went forth together for amusement, or for the severer duties of life. In the same manner the female sought the companionship of her own sex. Between the sexes there was but little sociality, as this term is understood in polished society. Such a thing as formal visiting was entirely unknown. When the unmarried of opposite sexes were casually brought together, there was little or no conversation between them. No attempts by the unmarried to please or gratify each other by acts of personal attention, were ever made. At the season of councils and religious festivals, there was more of actual intercourse and sociality, than at any other time; but this was confined to the dance, and was, in itself, limited. A solution of this singular problem is, in part, to be found in the absence of equality in the sexes. The Indian regarded woman as the inferior, the dependent, and the servant of man, and from nurture and habit, she actually considered herself to be so. This absence of equality in position, in addition to the force of custom, furnishes a satisfactory explanation of many of the peculiarities characteristic of Indian society. In the cultivation of the affections between the sexes, and in the development of kindred sentiments, is to be found the origin of the amenities and the mitigation of the asperities of life.

In intimate connection with the subject of marriage, is that of divorce. Polygamy was forbidden among the Iroquois, and never became a practice; but the right to put away the wife, or of voluntary separation, was allowed to all. The mothers of the married pair were responsible for their concord and harmony. If differences arose between them, it became their duty to effect a reconciliation, and by advice and counsel, to guard against a repetition of the difficulty. But if disturbances continued to follow reconciliations, and their dispositions were found to be too incongruous for domestic peace, a separation followed, either by mutual consent or the absolute refusal of one of the parties longer to recognize the marriage relation. As such a rupture in ancient times was regarded as discreditable to the parties, and brought them under the pressure of public censure, they were then unfrequent. In later days, however, the inviolability of the nuptial contract was less sacredly regarded, and the most frivolous reasons, or the caprice of the moment, were sufficient for breaking the marriage tie.

The husband and wife were never of the same tribe, as has been elsewhere more fully explained; and the children were of the tribe of their mother. No right in the father to the custody of their persons, or to their nurture, was recognized. As, after separation, he gave himself no farther trouble concerning them, nor interested himself in their future welfare, they became estranged as well as separated. Parental affection was much weaker, as is usually the fact, on the part of the father than on that of the mother. The Indian father seldom caressed his children, or by any outward acts manifested the least solicitude for their welfare; but when his sons grew up to maturity, he became more attached to them, making them his companions in the hunt and upon the war-path. The care of their infancy and childhood was intrusted to the watchful affection of the mother alone.

By the laws of the Iroquois, the nationality as well as the tribe of the individual was never lost, or merged in another. If a Cayuga woman married a Seneca, her children were Cayugas, and her descendants in the female line, to the latest posterity, continued to be Cayugas, although they resided with the Senecas, and by intermarriage with them had lost nearly every particle of Cayuga blood. In the same manner, if a Mohawk married a Delaware woman, her children were not only Delawares, but aliens, unless they were regularly adopted and christened as Mohawks, and the fact of adoption was announced in open council.

Property, both in amount and variety, was exceedingly limited; as would naturally be expected among a people living a hunter and semi-agricultural life, and making a mere subsistence the limit of their wants and of their ambition. But inconsiderable as it was in the aggregate, it was held, and subject to distribution, under fixed laws. Having neither currency nor trade, nor the love of gain, their property consisted merely of planting lots, orchards, houses, implements of the chase, weapons, articles of apparel, domestic utensils, personal ornaments, stores of grain, skins of animals, and those miscellaneous fabrics which the necessities of life led them to invent. The rights of property, of both husband and wife, were continued distinct during the existence of the marriage relation; the wife holding, and controlling her own, the same as her husband, and in case of separation, taking it with her. No individual could obtain the absolute title to land, as that was vested by the laws of the Iroquois in all the people; but he could reduce unoccupied lands to cultivation, to any extent he pleased; and so long as he continued to use them, his right to their enjoyment was protected and secured. He could also sell his improvements, or bequeath them to his wife or children. If the wife, either before or after marriage, inherited orchards, or planting lots, or reduced land to cultivation, she could dispose of them at her pleasure, and in case of her death they were inherited, together with her other effects, by her children. The rule of descent, on the death of the father, was different. His children, not being of his tribe, were out of the line of inheritance; for by their laws, property could not, by descent, pass out of the tribe. If he gave his planting lots, or any articles of property to his wife or children, in the presence of a witness, they were allowed to hold them. But if he made no disposition of his effects, they were handed over upon his decease, to the near relatives in his own tribe, who usually assigned to the family the house, and such other articles as they deemed advisable, and distributed the residue among themselves, as personal mementos of the deceased.

One of the most attractive features of Indian society was the spirit of hospitality by which it was pervaded. Perhaps no people ever carried this principle to the same degree of universality, as did the Iroquois. Their houses were not only open to each other, at all hours of the day and of the night, but also to the wayfarer and the stranger. Such entertainment as their means afforded was freely spread before him, with words of kindness and of welcome. Not unfrequently one of these houses contained from ten to twenty families, all bound together by the nearer ties of relationship, and constituting in effect one family. They carried the principle of "living in common" to its full extent. Whatever was taken in the chase, or raised in the fields, or gathered in its natural state by any member of the united families, enured to the benefit of all, for their stores of every description were common. They had regular hours for cooking through the whole establishment, and whatever was prepared was free to all. The Indian had no regular meal after the morning repast, but he allayed his appetite whenever the occasion offered. As they used no tables in ancient times, they took their food separately, and whenever it could be done with the least trouble, the males first, and the females afterwards. The care of the appetite was left entirely with the women, as the Indian never asked for food. Whenever the husband returned, at any hour of the day, it was the duty and the custom of the wife to set food before him. If a neighbor or a stranger entered her dwelling, a dish of hommony, or whatever else she had prepared, was immediately placed before him, with an invitation to partake. It made no difference at what hour of the day, or how numerous the calls, this courtesy was extended to every comer, and was the first act of attention bestowed. This custom was universal, in fact one of the laws of their social system; and a neglect on the part of the wife to observe it, was regarded both as a breach of hospitality, and as a personal affront. A neighbor, or a stranger, calling from house to house, through an Indian village, would be thus entertained at every dwelling he entered. If the appetite of the guest had thus been fully satisfied, he was yet bound in courtesy to taste of the dish presented, and to return the customary acknowledgment, *Hi-ne-ä'-weh*, " I thank you ;" an omission to do either being esteemed a violation of the usages of life. A stranger would be thus entertained without charge, as long as he was pleased to remain ; and a relation was entitled to a home among any'of his kindred, while he was disposed to claim it. Under the operation of such a simple and universal law of hospitality, hunger and destitution were entirely unknown among them. This method of dealing with the human appetite strikes the mind as novel ; but it was founded upon a principle of brotherhood, and of social intercourse, not much unlike the common table of the Spartans. The abounding supplies of corn yielded, with light cultivation, by their fruitful fields, and the simple fare of the Indian, rendered the prevailing hospitality an inconsiderable burden. It rested chiefly upon the industry, and therefore upon the natural kindness of the Indian woman ; who, by the cultivation of the maize, and their other plants, and the gathering of the wild fruits, provided the principal part of their subsistence,[85] for the warrior despised the toil of husbandry, and held all labor beneath him. But it was in exact accordance with the unparalleled generosity of the Indian character. He would surrender his dinner to feed the hungry, vacate his bed to refresh the weary, and give up his apparel to clothe the naked. No test of friendship was too severe, no sacrifice to repay a favor too great, no fidelity to an engagement too inflexible for the Indian character. With an innate knowledge of the freedom and the dignity of man, he has exhibited the noblest virtues of the heart, and the kindest deeds of humanity in those sylvan retreats, which we are wont to look back upon as vacant and frightful solitudes.[1]

---

[1] Canassatego, a distinguished Onondaga chief, who flourished about the middle of the last century, thus cuttingly contrasted the hospitality of the Iroquois with that of the whites, in a conversation with Conrad Weiser, an Indian interpreter. " You know our practice. If a white man, in travelling through our country, enters one of our cabins, we all treat him as I do you. We dry him if he is wet, we warm him if he is cold, and give him meat and drink that he may allay his hunger and thirst;

In their subsistence there was but a limited variety from the necessity of the case. Their principal articles of food were cracked corn, and skinned corn hommony, two or three varieties of corn bread, venison and other game, soups, succotash, charred and dried green corn prepared in different ways, wild fruit, ground nuts (*apios tuberosa*), resembling wild potatoes, beans and squashes. These were the staples of their consumption, furnishing a considerable diversity of dishes, but a limited range to the appetite. They had also several kinds of tea. A favorite beverage was made from the tips of hemlock boughs boiled in water, and seasoned with maple sugar. Maple tea was prepared by boiling sap, and seasoning it with sassafras root; and spice tea, by steeping a species of wild spice.

Crimes and offences were so unfrequent under their social system, that the Iroquois can scarcely be said to have had a criminal code. Yet there were certain misdemeanors which fell under the judicial cognizance of the sachems, and were punished by them in proportion to their magnitude. Witchcraft was punishable with death. Any person could take the life of a witch when discovered in the act. If this was not done, a council was called, and the witch arraigned before it, in the presence of the accuser. A full confession, with a promise of amendment, secured a discharge. But if the accusation was denied, witnesses

and we spread soft furs for him to rest and sleep on. We demand nothing in return. But if I go into a white man's house at Albany, and ask for victuals and drink, they say, ' Where is your money ? ' And if I have none, they say, ' *Get out, you Indian dog.* ' "

were called and examined concerning the circumstances of the case; and if they established the charge to the satisfaction of the council, which they rarely failed to do, condemnation followed, with a sentence of death. The witch was then delivered over to such executioners as volunteered for the purpose, and by them was led away to punishment. After the decision of the council, the relatives of the witch gave him up to his doom without a murmur.

Adultery was punished by whipping; but the punishment was inflicted upon the woman alone, who was supposed to be the only offender. A council passed upon the question, and if the charge was sustained, they ordered her to be publicly whipped by persons appointed for the purpose. This was the ancient custom, when such transgressions were exceedingly rare.

The greatest of all human crimes, murder, was punished with death; but the act was open to condonation. Unless the family were appeased, the murderer, as with the ancient Greeks, was given up to their private vengeance. They could take his life whenever they found him, even after the lapse of years, without being held accountable. A present of white wampum, sent on the part of the murderer to the family of his victim, when accepted, forever obliterated and wiped out the memory of the transaction. Immediately on the commission of a murder, the affair was taken up by the tribes to which the parties belonged, and strenuous efforts were made to effect a reconciliation, lest private retaliation should lead to disastrous consequences. If the criminal belonged to one of the first four tribes, and the deceased to one of the second four, these tribes assembled in separate councils,[57] to inquire into all the facts of the case. The question of the guilt or innocence of the accused was generally an easy matter to determine, when the consequences of guilt were open to condonation. The first council then ascertained whether the offender was willing to confess his crime, and to make atonement. If he was, the council immediately sent a belt of white wampum, in his name, to the other council, which contained a message to that effect. The latter then endeavored to pacify the family of the deceased, to quiet their excitement, and to induce them to accept the wampum in condonation. If this was not sent in due time, or the family resisted all persuasions to receive it, then their revenge was allowed to take its course. Had it chanced that both parties belonged to one of the four brother tribes, a council of this division alone would convene, to attempt an adjustment among themselves. If, however, the family continued implacable, the further interference of mutual friends was given over, leaving the question to be settled between the murderer and the kindred of his victim, according to the ancient usage. If the belt of wampum was received before the avenger had been appointed, and had left the lodge on his mission, it was usually accepted as a condonation, but if he had gone forth, the time for reparation had passed. The family then either took upon themselves jointly the obligation of taking what they deemed a just retribution, or appointed an avenger, who resolved never to rest until life had answered for life. In such cases, the murderer usually fled. As all quarrels were generally reconciled by the relatives of the parties, long-cherished animosities, and consequently homicides, were unfrequent in ancient times. The present of white wampum was not in the nature of a compensation for the life of the deceased, but of a regretful confession of the crime, with a petition for forgiveness. It was a peace-offering, the acceptance of which was pressed by mutual friends, and under such influences that a reconciliation was usually effected, except, perhaps, in aggravated cases of premeditated murder.

Theft, the most despicable of human crimes, was scarcely known among them. In the days of their primitive simplicity, a mercenary thought had not entered the Indian mind. After the commencement of their intercourse with the whites, the distribution of presents and of ardent spirits among them, and the creation of new kinds of property by the pursuits of trade, so far corrupted the habits of the Indian, that in some instances the vagrant and intemperate were led to the commission of this offence. But in justice to them it must be acknowledged, that no people ever possessed a higher sense of honor and self-respect in this particular, or looked down with greater disdain upon this shameful practice, than did the Iroquois. To this day, among their descendants, this offence is almost unknown. No locks, or bolts, or private repositories were ever necessary for the protection of property among themselves. The lash of public indignation, the severest punishment known to the red man, was the only penalty attached to this dereliction from the path of integrity.

These were the four principal crimes against society among our primitive inhabitants. The introduction of ardent spirits among them, in modern times, has changed the face of Indian society, and proved the fruitful source of all their calamities; aggravating those disorders which were incident to their social system, and introducing new ones entirely unknown in the days of their sylvan independence. Against this infamous traffic, their wise and good men, from the earliest period of their intercourse with us, have put forth incessant but unavailing protestations. The power of self-control, in this particular, was much weaker with the red man than the white; and the consequences of indulgence more lamentable and destructive. The "fire-water," as they have fitly termed it, has been a more invincible and devouring enemy than civilization itself, to both of which causes, about in equal degrees, they owe their displacement. It filled their villages with vagrancy, violence and bloodshed: it invaded the peace of the domestic fireside, stimulated the fiercest passions, introduced disease, contention and strife; thus wasting them away by violence, poverty and sickness, and by the casualties of hunger and cold. If there is any one act in our past intercourse with the Iroquois, for which we are more reprehensible than another, it was the permission, short of the penalty of hanging, of this most nefarious and inhuman traffic. A Mohawk chief, in 1754, thus addressed the governor of the province of New York upon this subject: "There is an affair about which our hearts tremble; this is the selling of rum in our castles. It destroys many both of the old and young people. We request of all the governors here present, that it may be forbidden to carry it among any of the Five Nations."[1] About the same time a representation was made to the British government, as follows: "They are supplied with rum by the traders, in vast and almost incredible quantities, the laws of the colonies now in force being insufficient to restrain the supply; and the Indians of every nation are frequently drunk, and abused in their trade, and their affections thereby alienated from the English. They often wound and murder each other in their liquor, and to avoid revenge flee to the French; and perhaps more have been lost by these means than by the French artifices."[2]

The love of truth was another marked trait of the Indian character. This inborn sentiment flourished in the period of their highest prosperity, in all the freshness of its primeval purity. On all occasions, and at whatever peril, the Iroquois spoke the truth without fear and without hesitation. Dissimulation was not an Indian habit. In fact, the language of the Iroquois does not admit of double speaking, or of the perversion of the words of the speaker. It is simple and direct, not admitting of those shades of meaning and those nice discriminations which pertain to polished languages. Subsequent to their discovery, in their intercourse with the whites, their native truthfulness was sometimes corrupted by traffic and intemperance, but, as a people, they have

[1] Doc. Hist. N. Y., ii. 591.   [2] Ib., ii. 610.

preserved to this day the same elevation of sentiment in this particular which characterized their ancestors.

To the faith of treaties the Iroquois adhered with unwavering fidelity. Having endured the severest trials of political disaster, this faith furnishes one of the proudest monuments of their national integrity. They held fast to the "covenant chain" with the British until they were themselves deserted, and their entire country became the forfeit of their fidelity. In their numerous transactions with the several provinces formed out of their ancient territories, no serious cause of complaint was found against them for the non-fulfilment of treaty stipulations, although they were shorn of their possessions by treaty after treaty, and oftentimes made the victims of deception and fraud. In their intercourse with Indian nations, they frequently entered into treaties, sometimes of amity and alliance, sometimes of protection only, and in some instances for special purposes. All of these national compacts were "talked into" strings of wampum, to use the Indian expression, after which these were delivered into the custody of *Ho-no-we-nă'-to*, the Onondaga sachem, who was made hereditary keeper of the Wampum, at the institution of the League; and from him and his successors, was to be sought their interpretation from generation to generation. Hence the expression — "This belt preserves my words," so frequently met with at the close of Indian speeches, on the presentation of a belt. Indian nations, after treating, always exchanged belts, which were not only the ratification, but the memorandum of the compact.

There was an ancient treaty between the Senecas and the *Gä-quä-ga'-o-no*,[1] or Eries, who resided upon the southern shore of Lake Erie, to the effect that the Genesee river should be the boundary between them, and that when a hostile band of either nation re-crossed this river into its own territories, it should be safe from further pursuit. An infraction of this treaty was one of the reasons of the long-cherished animosity of the Iroquois against them. A similar compact was once made with the *O-ya-dä'-go-o-no*,[2] or Cherokees, by which the Tennessee river was the limit of pursuit. If a war-party of the latter had returned and re-crossed the Tennessee before they were overtaken by the pursuing Iroquois, they were as safe from their attack, as if intrenched behind an impregnable rampart. The Iroquois band could still invade, if disposed, the territory of the enemy, but they passed the camp of the retreating war-party without offering the slightest molestation.

The Iroquois prided themselves upon their sacred regard for the public faith, and punished the want of it with severity when an occasion presented. An example is to be found in the case of the *Sag-a-na'-gä*, or Dela-

[1] This was the Iroquois name of the Erie nation, who were expelled by them about the year 1655. They were an offshoot of the Iroquois stock, and spoke a dialect of their language. Charlevoix calls them the " Cat Nation." Vol. ii. p. 62. It is a singular fact that the Neuter Nation, who dwelt on the banks of the Niagara river, and who were expelled by the Iroquois about the year 1643, was known among them as the *Je-go'-sä-sa*, or Cat Nation. The word signifies a wild-cat ; and from being the name of a woman of great influence among them,(14) it came to be the name of the nation. Charlevoix also speaks of the Neuter Nation. Vol. i. p. 377. It is quite probable that he transposed or confounded their aboriginal names.

[2] *O-ya-dä'-go-o-no*, the Iroquois name of the Cherokees, signifies " The people who dwell in caves."

wares.   After they had been subdued, and had acknowledged their dependence by sending the tributary
wampum, they made an inroad upon a western nation
under the protection of the Iroquois, notwithstanding
their knowledge of the treaty, and a prohibition against
its infringement.   A deputation of Iroquois chiefs went
immediately into the country of the Delawares, and
having assembled the people in council, they degraded
them from the rank of even a tributary nation.   Having reproved them for their want of faith, they forbade
them from ever after going out to war, divested them
of all civil powers, and declared that they should henceforth be as women.   This degradation they signified
in the figurative way of putting upon them the *Gä-
kä'-ah*, or skirt of the female, and placing in their
hands a corn-pounder, thus showing that their business ever after should be that of women.   The Delawares never emancipated themselves, after this act of
denationalization.[1]

---

[1] The Delawares, about the year 1742, having sold some of their lands
upon the Delaware river to Pennsylvania, without the knowledge or consent of the Iroquois, Canassetego, the Onondaga chief before mentioned,
reproved them in a speech, from which some extracts are subjoined in further illustration of the lordly manner in which the Iroquois conducted
themselves towards subjugated nations.   "Let this belt of wampum serve
to chastise you.* * How came you to take upon you to sell land at all?
We conquered you ; we made women of you; you know you are women,
and can no more sell land than women; nor is it fit that you should have
the power of selling lands, since you would abuse it. * * We therefore
assign you two places to go, either to Wyoming or Shamokin.   You may
go to either of these places, and then we shall have you more under our
eye, and shall see how you behave.   Don't deliberate, but remove, and
take this belt of wampum." * * Then taking another belt he continued:
"After our just reproof, and absolute order to depart from the land, you
are now to take notice of what we have further to say to you.   This

After war had been declared against any nation, either by the congress of sachems at Onondaga, or by an individual nation against a neighboring enemy, the existence of the war was indicated by a tomahawk painted red, ornamented with red feathers, and with black wampum, struck in the war-post in each village of the League. Any person was then at liberty to organize a band, and make an invasion. This was effected in a summary manner. Dressed in full costume, the war-chief who proposed to solicit volunteers and conduct the expedition, went through the village sounding the war-whoop to announce his intentions; after which he went to the war-post, *Gä-on-dote'*, and having struck into it his red tomahawk, he commenced the war-dance. A group gathered around him, and as their martial ardor was aroused by the dance, they enlisted, one after the other, by joining in its performance. In this manner a company was soon formed; the matrons of the village prepared their subsistence while the dance was performing; and at its close, while they were yet fired with enthusiasm for the enterprise, they immediately left the village, and turned their footsteps towards the country of the enemy. If the movement was simultaneous in several villages, these parties joined each other on their march, but each band continued under the direction of its own war-chief. Their subsistence was usually charred corn, parched a

string of wampum serves to forbid you, your children and your grandchildren to the latest posterity forever, meddling in land affairs; neither you, nor any who shall descend from you, are ever hereafter to presume to sell any land. For which purpose you are to preserve this string, in memory of what your uncles have this day given you in charge." Colden's Hist. Five Nations, Lond. Ed. 1750, pp. 80–81.

second time, pounded into fine flour, and mixed with maple-sugar, thus reducing it in bulk and lightness to such a degree that the warrior could carry without inconvenience in his bear-skin pocket a sufficient supply for a long and perilous expedition. The band took the war-path in single file, and moved with such rapidity that it was but five days' journey to the country of the Cherokees, upon the southern banks of the Tennessee. At their night encampments they cut upon the trees certain devices to indicate their numbers and destination. On their return, they did the same, showing also the number of captives, and the number slain. When the returning war-party reached the outskirts of their village, they sounded the war-whoop to announce their approach, and to summon the people to assemble for their reception. Then leading their captives, they entered the village in a dancing procession, as they had shortly before gone out. After they had reached the war-post in the centre of the place, a wise-man addressed them in a speech of welcome and congratulation; in reply to which, a speech was made by one of the band, descriptive of their adventures, after which the war-dance was again enjoyed.

The Iroquois never exchanged prisoners with Indian nations, nor ever sought to reclaim their own people from captivity among them. Adoption or the torture were the alternative chances of the captive. A distinguished war-chief would sometimes be released by them from admiration of his military achievements, and be restored to his people, with presents and other marks of favor. No pledges were exacted in these occasional instances of magnanimity, but the person thus discharged esteemed himself bound in honor never again to take the war-path against his generous enemy. If adopted, the allegiance and the affections of the captive were transferred to his adopted nation. When the Indian went forth to war, he emphatically took his life in his hand, knowing that if he should be taken it was forfeited by the laws of war; and if saved by adoption, his country, at least, was lost forever. From the foundation of the Confederacy, the custom of adoption has prevailed among the Iroquois, who carried this principle farther than other Indian nations. It was not confined to captives alone, but was extended to fragments of dismembered tribes, and even to the admission of independent nations into the League. It was a leading feature of their policy to subdue adjacent nations by conquest, and having absorbed them by naturalization, to mould them into one common family with themselves. Some fragments of tribes were adopted and distributed among the nations at large; some were received into the League as independent members, as the Tuscaroras, while others were taken under its shelter, like the Mohekunnucks, and assigned a territory within their own. The fruit of this system of policy was their gradual elevation to a universal supremacy; a supremacy which was spreading so rapidly at the epoch of their discovery, as to threaten the subjugation of all the nations east of the Mississippi.

A regular ceremony of adoption was performed in each case, to complete the naturalization.[5, 9, 104]

With captives, this ceremony was the gantlet, after which new names were assigned to them ; and at the next religious festival, their names, together with the tribe and family into which they were respectively adopted, were publicly announced. Upon the return of a war-party with captives, if they had lost any of their own number in the expedition, the families to which these belonged were first allowed an opportunity to supply from the captives the places made vacant in their households. Any family could then adopt out of the residue any who chanced to attract their favorable notice, or whom they wished to save. At the time appointed, which was usually three or four days after the return of the band, the women and children of the village arranged themselves in two parallel rows just without the place, each one having a whip with which to lash the captives as they passed between the lines. The male captives, who alone were required to undergo this test of their powers of endurance, were brought out, and each one was shown in turn the house in which he was to take refuge, and which was to be his future home, if he passed successfully through the ordeal. They were then taken to the head of this long avenue of whips, and were compelled, one after another, to run through it for their lives, and for the entertainment of the surrounding throng, exposed at every step, undefended, and with naked backs, to the merciless inflictions of the whip. Those who fell from exhaustion were immediately despatched as unworthy to be saved ; but those who emerged in safety from this test of their physical energies, were from that moment treated with the utmost affection and kindness. The effects of this contrast in behavior upon the mind of the captive must have been singular enough. During the slow progress of these arrangements, how many captives have listened to every sound, and watched every motion with the most intense solicitude. Carried into the heart of the country of the enemy, far away from all hope of succor, the question was about to be decided whether the clemency of their captors would bestow upon them the rights of citizenship, or their warlike frenzy lead them away to the torture. Its decision depended upon the most fickle impulses. Who shall relate our sylvan history ! To the red man compassion has seldom been ascribed, but yet these scenes in the forest oftentimes revealed the most generous traits of character. Admiration for the chivalric bearing of a captive, the recollection of a past favor, or a sudden impulse of compassion, were sufficient to decide the question of adoption. When the perils of the gantlet, which was an enviable lot compared with the fate of the rejected, were over, he ceased to be an enemy, and became an Iroquois. Not only so, but he was received into the family by which he was adopted with all the cordiality of affection, and into all the relations of the one whose place he was henceforth to fill. By these means all recollections of his distant kindred were gradually effaced, bound as he was by gratitude to those who had restored a life which was forfeited by the usages of war. If a captive, after adoption, became discontented, which is said to have been seldom the case, he was sometimes restored, with presents, to his nation, that they might know he had lost nothing by his captivity among them.

The rejected captives were then led away to the torture, and to death. It is not necessary to describe this horrible practice of our primitive inhabitants. It is sufficient to say that it was a test of courage. When the Indian went out upon the war-path, he prepared his mind for this very contingency, resolving to show the enemy, if captured, that his courage was equal to any trial, and above the power of death itself. The exhibitions of heroism and fortitude by the red man under the sufferings of martyrdom, almost surpass belief. They considered the character of their nation in their keeping, and the glory of the race as involved and illustrated in the manner of their death.

A slight notice of a few of their customs in relation to the hunt, will close this desultory chapter. The deer, the elk, the moose, the bear, and several species of wild fowl, furnished their principal game. At certain seasons of the year, the female of all animals was spared, by the provisions of their game-laws, lest there should be a diminution of the supply. Not having a species of dog adapted to the chase, they were obliged to resort to the still hunt, and seize the opportunity whenever it presented; thus rendering it necessary to success that the hunter should become well versed in the habits of animals. Sometimes they trapped both deer and bear, and spread nets for quails and other small fowl. One species of deer-trap was attached to a young tree bent over, and so adjusted that the springing of the trap fastened a loop around the hind legs of the deer, and at the same time released the tree, which drew him up, and held him suspended in the air. They practiced another method of taking deer, in herds. A large party of hunters was formed, and a brush fence was built in the shape of the letter V, two or three miles in length on each side. The woods were then fired in the rear at some miles' distance, so as to drive the deer towards the opening, into which they were guided by parties stationed upon either side. They followed the fence down to the angle, where the arrows of the unseen hunters soon brought them down one after the other. Sometimes a hundred were thus taken at one time. In the bear-hunt it was customary to tire out the animal by a long chase, as when fresh and vigorous he was too formidable to attack with the bow and arrow, or the hunting tomahawk; but when wearied out it was an easy matter to overcome him. The hunter selected the choice pieces of venison, and having removed the bone, and dried and cured the flesh before a fire, he packed it in small bark barrels, and thus carried it home upon his back. It was so much reduced in weight and bulk by the process of curing, that a hunter could thus transport, with ease, the substance of a dozen deer. Their skins were also dried and packed, and carried home in the same manner. When deer or bear were taken in winter, within a day's journey of their villages, bark sledges were prepared, on which they were drawn home, undressed, upon the snow crust.

Hunting was a passion with the red man. He pursued it for the excitement and employment it afforded, as well as for subsistence, frequently making long and toilsome expeditions. The Senecas, for example, in the season of the fall hunt, would leave their villages in small parties; some turning south, would encamp upon the Chemung river, and traverse the whole adjacent country; others, descending the Allegany, penetrated the inland regions of Ohio, which was a favorite hunting-ground, not only of the Senecas, but also of the other nations of the League; while still others encamped within the Niagara peninsula, which was formerly a place of great resort for the beaver-hunt. The Cayugas turned to the Susquehanna, which furnished them an inexhaustible store. They also ranged Pennsylvania; and with parties from the other nations, they not unfrequently roamed as far as the Potomac, which was within their ancient domain. Parties of the Onondagas descended the Chenango to the Susquehanna, or turning northward, perchance, crossed over into Canada. The Oneidas, for the fall hunt, descended the Unadilla, and also went northward, into the regions watered by the Black river. Lastly, the Mohawks, leaving their valley, found well-stocked hunting-grounds upon the head-waters of the Delaware and Susquehanna, and also in the wild and rugged regions of the north, and around lake Champlain.

About midwinter these widely scattered parties began to find their way back to their villages for the celebration of their annual jubilee; after which they surrendered themselves for a season to idleness, or to the amusements of the winter life. With the spring came the fishing season, in which for a time they found employment. The summer again was a season of repose, except when enlivened by councils, by their religious festivals, or by the adventures of the war-path.

In this round of occupations the Iroquois glided through the year. The progress of the seasons suggested their appropriate employments, if not marked in the exuberance of unsubdued nature, by the same attractive changes which pursue each other in regions beautified by cultivation. While with the fullest appreciation he enjoyed the grandeur of nature in her wild attire, and surrendered himself to her deepest inspirations, he yet knew nothing of her inexhaustible fruitfulness, or of those more delicate features of beauty which are revealed only by the hand of art. Aspiring to a freedom as boundless as the forest, satisfied with the martial pursuits, the amusements, the friendships and the social privileges of Indian life, and proud of their military achievements and of the fame of the League among Indian nations, the Iroquois measured out their days with all the happiness which these considerations could secure, and with all the contentment which could result from knowing no higher destiny.

VOLUME II

BOOK THIRD

INCIDENT TO THE LEAGUE

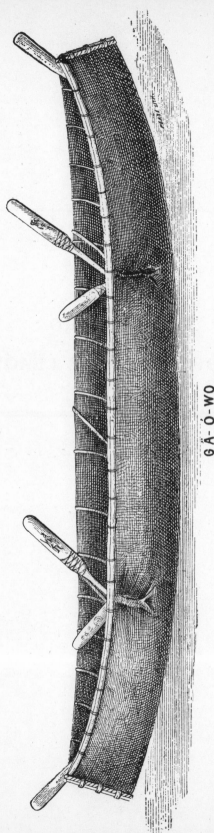

GÄ-Ó-WO
or
BARK CANOE.

BOOK III

INCIDENT TO THE LEAGUE

Chapter I

Fabrics of the Iroquois — Their Artisan Intellect — Indian Pottery — Earthen Vessels — Moccason — War Club — Tomahawk — Rope Making — Finger Weaving — Bark Vessels — Bark Canoe — Corn Mortar — Maize — Tobacco — Snow Shoe — Indian Saddle — Miscellaneous Inventions — Basket Making — Costumes — Wampum — Baby Frame — Diffusion of Indian Arts — Improvement of the Iroquois

THE fabrics of a people unlock their social history. They speak a language which is silent, but yet more eloquent than the written page. As memorials of former times, they commune directly with the beholder, opening the unwritten history of the period they represent, and clothing it with perpetual freshness. However rude the age, or uncultivated the people from whose hands they come, the products of human ingenuity are ever invested with a peculiar and even solemn interest. It is greatly to be regretted that so few remains of the skill and industry of the Iroquois have come down to the present age, to illustrate the era of Indian occupation. Although their fabrics are indicative of a low state of the useful arts, the artificial contrivances by which

3

they were surrounded are yet the indices of their social condition, and for this reason are not devoid of instruction. Further than this, it is but just to them to save from oblivion the fruits of their inventive intellect, however unpretending they may seem, that, in the general judgment pronounced upon their memory, they may not be defrauded of even their humblest inventions.

Since the commencement of European intercourse, and especially within the last century, great changes have been wrought among the Iroquois. Their primitive fabrics have mostly passed away, and with them, many of their original inventions. The introduction of articles of more skilful manufacture has led to the gradual disuse of many of their simple arts. At the present moment, therefore, much of the fruit of their inventive capacity is entirely lost. Fragments, it is true, are frequently disentombed from the resting-places to which they had been consigned by their burial rites, but they are mere vestiges of the past, and afford but a slight indication of their social condition, or of the range of their artisan intellect. It would now be extremely difficult to furnish a full description of their implements, domestic utensils, and miscellaneous fabrics. Many of the inventions of the earlier Iroquois are still preserved among their descendants now residing within our limits and in Canada ; but that portion of them which would especially serve to illustrate the condition of the hunter life have passed beyond our reach.

The remains of Indian art which are found scattered over the soil of New York are of two distinct kinds, and to be ascribed to widely different periods. The first class belong to the ante-Columbian period, or the era of the " Mound Builders,"   whose defensive works, mounds, and sacred enclosures are scattered so profusely throughout the west.[1] With the second period may be connected the name of the Iroquois.   It will also include the remains of the fugitive races, who, since the extermination of the " Mound Builders," have displaced each other in succession, until the period of the Iroquois commenced.

In the fabrics of the Iroquois a wide range is observable.   It reaches from the rudest specimens of pottery of the ancient, to the most delicate needlework of the modern Iroquois.   Since the era of the discovery, and the commencement of their intercourse with Europeans, a gradual revolution has been effected.   Their social condition has changed greatly, and is changing from day to day.   With equal pace their simple arts have been dropping from their hands, one after the other, as they have taken up agricultural pursuits, until at the present epoch the fabrics of the Iroquois contrast very strangely with those of their ancestors.   In their present advanced condition, a large proportion of their articles are of a mixed character.   They rather exhibit the application of Indian ingenuity to fabrics

---

[1] The remains of this period indicate a semi-civilization of the most imposing character, including a considerable development of the art of agriculture.   Exclusive of the mounds and enclosures, they have left implements of copper and chert, of stone, porphyry and earthen, some of which are elaborately and ingeniously wrought.   The fugitive specimens belonging to this period, which are occasionally found within the limits of our State, are much superior to any of the productions of the earlier Iroquois.

5

of foreign manufacture, as shown in their reduction into use, than originality of invention. But this class of articles are not without a peculiar interest. They furnish no slight indication of artisan capacity, and will serve as a species of substitute for those articles which they have displaced, and those inventions which they have hurried into forgetfulness.

One of the most ancient Indian arts was that of pottery. It was carried to considerable perfection by the Iroquois at an early day, as is shown by the specimens which are still occasionally disentombed from the burial-places, where they were deposited beside the dead; but the art itself has been so long disused that it is now entirely lost. Pipes, and earthen pots of various designs and sizes, are the principal articles thus found. Some of these specimens of black pottery, which is the best variety, are of so fine a texture as to admit of a tolerable polish, and so firm as to have the appearance of stone. Their common pottery is of a clay color, and is a compound of common clay and pulverized quartz.

This pipe is of black pottery, well finished, and nearly as hard as marble, and is also represented at its actual size. In some specimens the bowl is fronted with a human face, or with a wolf's or dog's head. Frequently these imitations are delicately, even exquisitely made. Another species of pipe, in use among the Iroquois in later times, was cut out of soapstone, which yields readily to metallic instruments. A representation of one of these pipes of Seneca manufacture, will be found in the plate (I. 105). It is fronted with a human face, and designed to be used with a stem-piece of reed. The other, in the same plate, is also a modern Iroquois pipe, made of Catlinite, or the

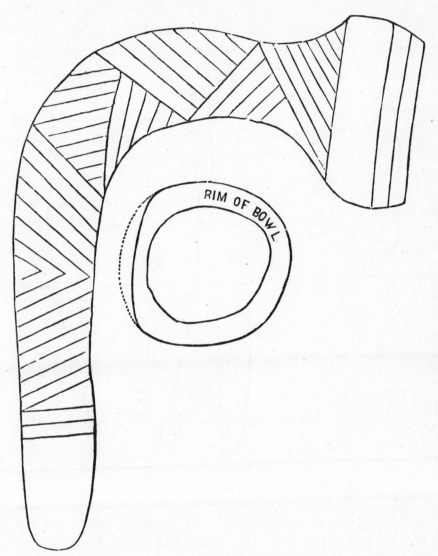

RIM OF BOWL

Ah-sc-quá'-tä, or Iroquois Pipe, Lima, Liv. Co., N. Y.

red Missouri pipe-stone. Pipes of this description are used chiefly among the Sioux, by whom they were introduced into use, and other western Indians; and were rather accidental than common among the Iroquois.

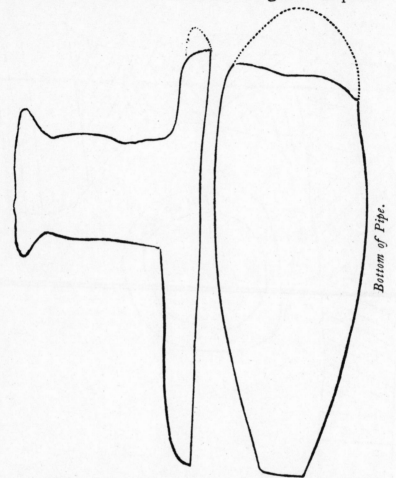

Bottom of Pipe.

Pipe of the Mound Builders, Valley of the Genesee.

This pipe is anomalous. It is of black marble, highly polished, with the bowl and stem bored with great precision. Doubtless it is a relic of the " Mound Builders," which, having found its way into the hands of a Seneca, was finally buried by his side in the valley of the Genesee, to be again brought to

8

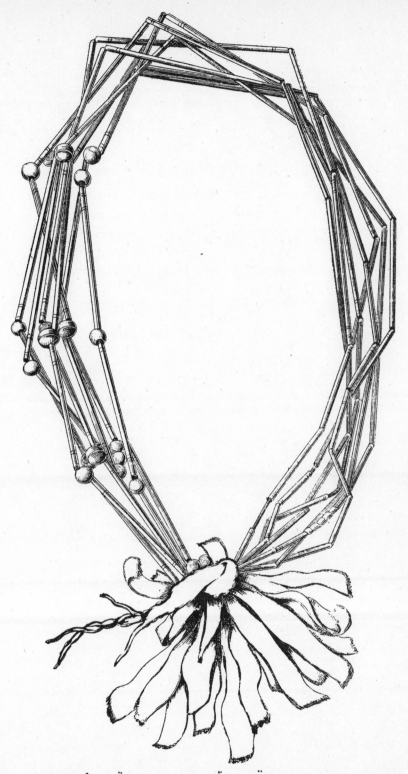

OUT-WIS-TÄ-NE-UN-DÄ-QUÄ or SILVER BEADS

light upon the excavation of the Valley canal. Like
the pipes of that era, it has the bowl in the central
part of the stone. In material, also, and in finish, it
is unlike, and superior to the pipes of the Iroquois.

Gä-jib', or Earthen Vessel.

Earthen pots of this description are frequently
found beside the remains of the Iroquois. They
are usually of sufficient capacity to contain from
two to six quarts. On exposure to the air, after dis-
interment, they are apt to crumble, being usually, if
not always, of the light-colored common pottery,
which is less firm and coherent than the black. In
these earthen vessels it was customary to deposit food
for the departed, while journeying to the realm of the
Great Spirit. These earthen dishes are still found in
Indian burial-places, where, perhaps, they had lain for
centuries; and the fragments of those which have
been broken by the plough, are also mingled with the
soil.

Metallic implements were unknown among them,
as they had not the use of metals. Rude knives of
chert were used for skinning deer, and similar purposes. For cutting trees and excavating canoes, and
corn mortars, in a word, for those necessary purposes

9

for which the axe would seem to be indispensable, the Iroquois used the stone chisel, *Uh'-ga-o-gwät'-hä.* In cutting trees, fire was applied at the foot, and the chisel used to clear away the coal. By a repetition of the process, trees were felled and cut to pieces. Wooden vessels were hollowed out by the same means. Fire and the chisel were the substitutes for the axe. The chisel was usually about six inches long, three wide, and two thick; the lower end being fashioned like the edge of an axe. Stone gouges in the form of a convex chisel, were also used when a more regular concavity of the vessel was desired. Stone mortars for pounding corn, grinding mineral paint, and for pulverizing roots and barks for medicines, were also among their utensils.

Arrow-heads of chert, or flint, were so common that it is scarcely necessary to refer to them. Occasionally they are found with a twist to make the arrow revolve in its flight. It is well known that the Indian always feathered his arrow for the same purpose. It is not uncommon to find the places where these arrow-heads were manufactured, which is indicated by the fragments of chert which had been made by cleavage. In the western mounds rows of similar chert heads have been found lying side by side, like teeth, the row being about two feet long. This has suggested the idea that they were set in a frame and fastened with thongs, thus making a species of sword. Their discovery in those mounds also establishes the great antiquity of the art.

In ancient times the Iroquois used the stone tomahawk. It was fashioned something like an axe, but in place of an eye for the helve, a deep groove was cut around the outside, by means of which the handle was firmly attached with a withe or thong. Oval stones, with grooves around their greatest circumference, were also secured in the head of war-clubs, and thus made dangerous weapons. Other implements and utensils of stone, some of which were very ingeniously worked, were in use among the Iroquois; and also personal ornaments of the same material, but a sufficient number have been brought under notice.

O-sque'-sont, or Stone Tomahawk.

The moccason (see plates I. 35, 44, 79) is preëminently an Indian invention, and one of the highest antiquity. It is true to nature in its adjustment to the foot, beautiful in its materials and finish, and durable as an article of apparel. It will compare favorably with the best single article for the protection and adornment of the foot ever invented, either in ancient or modern times. With the sanction of fashion, it would supersede among us a long list of similar inventions. Other nations have fallen behind the Indian, in this one particular at least. The masses of the Romans wore the calceus ligneus, or wooden shoe; the masses of Germany and Ireland, and of many of the European nations, formerly wore the same. With the cothurnus and sandal of the ancients, and the boot of the moderns, the moccason admits of no unfavorable comparison. It deserves to be classed among the highest articles of apparel ever invented, both in usefulness, durability, and beauty.

The moccason is made of one piece of deer-skin. It is seamed up at the heel, and also in front, above the foot, leaving the bottom of the moccason without a seam. In front the deer-skin is gathered, in place of being crimped; over this part porcupine quills or beads are worked, in various patterns. The plain moccason rises several inches above the ankle, like the Roman cothurnus, and is fastened with deer strings; but usually this part is turned down, so as to expose a part of the instep, and is ornamented with bead-work, as represented in the plates. A small bone near the ankle joint of the deer, has furnished the moccason needle from time immemorial; and the sinews of the animal the thread. These bone needles are found in the mounds of the West, and beside the skeletons of the Iroquois, where they were deposited with religious care. This isolated fact would seem to indicate an affinity, in one art at least, between the Iroquois and the Mound Builders, whose name, and era of occupation and destiny are entirely lost.

In ancient times the Iroquois used another shoe, made of the skin of the elk. They cut the skin above and below the gambrel joint, and then took it off entire. As the hind leg of the elk inclines at this joint, nearly at a right angle, it was naturally adapted to the foot. The lower end was sewed firmly with sinew, and the upper part secured above the ankle with deer strings.

In connection with this subject is the art of tanning deer-skins; as they still tan them after the ancient method. It is done with the brain of the deer, the tanning properties of which, according to a tradition, were discovered by accident. The brain is mingled with moss, to make it adhere sufficiently to be formed into a cake, which is afterwards hung by the fire to dry. It is thus preserved for years. When the deer-skin is fresh, the hair, and also the grain of the skin are taken off, over a cylindrical beam, with a wooden blade or stone scraper. A solution is then made by boiling a cake of the brain in water, and the moss, which is of no use, being removed, the skin is soaked in it for a few hours. It is then wrung out and stretched, until it becomes dry and pliable. Should it be a thick one, it would be necessary to repeat the process until it becomes thoroughly penetrated by the solution. The skin is still porous and easily torn. To correct both, a smoke is made, and the skin placed over it in such a manner as to enclose it entirely. Each side is smoked in this way until the pores are closed, and the skin has become thoroughly toughened, with its color changed from white to a kind of brown. It is then ready for use.

They also use the brain of other animals, and sometimes the back-bone of the eel, which, pounded up and boiled, possesses nearly the same properties for tanning. Bear-skins were never tanned. They were scraped and softened, after which they were dried, and used without removing the hair, either as an article of apparel, or as a mattress to sleep upon.

Before the tomahawk came into use among the

Iroquois, their principal weapons were the bow, the stone tomahawk, and the war-club. The *Gä-je'-wä* was a heavy weapon, usually made of ironwood, with

Gä-je'-wä, or War-club.

a large ball of knot at the head. It was usually about two feet in length, and the ball five or six inches in diameter. In close combat it would prove a formidable weapon. They wore it in the belt, in front.

Ga-ne-u'-ga-o-dus-ha, or Deer-horn War-club.

This species of war-club was also much used. It was made of hard wood, elaborately carved, painted and ornamented with feathers at the ends. In the lower edge, a sharp-pointed deer's horn, about four inches in length, was inserted. It was thus rendered a dangerous weapon in close combat, and would inflict a deeper wound than the former. They wore it in the girdle. At a later period they used the same species of club, substituting a steel or iron blade resembling a spearhead, in the place of the horn. War-clubs of this description are still to be found among the Iroquois, preserved as relics of past exploits. It is not probable, however, that these two varieties were peculiar to them; they were doubtless common over the continent.

The tomahawk succeeded the war-club, as the rifle did the bow. With the invention of this terrible implement of warfare the red man had nothing to do, except in having it so fashioned as to be adapted to his taste and usage. The tomahawk is known as widely as the Indian, and the two names have become

O-sque'-sont, or Tomahawk.

apparently inseparable. They are made of steel, brass, or iron. The choicer articles are surmounted by a pipe-bowl, and have a perforated handle, that they may answer the double purpose of ornament and use. In such the handle, and often the blade itself, are richly inlaid with silver. It is worn in the girdle, and behind the back, except when in actual battle. They used it in close combat with terrible effect, and also threw it with unerring certainty at distant objects, making it revolve in the air in its flight. With the

15

Indian, the tomahawk is the emblem of war itself. To bury it, is peace ; to raise it, is to declare the most deadly warfare.

Rope-making, from filaments of bark, is also an Indian art. The deer string answers a multitude of pur-

Ose-gă, or Skein of Slippery Elm Filaments.

poses in their domestic economy ; but it could not supply them all. Bark-rope (*Gä-a'-sken-dä*) has been fabricated among them from time immemorial. In its manufacture, they use the bark of the slippery-elm, the red-elm, and the bass-wood. Having removed the outer surface of the bark, they divide it into narrow strips,

Gus-ha'-äh, or Burden Strap.

and then boil it in ashes and water. After it is dried it is easily separated into small filaments, the strings running with the grain several feet without breaking. These filaments are then put up in skeins and laid aside for use. Slippery-elm makes the most pliable rope ; it is soft to the touch, can be closely braided, and is very durable. The burden strap is worn around the

forehead, and lashed to a litter, which is borne by Indian women on their back. It is usually about fifteen
feet in length, and braided into a belt in the centre,
three or four inches wide. Some of them are entirely
covered upon one side with porcupine-quills-work, after
various devices, and are in themselves remarkable
products of skilful industry. The braiding or
knitting of the bark threads is effected with a single
needle of hickory. In other specimens, the quill-work
is sprinkled over the belt for ornament, the quills in
all cases being of divers colors. Of all their fabrics,
there is no one, perhaps, which surpasses the porcupine-quill burden strap, in skill of manufacture, richness of material, or beauty of workmanship. In this
species of work, the Iroquois female excelled. They
also made a common bark rope for ordinary uses,
which consisted of three strands, hard twisted ; a single
rope being frequently forty or fifty feet in length. The
art of rope-making, like many others, has mostly fallen
into disuse among the present Iroquois. But few Indian families now provide themselves with skeins of
bark thread, or make any ropes of this description.

In the manufacture of the several species of burden
strap, more skill, ingenuity, and patient industry are
exhibited, perhaps, than in any other single article
fabricated by the Iroquois. The strap consists of a
belt in the centre about two feet in length by two
and a half inches in width, with ropes at each end
about seven feet each ; thus making its entire length
from fifteen to twenty feet. It is used attached to
the litter or burden frame, to the baby frame, and to
the basket, when these burdens are to be borne on the

back; in which cases the belt is passed around the forehead. Fifteen or twenty small cords are first made, about three feet in length, by twisting the filaments of bark by hand. These cords, which make the warp, or substance of the belt, are then placed parallel with each other, and side by side; after which finer threads of the same material, usually colored, are prepared for the filling, to be passed across the cords over and under each alternately from side to side and back again. The fine thread, or filling, is twisted in the first instance, and also again as it is braided or woven in with the warp while being passed across from side to side. As the work is all done by hand, it is a slow and laborious process, but the specimen will show how successfully it is accomplished. After the filling has thus been braided in with the warp, each of the main cords, although covered on both sides, literally wound with the finer threads in crossing and returning, is still distinctly visible, giving to the belt the appearance of being ribbed. The whole process is exactly the same as the modern process of weaving, the main difference consisting in this, that in the latter the warp and filling are nearly equal in the size of the threads, while in the Indian art the warp is several times larger than the filling.

Towards the ends the belt is narrowed gradually by joining two of the cords in one, until its width is diminished about one-third. The cords are then lengthened out by adding new filaments, and braided into an open-work band or bark rope about an inch wide, and flat; the band consisting of as many strands as there were cords at the end of the belt. The surface of these belts is generally smooth and even, and the belt itself so closely braided as to leave no interstices through which the eye could penetrate. When threads of different colors were used, the belt was variegated simply, or small figures were woven in it for ornament.

Another species of burden strap, of more expeditious manufacture, was made by placing the warp cords side by side, and stitching them through and through with bark thread, in which case the cords themselves were made larger than in the ordinary burden strap. For stitching, a hickory or bone needle, without an eye, was used in ancient times. As the cords consisted of two strong threads twisted into one, the stitching thread was passed through each cord, between its two parts, from one side to the other and back again. Ropes were then attached to the ends of the belt, and the work was completed.

O–Ä–TA–OSE–KÄ, OR MOOSE HAIR BURDEN STRAP
GUS–HÄ–AH, OR DEER HAIR BURDEN STRAP
See PLATE facing page 20

Near the rump of the moose (*Yen-dä-ne*), and near the neck between the shoulders, there are small tufts of white hair, about four inches in length, each yielding a small handful. These hairs were carefully preserved, dyed red, blue and yellow, and used in the manufacture of the finest varieties of burden straps. Similar tufts of hair, but inferior in quality, are found upon the elk (*Jo-rǎ-dä*), and in the tail of the deer (*Na-o-geh*). The moose hair burden strap is made in all respects as above described, except that the thread, which serves as the filling, is wound with this hair upon one side of the belt, in such a way as either to cover the whole face of the belt, or to sprinkle it through with small figures at the pleasure of the maker. The one represented in the plate is a very perfect and beautiful piece of work, nearly the whole upper surface of the belt being covered with moose hair, white, yellow, red and blue, which is woven into the belt in a regular figure. It was made by an Onondaga woman on Grand river in Upper Canada, where it was purchased in October last. Although it has been used many years, and the colors have lost some portion of their original brilliancy, it is yet wholly unimpaired, and a remarkable specimen of finger weaving, as well as of artisan skill. It is not only woven compactly, but with such evenness of thread as to present a smooth surface and uniform texture. It is difficult to believe, upon an examination of the under side of the belt, that it is manufactured with bark threads; and perhaps still more incredible, that in the mechanism of this belt can be found the primary elements of the art of weaving.

GÄ–NE–KO–WÄ–AH, BURDEN FRAME, OR LITTER

This is an ancient contrivance to assist in carrying burdens. Game, cooking utensils, wood, bark, in fact, everything which could be transported by hand could be borne upon this frame. They were a necessary appendage to every house, to the traveller, and to the hunter. Sometimes they were elaborately carved

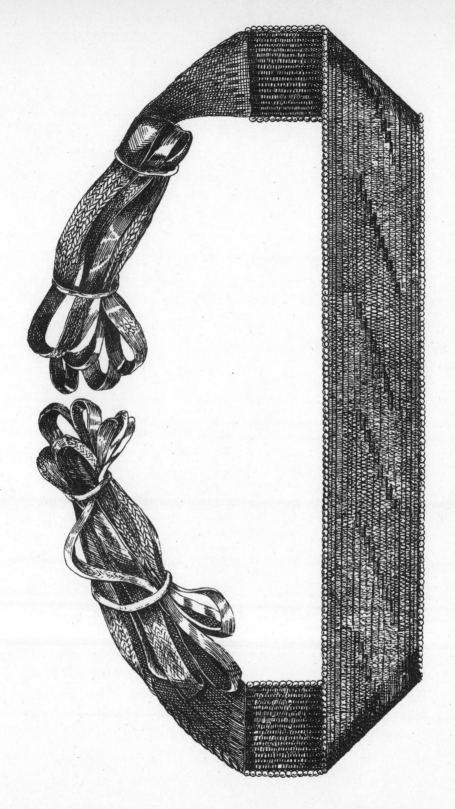

O-Ă-TA-OSE-KÄ OR MOOSE HAIR BURDEN STRAP.

and finished, but more frequently were of a plain piece of hickory, like the one represented in the figure, and made with the quickest despatch. The frame consists of two bows of hickory, brought to-

Gä-ne-ko-wä-ah, Burden Frame, or Litter.

gether at right angles, and fastened to each other by means of an eye and head. The upright part of the frame is the same as the horizontal in all particulars, except its greater length. Strips from the inner rind of basswood bark were then passed between the bows both length and crosswise, and fastened to the rim pieces. A burden strap was then attached to the frame at the point where the strip of bark passed across the upright bow from side to side; and from

thence it passed diagonally across to the horizontal
part of the frame, to the point where the lower strip
of bark crossed that part of the frame. There were
several feet of rope at each end, reserved to lash
around whatever burden was placed upon the frame;
but when the frame was empty, as it is shown
above, these ropes were passed up to the top of the
frame and there secured. After being loaded the
frame was placed upon the back, and the burden
strap passed over the head and placed across the
chest. If the burden was very heavy it was customary to use two straps, one across the chest, and
the other against the forehead. At the present day
the burden frame is still in use.

Bark vessels and dishes of various kinds were in common use among them. The bark barrel, *Gä-no'-quǎ*,
was of the number. It was made of the inner
rind of red-elm bark, or of black-ash bark, the grain
running around the barrel. Up the side it was stitched
firmly, and had a bottom and a lid secured in the same
manner. Such barrels were used to store charred
corn, beans, dried fruit, seeds, and a great variety of
articles.

When corn was buried in pits or caches, it was
usually put in bark barrels of this description. During the war of 1812, when the British forces were
expected over the frontier, the Senecas at Tonawanda,
who had enlisted in the American army, buried their
corn in bark barrels, after the ancient custom. These
barrels were made of all sizes, from those of sufficient
capacity to hold three bushels, to those large enough for
a peck. Such barrels were found in every family in

ancient times, and among other purposes to which they were devoted, they were made repositories for articles of apparel and personal ornaments. They

Gä-snä Gä-ose-hă, or Bark Barrel.

were very durable, and when properly taken care of would last a hundred years.

GÄ–O–WO', OR BARK TRAY

Trays of this description are found in every Indian family. They serve a variety of purposes, but are chiefly used for kneading, or rather preparing corn bread. A strip of elm-bark, of the requisite dimensions, was rounded and gathered up at the ends, so as to form a shallow concavity. Around the rim, both outside and in, splints of hickory were adjusted, and stitched through and through with the bark. These trays were of all sizes, from those of sufficient capacity to contain one, to those large enough for ten pecks. The rough bark was removed from the outside, and the vessel within became smooth with usage. They

Gä-o-wo', or Bark Tray.

made durable and convenient articles for holding corn meal, for preparing corn bread, and for many other purposes.

Trapping game of all kinds, from the bear and deer to the quail and snipe, was a common practice. For deer, a young tree was bent over and held in this position by the mechanism of the trap. When sprung a noose was fastened around the hind leg of the deer, and he was drawn up in the air by the unsprung tree. Bear traps were constructed in such a way as to let down a heavy timber upon the back of the animal, when sprung, and thus pin him to the earth. Nets of bark twine were also spread for pigeons and quails. A simple bird trap for small birds consists of a rounding strip of elm bark about eight inches long by four wide, with an eye cut in one end and a piece of bark twine with a noose at the end of it, attached to the other. After the bark is secured upon the ground, a few kernels of corn are dropped through the eye upon the ground, and a noose adjusted around it. When a bird attempts to pick up the corn the ruffled plumage of the neck takes up the string, and brings

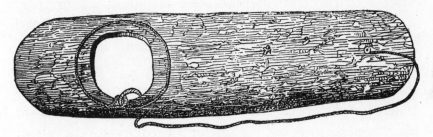

Bird Trap.

the noose around the neck, which is tightened the moment the bird attempts to fly, and either strangles or holds it in captivity. The trap is said to be very successful.

GA–SNÄ′ GÄ–O–WO′, OR BARK CANOE

In the construction of the bark canoe, the Iroquois exercised considerable taste and skill. The art appears to have been common to all the Indian races within the limits of the republic, and the mode of construction much the same. Birch bark was the best material; but as the canoe birch did not grow within the home territories of the Iroquois, they generally used the red-elm, and bitternut-hickory. The canoe figured in the plate (II. 3), is made of the bark of the red-elm, and consists of but one piece. Having taken

off a bark of the requisite length and width, and removed the rough outside, it was shaped in the canoe
form.   Rim pieces of white-ash, or other elastic wood,
of the width of the hand, were then run around the
edge, outside and in, and stitched through and through
with the bark itself.   In stitching, they used bark
thread or twine, and splints.   The ribs consisted of
narrow strips of ash, which were set about a foot apart
along the bottom of the canoe, and having been turned
up the sides, were secured under the rim.   Each end of
the canoe was fashioned alike, the two side pieces inclining towards each other until they united, and formed
a sharp and vertical prow.   In size, these canoes varied
from twelve feet, with sufficient capacity to carry two
men, to forty feet with sufficient capacity for thirty.
The one figured in the plate is about twenty-five feet
in length, and its tonnage estimated at two tons, about
half that of the ordinary bateau.   Birch bark retained
its place without warping, but the elm and hickory
bark canoes were exposed to this objection.   After
being used, they were drawn out of the water to dry.
One of the chief advantages of these canoes, especially
the birch bark, was their extreme lightness, which often
became a matter of some moment from the flood wood
and water-falls, which obstructed the navigation of the
inland rivers.   Two men could easily transport these
light vessels around these obstacles, and even from one
river to another when the portage was not long.

For short excursions one person usually paddled the
canoe, standing up in the stern ; if more than two, and
on a long expedition, they were seated at equal distances
upon each side alternately.   In the fur trade these

canoes were extensively used. They coasted lakes Erie and Ontario, and turning up the Oswego river into the Oneida lake, they went from thence over the carrying place into the Mohawk, which they descended to Schenectady. They would usually carry about twelve hundred pounds of fur. At the period of the invasions of the Iroquois territories by the French, large fleets of these canoes were formed for the conveyance of troops and provisions. With careful usage they would last several years.

Gä-o-wo', or Bark Sap-tub.

Our Indian population have been long in the habit of manufacturing sugar from the maple. Whether they learned the art from us, or we received it from them, is uncertain. One evidence, at least, of its antiquity among them, is to be found in one of their ancient religious festivals, instituted to the maple, and called the Maple dance. The sap-tub is a very neat contrivance, and surpasses all other articles of this description. Our farmers may safely borrow, in this one particular, and with profit substitute this Indian invention for the rough and wasteful one of their own contrivance.

A strip of bark about three feet in length by two in width, makes the tub. The rough bark is left upon the bottom and sides. At the point where the bark is to be turned up to form the ends, the outer bark is removed; the inner rind is then turned up, gathered together in small folds at the top, and tied around with a splint. It is then ready for use, and will last several seasons. Aside from the natural fact that the sap would be quite at home in the bark tub, and its flavor preserved untainted, it is more durable and capacious than the wooden one, and more readily made.

The Senecas use three varieties of corn: the White (*O-na-o'-ga-ant*), the Red (*Tic'-ne*), and the White Flint (*Ha-go'-wä*). Corn is, and always has been, their staple article of food. When ready to be harvested, they pick the ears, strip down the husks, and braid them together in bunches, with about twenty ears in each. They are then hung up ready for use. The white flint ripens first, and is the favorite corn for hommony; the red next, and is used principally for charring and drying; the white last, and is the corn most esteemed by the Indians. It is used for bread, and supplies the same place with them that wheat does with us. They shell their corn by hand, and pound it into flour in wooden mortars. In two hours from the time the corn is taken from the ear it is ready to eat, in the form of unleavened bread. It is hulled in the first instance, by boiling in ashes and water; after the skin is thus removed from each kernel, it is thoroughly washed, and pounded into flour or meal in a mortar, of which a representation will be found above. Having been passed through a sieve basket, to remove the

CORN MORTAR

Gä-ne'-gä-tä, or Corn Mortar.

Mortar, 2 feet in diameter.   Pounder, 4 feet in length.

chit and coarser grains, it is made into loaves or cakes
about an inch in thickness, and six inches in diameter;
which are cooked by boiling them in water. The

Ya-ă-go-gen-tä-quä, or Bread Turner.
3 ½ feet.

bread turner is used, as its name indicates, to handle
these loaves while under the process of cooking. Upon
bread of this description, and upon the fruits of the
chase, the Indian has principally subsisted from time
immemorial.

The practice of charring corn is of great antiquity
among the red races. In this condition it is preserved
for years without injury. Caches or pits of charred
corn have been found in various parts of the country.
The Iroquois were in the habit of charring corn to
preserve it for domestic use. The Senecas still do the
same. For this use the red corn is preferred. When
green the corn is picked, and roasted in the field before
a long fire, the ears being set up on end in a row. It
is not charred or blackened entirely, but roasted sufficiently to dry up the moisture in each kernel. It is
then shelled and dried in the sun. The splint sieve
represented in the figure was used to sift out the fine
ashes which might adhere to the kernel. In this state
the corn is chiefly used by hunting parties, and for sub-

YA·WA·O·DÄ·QUA or NEEDLE BOOK

sistence on distant excursions. Its bulk and weight having been diminished about half by the two processes, its transportation became less burdensome. The

Yun-des-ho-yon-dä-gwat-hä, or Pop-corn Sieve.

red races seldom formed magazines of grain to guard against distant wants. It is probable, therefore, that these pits of charred corn owe their origin to the sudden flight of the inhabitants, who buried their dried corn because they could not remove it, rather than to a desire to provide against a failure of the harvest.

There was another method of curing corn in its green state, quite as prevalent as the former. The corn was shaved off into small particles, and having been baked over the fire in pans or earthen dishes, it was then dried in the sun. In this condition it was preserved for winter use.

A favorite article of subsistence was prepared from the charred corn. It was parched a second time, after which, having been mixed with about a third part of maple sugar, it was pounded into a fine flour. This was carried in the bear-skin pocket of the hunter, and upon it alone he subsisted for days together.

This noble grain, one of the gifts of the Indian to

the world, is destined, eventually, to become one of the staple articles of human consumption. More than half of our republic lies within the embrace of the tributaries of the Mississippi. Upon their banks are the corn-growing districts of the country; and there, also, at no distant day, will be seated the millions of our race. Experience demonstrates that no people can rely wholly upon exchanges for the substance of their bread-stuffs, but that they must look chiefly to the soil they cultivate. This law of production and consumption is destined to introduce the gradual use of corn flour, as a partial substitute at least, for its superior rival, in those districts where it is the natural product of the soil. In the southern portions of our country this principle is already attested, by the fact that corn bread enters as largely into human consumption as wheaten. Next to wheat, this grain, perhaps, contains the largest amount of nutriment. It is the cheapest and surest of all the grains to cultivate; and is, also, the cheapest article of subsistence known among men. Although wheat can be cultivated in nearly all the sections of the country; although its production can be increased to an unlimited degree by a higher agriculture; we have yet great reason to be thankful for this secondary grain, whose reproductive energy is so unmeasured as to secure our entire race, through all coming time, against the dangers of scarcity, or the pressure of want.

O-YEH'-GWÄ-Ä-WEH, OR INDIAN TOBACCO

Tobacco is another gift of the Indian to the world; but a gift, it must be admitted, of questionable utility.

We call both corn and tobacco the legacy of the red man ; as these indigenous plants, but for his nurture and culture through so many ages, might have perished, like other varieties of the fruits of the earth. Many of our choicest fruits owe their origin to vegetable combinations entirely fortuitous. They spring up spontaneously, flourish for a season, and become extinct, but for the watchful care of man. Nature literally pours forth her vegetable wealth, and buries beneath her advancing exuberance the products of the past. But few of the fruits and plants and flowers of the ancient world have come down to us unchanged ; and still other plants, perhaps, have perished, unknown, in the openings of the forest, which contained within their shrivelled and stinted foliage the germ of some fruit, or grain, or plant, which might have nourished or clothed the whole human family. We may therefore, perchance, owe a debt to the Indian, in these particulars, beyond our utmost acknowledgments.

The Senecas still cultivate tobacco. Its name signifies " *The only Tobacco*," because they considered this variety superior to all others. It is raised from the seed, which is sown or planted in the spring, and requires but little cultivation. The leaves are picked early in the fall, when their color first changes with the frost, and when dried are ready for use. After the first year it grows spontaneously, from the seed shed by the plant when fully ripened. If the plants become too thick, which is frequently the case, from their vigorous growth, it becomes necessary to thin them out, as the leaves diminish in size with their increase in number. This tobacco is used exclusively for smoking. The custom of chewing the article appears to have been derived from us. Although this tobacco is exceedingly mild, they mingle with it the leaves of the sumac, to diminish its stimulating properties. The sumac has been used by the Indian to temper tobacco from time immemorial.

Several varieties of the bean and of the squash were also cultivated by the Iroquois, and were indigenous in the American soil. They regarded the corn, the bean, and the squash as the special gift of the Great Spirit, and associated them together under the name of the Three Sisters. They also used the ground-nut (*apios tuberosa*), as a species of potato, gathering it in its wild state.

The snow-shoe is an Indian invention. Upon the deep snows which accumulate in the forest, it would be nearly impossible to travel without them. They were used in the hunt, and in warlike expeditions undertaken in the season of winter.

GA–WEH'–GÄ, OR SNOW–SHOE

The snow-shoe is nearly three feet in length, by about sixteen inches in width. A rim of hickory, bent round with an arching front, and brought to a point at the heel, constituted the frame, with the addition of cross pieces to determine its spread. Within the area, with the exception of an opening for the toe, was woven a net-work of deer strings, with interstices about an inch square. The ball of the foot was lashed at the edge of this opening with thongs, which passed around the heel for the support of the foot. The heel was left free to work up and down, and the opening was designed to allow the toe of the foot to descend below the surface of the shoe, as the heel is raised in the act of walking. It is a very simple invention, but exactly adapted for its uses. A person familiar with the snow-shoe can walk as rapidly

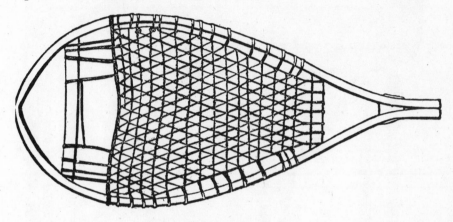

Ga-weh'-gä, or Snow-shoe.
2 feet 10 inches.

upon the snow as without it upon the ground. The Senecas affirm that they can walk fifty miles per day upon the snow-shoe, and with much greater rapidity than without it, in consequence of the length and uniformity of the step. In the bear-hunt, especially, it is of the greatest service, as the hunter can speedily overtake the bear, who, breaking through the crust, is enabled to move but slowly.

AH-DÄ-DÄ'-QUÄ, OR INDIAN SADDLE

This is an Indian invention, but came originally from the west. It closely resembles the saddle of the native Mexicans in its general plan, but its pommel is not as high, and its side-pieces are longer. It is

still used among the Indian tribes of the west. The frame is made of four pieces of wood, firmly set together, over which is a covering of raw hide. The side-pieces are about eighteen inches in length, six in width, and about an inch in thickness, at the centre, but terminating in a sharp edge above and below. In front the pommel rises about five inches above the side-pieces. It is made of a stick having a natural fork, which is so adjusted as to embrace the side-pieces, and determine the spread of the saddle. Another piece, in the same manner, embraced the side-pieces at the opposite end, rising several inches above, and descending nearly to their lower edges. These side-pieces at the top are about three inches apart, leaving a space for the back-bone of the horse. The fastenings of the saddle, including those of the stirrup, were originally of ropes, made of buffalo's hair. Triangular stirrups of wood completed the trappings of the saddle. As the Iroquois seldom made use of the Indian horse, the saddle with them was rather an accidental, than a usual article. The specimen above represented is of Seneca manufacture.

Gä-ga-an-dä, or Air-gun; and Gä-no¹, or Arrow.

Air-gun, 6 feet. Arrow, 2 feet.

The air-gun is claimed as an Indian invention. It is a simple tube or barrel, about six feet in length, and an inch in diameter, and having a half-inch bore. It is made of alder, and also of other wood, which is bored by some artificial contrivance. A very slender arrow, about two feet in length, with a sharp point, is the missile. Upon the foot of the arrow, the down or floss of the thistle is fastened on entire, with sinew. This down is soft and yielding, and when the arrow is placed in the barrel, fills it air-tight. The arrow is then discharged by blowing. It is used for bird-shooting.

Yä-o'-dä-was-tä, or Indian Flute.
1 ½ feet.

This instrument is unlike any known among us, but it clearly resembles the clarionet. Its name signifies " a blow pipe." It is usually made of red cedar, is about eighteen inches in length, and above an inch in diameter. The finger holes, six in number, are equidistant. Between them and the mouth-piece, which is at the end, is the whistle, contrived much upon the same principle as the common whistle. It makes six consecutive notes, from the lowest, on a rising scale. The seventh note is wanting, but the three or four next above are regularly made. This is the whole compass of the instrument. As played by the Indians it affords a species of wild and plaintive music. It is claimed as an Indian invention.

Yun-gä'-sa, or Tobacco Pouch.

The tobacco pouch is made of the skin of some small animal, which is taken off entire. It was anciently an indispensable article, and was worn in the girdle. They were usually made of white weasel, mink, squirrel, and fisher skin.

Bags or pockets of this description, made of the

skins of animals, were in constant use among the Iroquois in ancient times. They were hung to the girdle of the warrior and the hunter, and would contain

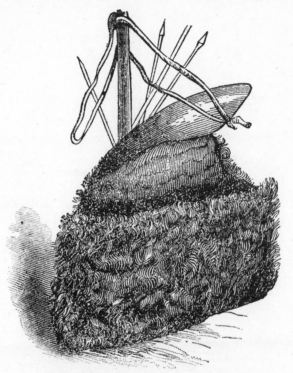

Gìs-tät-he-o Gä-yä-ah, or Fawn Skin Bag.

within their narrow folds sufficient subsistence for a long expedition, thus answering very perfectly the purposes of the knapsack. At home they were used as repositories for the safe keeping of choice articles.

The *Da-ya-yä-dä-gä'-neä-tä* is an Indian invention, of great antiquity. Its rudeness may excite a smile, in this day of lucifer matches, but yet the step backward to the steel and flint is about the same, as from the latter to the contrivance in question. Not knowing the use of metals or of chemicals, it was the only method of creating fire known to the red man. It consisted of an upright shaft, about four feet in length, and an

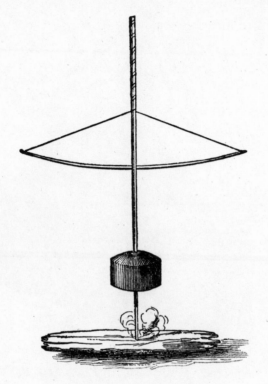

Da-ya-yä-dä-gä'-neä-tä.

inch in diameter, with a small wheel set upon the lower part, to give it momentum. In a notch at the top of the shaft was set a string, attached to a bow about three feet in length. The lower point rested upon a block of dry wood, near which are placed small pieces of punk. When ready to use, the string is first coiled around the shaft, by turning it with the hand. The bow is then pulled downwards, thus uncoiling the string, and revolving the shaft towards the

40

left. By the momentum given to the wheel, the string is again coiled up in a reverse manner, and the bow again drawn up. The bow is again pulled downwards, and the revolution of the shaft reversed, uncoiling the string, and recoiling it as before. This alternate revolution of the shaft is continued, until sparks are emitted from the point where it rests upon the piece of dry wood below. Sparks are produced in a few moments by the intensity of the friction, and ignite the punk, which speedily furnishes a fire.

O-no-neä Gos-ha'-dä, or Corn-husk Salt Bottle.

In the art of basket-work, in all its varieties, the Indian women also excel. Their baskets are made with a neatness, ingenuity, and simplicity which deserve the highest praise. Splint is the chief material, but they likewise use a species of flag, and also cornhusks. Among these various patterns, which are as diversified as convenience or ingenuity could suggest, the most perfectly finished is the sieve basket. It is designed for sifting corn meal to remove the chit, and coarser particles, after the corn has been pounded into flour. The bottom of the basket is wove in such fine checks as to answer very perfectly all the ends of the wire sieve. Another variety of open basket was made of corn-husks and flags, very closely and ingeniously braided. In their domestic economy, the basket answered a multitude of purposes. Bottles for salt were made of corn-husks in the forms represented in the figures.

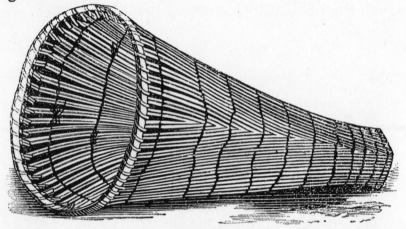

Yont-kä-do-quä, or Basket Fish Net.
3 feet.

The basket net was made of splint in a conical form, about three feet in length, fifteen inches in diameter at the mouth, and six at the small end. In using it, the fisherman stood in the rapids of the creek or river, where the water rippled over the stony bottom, and with a stick or rod managed to direct the fish into the partly submerged basket, as they attempted to shoot down the rapid. When one was heard to flutter in the basket, it was at once raised from the water, and the fish was found secure within it. In those forest days, when fish abounded in every stream, it was an easy matter thus to capture them in large numbers.

Black-ash furnishes the only splint used by the Iroquois, and perhaps the same may be said of all other Indians. They choose a tree about a foot in diameter and free from limbs, after which they cut off a stick about six feet in length. After removing the bark they pound the stick with some heavy implement to start the splints, which can thus be made to run off with the utmost regularity and uniformity of thickness. This process is continued until the log is stripped down to the heart. These splints, which are about three inches wide and an eighth of an inch thick, are afterwards subdivided both ways until reduced to the required width and thickness. When resplit into thinner strips the splints have a white and smooth surface. If the baskets are to be variegated, the splints are dyed upon one side before they are woven, and are also moistened to make them pliable before they are used. The patient industry of the Indian female while engaged in this manual labor, and her skill and taste are alike exemplified in this interesting manufacture.

Their wooden implements were often elaborately carved. Those upon which the most labor was expended were the ladles, *Ah-do-quä'-să*, of various sizes, used for eating hommony and soup. They were their substitute for the spoon, and hence every Indian family was supplied with a number. The end of the handle was usually surmounted with the figure of an animal, as a squirrel, a hawk, or a beaver, some of them with a human figure in a sitting posture, others with a group of such figures in various attitudes, as those of wrestling or embracing. These figures are carved with considerable skill and correctness of proportion.

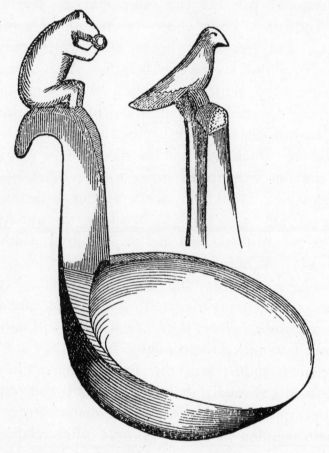

Ah-do-quä-să, or Ladle.

Upon the hommony-stirrer, *Got'-go-ne-os-hă*, an article used in every Indian household for making hommony, succotash or soup and for many other purposes, similar ornaments were bestowed. It is usually from three to four feet in length, and made of hard maple, or other tough wood, in the general form of the one represented in the figure. This hommony blade is made out of one piece of wood, although the end piece is attached to the blade by a link. In the end piece are two wooden balls, also cut out of the solid

Got'-go-ne-os-hă', or Hommony Blade.
4 feet.

wood within the frame in which they are confined. For a wooden utensil it is beautifully made. Bowls, pitchers and other vessels of knot are common in Indian families, and are worked out with great labor and care. In ancient times the aged and infirm were wont to assist themselves in walking with a simple staff, but in later times the cane, *Ah-dä-dis-hă*, has been substituted. Like their other utensils of wood, the modern cane is elaborately carved.

The original ladle was of bark and a very simple contrivance, as will appear from the representation. It was made of red elm bark, and would hold but little more than the common spoon. In ancient times ladles of this description only were used; but they were laid aside when the possession of metallic im-

45

plements enabled them to substitute the present one of wood. The ladle is, without doubt, an original Indian

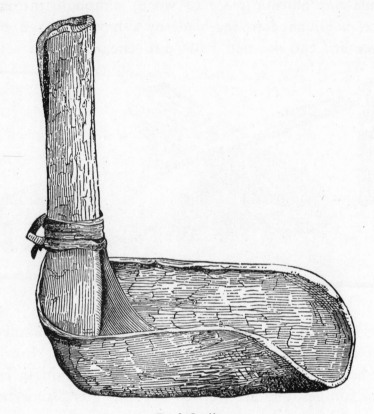

Bark Ladle.

utensil, and in all probability the origin of the common wooden ladle still in general use among our own people.

GÄ–KÄ'–AH, OR SKIRT
See Plate, I. 122

The modern female costume of the Iroquois is both striking and graceful. Some of them would excite admiration by the exactness of their adjustment and the delicacy, even brilliancy of their bead-work embroidery. They use, to this day, the same articles of apparel in form and fashion, as in ancient times, but they have substituted materials of foreign manufacture. The porcupine quill has given place to the bead, and the skins of animals to the cotton fabric and the broadcloth. Much taste is exhibited in the bead-work, which is so conspicuous in the female costume. The colors are blended harmoniously, and the patterns are ingeniously devised and skilfully executed. It is sufficiently evident, from the specimens of their handiwork, that the Indian female can be taught to excel with the needle. The *Gä-kä'-ah*, or Skirt, of one of which the plate (I. 122) is an accurate copy, is usually of blue broadcloth, and elaborately embroidered with bead-work. It requires two yards of cloth, which is worn with the selvedge at the top and bottom ; the skirt being secured about the waist, and descending nearly to the moccason. Around the lower edge, and part way up the centre in front, it is tastefully and beautifully embroidered. In one of the angles a figure is worked representing a tree or flower. The cloth skirt is universally worn among the present Iroquois, but they are not usually as richly embroidered, or of as fine material as the one represented in the plate. This is of Seneca workmanship, and is a rare specimen of Indian needlework.

The skirt shown in this plate (II. 47) is without question the finest specimen of Indian bead-work ever exhibited. Next to the article itself the plate will furnish the best description. It was made by Miss Caroline G. Parker (*Gä-hä'-no*), a Seneca Indian girl, now being educated in the State Normal School, to whose finished taste and patient industry the State is indebted for most of the many beautiful specimens of bead-work embroidery now in the Indian collection.[14]

In doing this work, the eye and the taste are the chief reliances, as they use no patterns except as they may have seen them in the works of others. In combining colors certain general rules, the result of experience and observation are followed, but beyond them each one pursues her own fancy. They never seek for strong contrasts, but break the force of them by interposing white, that the colors may blend harmoniously. Thus light blue and pink beads, with white beads between them, is a favorable combination ; dark blue and yellow, with white between, is another ; red and light blue, with white between, is another ; and light purple and dark purple, with white between, is a fourth. Others might be added were it necessary. If this bead-work is critically examined it will be found that these general rules are strictly observed ; and in so far bead-work embroidery may be called a systematic art. The art of flowering, as they term it, is the most difficult part of bead-work, as it requires an accurate knowledge of the appearance of the flower, and the structure and condition of the plant at the stage in which it is represented. These imitations are frequently made with great delicacy, of which a very favorable exhibition may be seen in the plate, in the flower introduced at the angle of the skirt.

GÄ-KÄ-AH OR SKIRT.

GISE'-HĂ, OR PANTALETTE

See Plate, I. 274

This article of female apparel is also universally worn. It is usually made of red broadcloth, and ornamented with a border of bead-work around the lower edge, and also part way up the side at the point which becomes the front of the pantalette. It is secured above the knee, and falls down upon the moccason. In ancient times the *Gise'-hă* was made of deer-skin and embroidered with porcupine-quill work. As the moccason is elsewhere described, nothing further need be said in relation to it as a part of the female costume.

AH–DE–A'–DA–WE–SA, OR OVER–DRESS

See Plates, I. 190, 191

The over-dress is usually of muslin or calico of the highest colors. It is loosely adjusted to the person, gathered slightly at the waist, and falls part way down the skirt. Around the lower edge is a narrow border of bead-work. In front it is generally buttoned with silver broaches, arranged as represented in the plate. They are usually larger in size, and arranged in parallel rows, as represented in the female costume in the frontispiece. The Indian female delights in a profusion of silver ornaments, consisting of silver broaches of various patterns and sizes, from those which are six inches in diameter, and worth as many dollars, down to those of the smallest size, valued at a sixpence. Silver ear-rings and finger-rings of various designs, silver beads, hat bands and crosses, are also found in their paraphernalia. These crosses, relics of Jesuit influence, are frequently eight inches in length, of solid silver, and very valuable, but they are looked upon by them simply in the light of ornaments.

Finger and ear rings of the same material, specimens of which may be seen in the plate (II. 50), were also very common. The most of these silver ornaments in later years have been made by Indian silversmiths, one of whom may be found in nearly every Indian village. They are either made of brass, of silver, or from silver coins pounded out, and then cut into patterns with metallic instruments. The ear rings figured in the plate were made out of bar silver, by an Onondaga silversmith on Grand river, under the direction of the writer.

E'-YOSE, OR BLANKET

This indispensable and graceful garment is of blue or green broadcloth, of which it requires two yards. It falls from the head or neck in natural folds the width of the cloth, as the selvedges are at the top and bottom, and it is gathered round the person like a shawl. It is worn very gracefully by the Indian female, and makes a becoming article of apparel.

By some singular impulse of fancy, the fur hat has been appropriated by the women as a part of the female costume, until among the modern Iroquois it is more common to see this part of the white man's apparel upon the head of the Indian female than upon that of the warrior. Hat bands of silver, or of broaches strung together, or of long silver beads, are indispensable ornaments on public occasions. Sometimes, but rarely, clusters of feathers are attached to the hat.

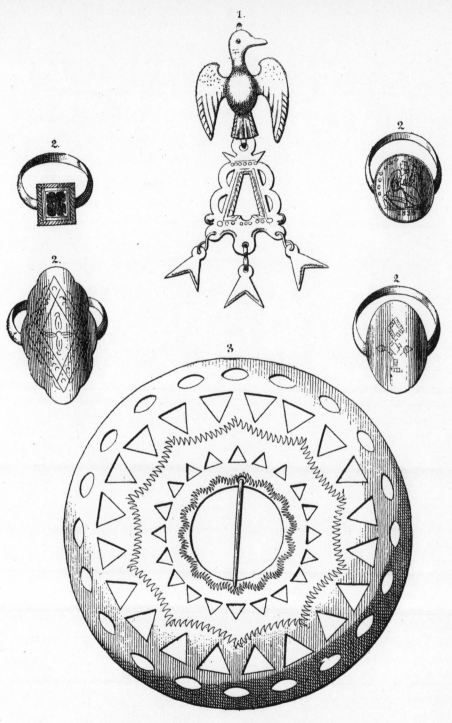

1. AH-WAS-HA or SILVER EAR RING

2. AH-NE-A-HUS-HA SILVER FINGER RINGS

3. AN-NE-ÄS-GA or SILVER BROACH

GÄ'-TE-AS-HĂ', OR NECKLACE
See Plate, I. 254

The necklace is made of silver and wampum beads, and has a silver cross suspended. The beads usually worn by Indian women are of common glass. In ancient times it was customary to wear necklaces of the teeth of animals, but such barbarous ornaments were long since repudiated by the Iroquois. A species of shoulder ornament in the nature of a necklace made of a fragrant marsh grass, called by the Senecas *Gä-a-o'-tä-ges*, is very generally worn. Several strands or cords are braided from this grass, of the requisite length, and tied into one string. At intervals of three or four inches, small round discs, made of the same material, sometimes covered upon the upper face with bead-work, are attached. It thus makes a conspicuous ornament, and emits an agreeable odor, furnishing a substitute for perfumery.

GÄ–SWEH–TÄ OTE–KO–Ă, OR BELT OF WAMPUM

OTE–KO–Ă, OR STRING OF WAMPUM
See Plate, II. 52, Figures 1 and 2

The use of wampum reaches back to a remote period upon this continent. It was an original Indian notion which prevailed among the Iroquois as early, at least, as the formation of the League. The primitive wampum of the Iroquois consisted of strings of a small fresh water spiral shell, called in the Seneca dialect *Ote-ko-ă*, the name of which has been bestowed upon the modern wampum. When

Da-gä-no-weّ-dä, the founder of the League, had perfected its organic provisions, he produced several
strings of this ancient wampum of his own arranging, and taught them its use in recording the provisions of the compact by which the several nations
were united into one people. At a subsequent day
the wampum in present use was introduced among
them by the Dutch, who in the manufactured shell
bead offered an acceptable substitute for the less
convenient one of the spiral shell. These beads, as
shown in the plate, are purple and white, about a
quarter of an inch in length, an eighth in diameter,
and perforated lengthwise so as to be strung on sinew
or bark thread. The white bead was manufactured
from the great conch sea shell, and the purple from
the muscle shell. They are woven into belts, or
used in strings simply, in both of which conditions
they are employed to record treaty stipulations, to
convey messages, and to subserve many religious and
social purposes. The word *wampum* is not of
Iroquois origin. Baylie, in his History of New Ply-
mouth, informs us that it was first known in New-
England as *Wampumpeag*, from which its Algonquin
derivation is to be inferred; and Hutchinson says that
the art of making it was obtained from the Dutch
about the year 1627.

Wampum beads are rarely worn, as they are scarce
and held at high rates. These beads are used
chiefly for religious purposes, and to preserve laws and
treaties. They are made of the conch shell, which
yields both a white and a purple bead, the former of
which is used for religious, and the latter for politi-

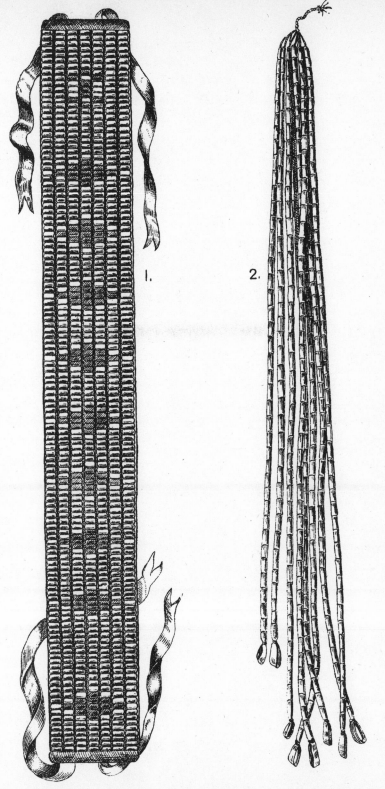

1. GÄ-SWEH-TÄ OTE-KO-Ă or BELT OF WAMPUM.
2. OTE-KO-Ă or STRING OF WAMPUM.

cal purposes. A full string of wampum is usually three feet long, and contains a dozen or more strands. White wampum was the Iroquois emblem of purity and of faith. It was hung around the neck of the White Dog before it was burned; it was used before the periodical religious festivals for the confession of sins, no confession being regarded as sincere unless recorded with white wampum; further than this, it was the customary offering in condonation of murder, although the purple was sometimes employed. In ancient times, six of these strands was the value of a life, the amount paid in condonation for a murder. Wampum has frequently been called the money of the Indian; but there is no sufficient reason for supposing that they ever made it an exclusive currency, or a currency in any sense, more than silver or other ornaments. All personal ornaments, and most other articles of personal property passed from hand to hand at a fixed value; but they appear to have had no common standard of value until they found it in our currency. If wampum had been their currency it would have had a settled value to which all other articles would have been referred. There is no doubt that it came nearer to a currency than any other species of property among them, because its uses were so general, and its transit from hand to hand so easy, that every one could be said to need it. When sold, the strings were counted and reckoned at half a cent a bead. Wampum belts were made by covering one side of a deer-skin belt with these beads, arranged after various devices, and with most laborious skill. As a belt four or five feet long by four inches wide would require

several thousands of these beads, they were estimated
at a great price. In making a belt no particular pattern
was followed: sometimes they are of the width of
three fingers and three feet long, in other instances as
wide as the hand, and over three feet in length;
sometimes they are all of one color, in others variegated, and in still others woven with the figures
of men to symbolize, by their attitudes, the objects
or events they were designed to commemorate. The
most common width was three fingers, or the width
of seven beads, the length ranging from two to six
feet. In belt making, which is a simple process,
eight strands or cords of bark thread are first twisted,
from filaments of slippery elm, of the requisite length
and size; after which they are passed through a strip
of deer-skin to separate them at equal distances from
each other in parallel lines. A piece of splint is then
sprung in the form of a bow, to which each end of
the several strings is secured, and by which all of
them are held in tension, like warp threads in a weaving machine. Seven beads, these making the intended
width of the belt, are then run upon a thread by
means of a needle, and are passed under the cords
at right angles, so as to bring one bead lengthwise
between each cord, and the one next in position.
The thread is then passed back again along the
upper side of the cords and again through each of
the beads; so that each bead is held firmly in its
place by means of two threads, one passing under
and one above the cords. This process is continued
until the belt reaches its intended length, when the
ends of the cords are tied, the end of the belt cov-

ered, and afterwards trimmed with ribbons. In ancient times both the cords and the thread were of sinew.

The belt possesses an additional interest from the fact that the beads of which it is composed, formerly

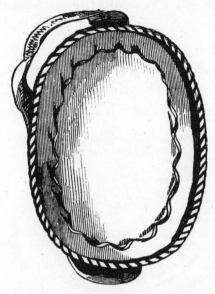

Ont-wis'-dä-ga-dust-hä', or Silver Medal.

belonged to the celebrated Mohawk Chief, Joseph Brant, *Tä-yen-dä-na'-ga.* They were purchased, by the writer, of his youngest daughter Catharine in October last, at the reservation on Grand river in Upper Canada before referred to; and were afterwards taken to Tonawanda in this State and made into the present belt. In this form it will be most convenient to preserve them as a relic of the distinguished war captain of the Mohawks.

The government has long been in the habit of presenting silver medals to the chiefs of the various Indian tribes at the formation of treaties, and on the occasion of their visit to the seat of government. These medals are held in the highest estimation. Red Jacket, Corn Planter, Farmer's Brother, and several other distinguished Seneca chiefs have received medals of this description. Washington presented a medal to Red Jacket in 1792. It is an elliptical plate of silver, surrounded by a rim, as represented in the figure, and is about six inches in its greatest diameter. On each side it is engraved with various devices. The medal is now worn by *Sose-ha'-wä* (Johnson), a Seneca chief.

Gä-nuh'-så, or Sea-shell Medal.

Medals of sea-shell, inlaid with silver, as represented in the figure, were also worn suspended from the neck as personal ornaments. They were made of the conch-shell, and were highly valued.

A few plates further to illustrate the handiwork of the Indian female in bead-work are introduced in this volume. The figures themselves will dispense with the necessity of any description, although they should be colored to give a full impression of their character. The patient industry of the Indian female is quite remarkable, when seen in contrast with the impatience of labor in the warrior himself. In the work of their reclamation and gradual induction into industrial pursuits, this fact furnishes no small degree of encouragement.

GĂ–OSE–HĂ', OR BABY–FRAME
See PLATE, II. 58

This is likewise an Indian invention. It appears to have been designed rather as a convenience to the Indian mother for the transportation of her infant, than, as has generally been supposed, to secure an erect figure. The frame is about two feet in length, by about fourteen inches in width, with a carved footboard at the small end, and a hoop or bow at the head, arching over at right angles. After being enclosed in a blanket, the infant is lashed upon the frame with belts of bead-work, which firmly secure and cover its person, with the exception of the face. A separate article for covering the face is then drawn over the bow, and the child is wholly protected. When carried, the burden-strap attached to the frame is placed around the forehead of the mother, and the *Gă-osé-hă* upon her back. This frame is often elaborately carved, and its ornaments are of the choicest description.

The figure is introduced to show the frame divested of the belts and drapery by which, when in actual use, it is entirely concealed. It consists of but three principal pieces of wood, the bow, bottom board and foot board, upon the first and last of which the most labor was bestowed. They are always carved, and frequently inlaid with silver, or with wood of different colors and in various figures. The bow, which arches over, is held to the bottom board by means of a cross piece, passing under it, into which the ends of the bow are inserted. It is further secured in its perpendicular position by means of side pieces in which the bow is embedded. The foot board at the small end of the frame is also carved, and often inlaid,

Gă-ose-hă, or Baby-frame.

it being the only part of it which is exposed when the infant is lashed upon the frame. Deer strings are run along the outer edges of the bottom board under which the belts are passed from side to side, passing over the body of the child. As a whole the *Gă-ose'-hă*, with its embroidered belts, and other decorations, is one of the most conspicuous articles pertaining to their social life.

When cultivating the maize, or engaged in any outdoor occupation, the *Gă-ose'-hă* is hung upon a limb of the nearest tree, and left to swing in the breeze. The

GA-ON-SEH OR BABY FRAME.

patience and quiet of the Indian child in this close confinement are quite remarkable. It will hang thus suspended for hours, without uttering a complaint.

Many other articles might be introduced further to illustrate the social life of the Iroquois, did space permit, but sufficient has been given to exhibit the general character of their fabrics, implements and utensils. A portion of them, which appeared particularly calculated to exhibit their artisan intellect, have been noticed minutely, for it is in this view that they are chiefly interesting.

Such is the diffusion of Indian arts and Indian inventions among the red races, that it is impossible to ascertain with what nation or tribe they in fact originated. Many of them were common to all, from Maine to Oregon, and from the St. Lawrence to the peninsula of Florida. To this day Indian life is about the same over the whole republic. If we wished to discover the inventions of the Iroquois, we might expect to find them as well among the Sioux of the upper Mississippi as among the descendants of the Iroquois themselves. It is for this reason that in describing the fabrics which illustrate the era of Indian occupation, we should take in the whole range of Indian life, from the wild tribes dwelling in the seclusions of Oregon, to the present semi-agricultural Iroquois who reside among ourselves. They have passed through all the intermediate stages, from extreme rudeness to comparative civilization. If we wish to connect the fabrics of the former with those of our own primitive inhabitants, we may find that connection in the fact that similar implements and similar fabrics, at no remote period, were in the hands, and of the manufacture of the Iroquois themselves. Many of the relics disentombed from the soil of New York relate back to the period of the Mound Builders of the west, and belong to a race of men and an age which have passed beyond the ken of Indian tradition. Our first Indian epoch is thus connected with that of the Mound Builders. In the same manner, the fabrics of the Iroquois are intimately connected with those of all the tribes now resident within the republic. One system of trails belted the whole face of the territory from the Atlantic to the Pacific; and the intercourse between the multitude of nations who dwelt within these boundless domains was constant, and much more extensive than has ever been supposed. If any one, therefore, desires a picture of Iroquois life before Hendrick Hudson sailed up the river upon whose banks rested the eastern end of their " Long House," he should look for it in Catlin's Scenes at the skirts of the Rocky Mountains. There are diversities, it is true, but Indian life is essentially the same.

In the fabrics of the modern Iroquois, there is much to inspire confidence in their teachableness in the useful arts. When their minds are unfolded by education, and their attention is attracted by habit to agricultural pursuits, as has already become the case, to some extent, there is great promise that a portion, at least, of this gifted race will be reclaimed, and raised, eventually, to a citizenship among ourselves. It would be a grateful spectacle, yet to behold the children of our primeval forests cultivating the fields over which their fathers roamed in sylvan independence.

Chapter II

Language of the Iroquois — Alphabet — The Noun — Adjective — Comparison — Article — Adverb — Preposition — Species of De- clension — The Verb — Fulness of Conjugation — Formation of Sentences — The Lord's Prayer

THE language of the Iroquois, like all un- written languages, is imperfect in its construc- tion, and scarcely admits of comparison, except on general principles, with those which have been systematized and perfected. It would doubtless be characterized by the schoolman as a barbarous jar- gon, although entitled to some portion of the indul- gence which is due to all primitive or uncompounded languages, in the early stages of their formation.

To us, however, there is an interest incident to these dialects, which rises above mere literary curiosity. Through all generations, their language will continue to be spoken in our geographical terms : " their names are on our waters, we may not wash them out." The face of nature, indeed, changes its appearance, *mutat terra vices*, but its landmarks remain essentially the same. Within our borders, the Iroquois have written them over with such a permanent imprint, that to the most distant ages will our hills and vales and ever-flowing rivers speak

" Their dialect of yore."

The *Ho-de'-no-sau-nee* were eminently fortunate in engrafting their names upon the features of nature, if

61

they were desirous of a living remembrance. No one can turn to the lake, or river, or streamlet, to which they have bequeathed an appellation, without confessing that the Indian has perpetuated himself by a monument more eloquent and imperishable than could be fabricated by human hands.

From considerations of this description, there arises a sufficient interest in the language of our predecessors, to invite an inquiry into its principal features.

Of the six dialects in which it is now spoken, the Mohawk and Oneida have a close resemblance to each other; the Cayuga and Seneca the same; while the Onondaga and Tuscarora are not only unlike each other, but are also distinguished from the other four by strong dialectical differences. In the estimation of the Iroquois, the Onondaga dialect is the most finished and majestic, and the Oneida the least vigorous in its expressions; but to the American ear, the former is harsh and pointed, and the latter is liquid, harmonious, and musical. The Tuscarora is admitted to be a dialect of the Iroquois language, but it has not such a close affinity to either of the remaining five, as the latter have to each other. In conversation they are all able to understand each other with readiness, unless words intervene which have been naturalized into one of their dialects from foreign languages. A comparison of these dialects will be found in the table.

The alphabet common to the six dialects consists of nineteen letters: A, C, D, E, G, H, I, J, K, N, O, Q, R, S, T, U, W, X, and Y. In addition to several elementary sounds which require a combination of letters, the Senecas occasionally employ the sound of Z; but it is so closely allied with the sound of S, as not to be distinguishable, except by careful observation. The Mohawks and Oneidas use the liquid L, and the Tuscaroras occasionally employ the sound of F; but these letters are not common to all the dialects. It has been customary to exclude the liquid R from the Iroquois alphabet, as not common to the several dialects, but this is clearly erroneous. Although it is principally found in the Mohawk, Seneca, and Cayuga, it is yet occasionally discovered in each of the others. Some of the ancient writers affirmed that this letter was not to be found in the Oneida tongue, and that the word Rebecca, for example, would be pronounced, by an Oneida, Lequecca. It is possible that the presence of the consonant *b*, which is unknown in their language, may have rendered the substitution of L necessary to effect the whole pronunciation; but it is certain that in some of their words the R is found, as, for example, in the name of Schoharie creek, *O-sko'-harl*. This letter is found in the Onondaga dialect, in the same geographical name, which, in the latter, is *Sko̞'-har*. In the Tuscarora, this letter is frequently found, as, for instance, in the name of Buffalo, *Ne-o-thro'-rä*, and of Niagara, *O-ne-a'-cars*.

The number of their elementary sounds, as at present ascertained, is below that of the English language, but twenty-three having been determined in the Seneca tongue, while in the former it is well known that there are thirty-eight. A more critical analysis would doubtless discover additional sounds, as in the guttural and nasal tones they take a wider range than the English voice.

In illustrating the parts of speech by a cursory examination, and in elucidating the declensions and conjugations, the words introduced as specimens will be taken from the Seneca language.

It is supposed by those who have inquired philosophically into the formation of language, that the noun substantive would be the first part of speech in the order of origination, inasmuch as the objects in nature must be named, and perhaps classed, before relations between them are suggested, or actions concerning them are expressed. Much of the beauty of a language depends upon this part of speech. Nouns of one syllable are rarely, if ever, found in either of the dialects; those of two syllables are not very numerous; those of three and four syllables embrace the great mass of words which belong to this part of speech. As specimens of the language, the following examples are given : —

NOUNS OF TWO SYLLABLES.

An-da',	Day.	Gă-ee',	Tree.
So-a',	Night.	Ha-ace',	Panther.
Gă-o',	Wind.	Je-yeh',	Dog.
Gus-no',	Bark.	Gen-joh',	Fish.

NOUNS OF THREE SYLLABLES.

Ah-wă'-o,	Rose.	O-o'-ză,	Bass-wood.
O-gis'-tä,	Fire.	O-āne'-dä,	Shrub.
O-we'-ză,	Ice.	O-nă'-tä,	Leaf.
O-dus'-hote,	A spring.	Gă-ha'-neh,	Summer.
Gä-hä-'dä,	Forest.	O-gă̆s'-ah,	Evening.
O-eke'-tä,	Thistle.	Gä-o'-wo,	Canoe.

NOUNS OF FOUR SYLLABLES.

O-na-gä'-nose,	Water.	Ong-wa-o'-weh,	Indian.
Gä-a-nun'-da,	Mountain.	Gä-gä-neäs'-heh,	Knife.
Gä-gwe-dake'-neh,	Spring.	O-gwen-nis'-hă,	Copper.
Sä-da'-che'-ah,	Morning.	Ah-tă-gwen'-dä,	Flint.
Gä-a-o'-dä,	Gun.		

NOUNS OF FIVE SYLLABLES.

Sä-da'-wä-sun-teh,	Midnight.	So-a'-kä-gă-gwä,	Moon.
O-wis'-tä-no-o,	Silver.	Gä-ne-o'-us-heh,	Iron.
An-da'-kä-gă-gwä,	Sun.	O-dä'-wä-an-do,	Otter.

In most, if not all languages, the idea of singular and plural is conveyed by an inflection of the word itself, or by some addition. To illustrate from the language under consideration, which forms the plural in several ways by inflection, the subjoined examples are introduced.

Singular.		Plural.	
O-on'-dote,	A tree.	O-on-do'-do,	Trees.
Gä-no'-sote,	A house.	Gä-no-so'-do,	Houses.
Gä-ne-o'-wa-o,	A brook.	Gä-ne-o-wa-o'-neo,	Brooks.
Je-dä'-o,	A bird.	Je-dä-o'-suh-uh,	Birds.
O-an'-nuh,	A pole.	O-an'-nuh-suh,	Poles.
Ga-hun'-da,	A creek.	Ga-hun-da'-neo,	Creeks.

There are several other terminations by which the plural is indicated.

It is said that the dual number originated in the difficulty of inventing the numerals, one, two, three, &c., which are in themselves extremely abstract conceptions. The ideas of *one*, *two* and *more*, which correspond with singular, dual and plural, would be far more easily formed in the mind, than the idea of number in general; and the most simple mode of expressing them would be by a variation of the word itself. Hence in the Hebrew and Greek, which are original or uncompounded languages, in the general sense, the dual is found to exist, while in the Latin, and in modern languages, which are compounds, and were formed subsequent to the invention of numerals, the dual number is discarded. The Iroquois, so far as we know, is an original and uncompounded language, and it has the dual number, both in its verbs and nouns.

Gender was very happily indicated in the Latin and Greek by final letters or terminations. In the English, by giving up the ancient declensions, this mode of designating gender was also laid aside, and two or three modes substituted; thus, that of varying the word itself, as tiger, tigress, of giving the same animal names entirely different, as buck and doe, and more frequently still that of prefixing words which signify male and female. The Iroquois nouns have three genders, which are indicated in the manner last mentioned. Unlike the provisions of other languages, all inanimate objects, without distinction, were placed in the neuter gender.

In some respects the adjective would be a simple part of speech to invent, as quality is an object of external sense, and is always in concrete with the subject. But to discover and adopt a classification, founded upon the similitudes of objects, would be more difficult, since both generalisation and abstraction would be required. The dialects of the *Ho-de'-no-sau-nee* appear to be amply furnished with this part of speech, on which so much of the beauty of a language is known to depend, to express nearly every shade of quality in objects. Comparison, of which they have the three degrees, is effected by adding another word, and not by an inflection of the word itself, in the following manner:

Positive.		Comparative.	Superlative.
Great,	Go-wä-na′,	Ah-gwus′-go-wä-na,	Ha-yo-go-sote′-go-wä-na.
Good,	We-yo′,	Ah-gwus′-we-yo,	Ha-yo-go-sote′-we-yo.
Sweet,	O-gä-uh′,	Ah-gwus′-o-gä-uh,	Ha-yo-go-sote′-o-gä-uh.
Small,	Ne-wä-ah′,	Ah-gwus′-ne-wä-ah,	Ha-yo-go-sote′-ne-wä-ah.

But in connecting the adjective with the noun, the two words usually enter into combination, and lose one or more syllables. This principle, or species of contraction, is carried throughout the language, and to some extent prevents prolixity. The language has but few primitive words, or ultimate roots; and when these are mastered, their presence is readily detected and understood, through all the elaborate and intricate combinations in which they are used. To illustrate the manner of compounding the adjective with the substantive, the following examples may be taken: *O-yä̀*, fruit; *O-gä-uh′*, sweet; *O-yä̀-gä-uh*, sweet fruit; *O*, the first syllable of sweet, being dropped. Again, *E′-yose*, a blanket; *Gä′-geh-ant*, white; *Yose-ä-geh′-ant*, white blanket; *Gä-no′-sote*, a house; *We-yo′*, good; *Gä-no′-se-yo*, a good house; literally fruit sweet, blanket white, and house good, illustrative of that natural impulse in man which leads him to place the object before the quality. In other instances the adjective is divided, and one part prefixed and the other suffixed to the noun thus: *Gä-nun′-dä-yeh*, a village; *Ne-wä-ah*, small; *Ne-gä-nun-dä′-ah*, a small village; *Ah-tä′-quä-o-weh*, a moccason; *Ne-wä′-tä-quä-ah*, a·small moccason.   The adjective is also frequently used un-compounded with the noun, as *Ga-na'-dike-ho E'-yose*, a green blanket.

The indefinite article, *a* or *an*, is entirely unknown in the language of the Iroquois.   There are numerous particles, as in the Greek, which, without significance in themselves separately, are employed for euphony, and to connect other words.   These particles qualify and sometimes limit the signification of words; but yet if they should be submitted to a critical examination, none of them would answer the idea of the article *a*, or *an*.   The existence in completeness of this refined part of speech would indicate a greater maturity and finish than the dialects of the Iroquois possessed. But the definite article *na*, *the*, is found in the language.   It is not as distinctly defined, and perfectly used, as in more polished languages, but it is usually prefixed to substantives, as with us, to indicate the thing intended.

Of the adverb nothing need be introduced, except to remark that the language is furnished with the usual variety.   A few specimens may be added, *Nake-ho'*, here; *O-nă'*, now; *Ta-dă'*, yesterday; *Skă-no'*, well.

The preposition is allowed to be so abstract and metaphysical in its nature, that it would be one of the last and most difficult parts of speech to invent. It expresses relation "considered in concrete with the correlative object;" and is of necessity very abstruse.   The prepositions, *of*, *to*, and *for*, are regarded as the most abstract, from the character of the relations which they indicate.   Declension, it is supposed, was resorted to by the Greeks, and adopted by the Latins, to evade the necessity of inventing these prepositions ; as it would be much easier to express the idea by the variation of the noun, than to ascertain some word which would convey such an abstract relation as that indicated by *of* or *to*. By the ancient cases, this difficulty was surmounted, and the preposition was blended with the correlative object, as in *Sermonis*, of a speech ; *Sermoni*, to a speech. Modern languages have laid aside the ancient cases, for the reason, it is said, that the invention of prepositions rendered them unnecessary. In the Iroquois language, the prepositions above mentioned are not to be found ; neither have its nouns a declension, like the Greek and Latin. Some traces of a declension are discoverable ; but the cases are too imperfect to be compared with those of the ancient languages, or to answer fully the ends of the prepositions. This part of speech is the most imperfectly developed of any in the language ; and the contrivances resorted to, to express such of these relations as were of absolute necessity, are too complex to be easily understood.

The language, however, contains the simple prepositions, as *Da-ga'-o*, across ; *No'-gă*, after ; *Nă'-ho*, at ; *O'-an-do*, before ; *Dose-gă'-o*, near, &c. It must be inferred that the framers of the language had no distinct idea of the relations conveyed by the deficient prepositions, otherwise they would be found in the language. From the number of particles employed in the language, and the complexity of their combinations, it would be impossible to analyze the word, or phrase, for example, in which *on* occurs, and take out the specific fragment which has the force of the preposition.

In the imperfect declensions through which the Iroquois substantives are passed, pronouns, as well as prepositions, are interwoven by inflection. These declensions are not reduceable to regular forms, but admit of great diversities, thus rendering the language itself, like all simple and original languages, exceedingly intricate in its inflections. The following examples will exhibit the ordinary variations of the noun.

Gä-no'-sote,	A house.
Ho-no'-sote,	His house.
Hă-to-no'-sote,	Of, to, from, or at his house.
Ho-no'-sa-go,	In his house.
A-so'-gwä-tä,	A pipe.
Ho-so'-gwä-tä,	His pipe.
Na-no-so'-gwä-tä,	Of his pipe.
Ho-so'-gwä-tä-go,	In his pipe.
O-on-dote',	A tree.
Ho-on-dä',	His tree.
Hä'-to-de-on-dote,	Of, to, from, or at his tree.
O-yä',	Fruit.
Ho-yä',	His fruit.
Ho-dä-yä',	Of, to, from, or at his fruit.
Wä-nis'-heh-da,	Day.
Dwen-nis'-heh-dake,	At a day past.
Dwen-nis'-heh-deh,	At a day future.
Sä-wen-nis'-hăt,	With the day.
Wä-sun'-dä-da,	Night.
Dwä-sun'-dä-dake,	At a night past.
Dwä-sun'-dä-da,	At a night future.
Sä-wä-sun'-dart,	With the night.

Of the pronouns but little need be added, except that they are very defective: thus *E* signifies I, we, me, and us; *Ese,* thou, ye or you, and thee. *He* and *they* are wanting, except as expressed in the verb by its inflection. The personal pronouns make the possessive case very regularly, thus: *Ah-gä-weh',* mine; *Sä-weh',* thine; *Ho-weh',* his; *Go-weh',* hers; *Ung-gwä-weh',* ours; *Swä-weh',* yours; *Ho-nau-weh',* theirs. Similar variations can be made on some of the relative pronouns.

Interjections are extremely numerous in this language, and appear to be adapted to all the passions. It has also the ordinary conjunctions.

Next and last the verb presents itself. This part of speech, in the nature of things, must have been one of the first invented, as without its aid, there could be no affirmation, no expression of action or passion. Among primitive languages, the conjugation of the verb is extremely complex. Grammarians assign as a reason, that the tenses and moods of the verb would be more easily indicated by its inflection, than by contriving or inventing the substantive verb, I am; the possessive verb, I have; and the auxiliaries, do, will, would, shall, can, and may; all of which are necessary in the conjugation of an English verb. It will be remembered that the English verb admits of but three variations in itself, as *press, pressed, pressing;* and its conjugation is completed by the auxiliary verbs above-mentioned; while the Greek, Latin, and Iroquois verbs are conjugated, except some part of the passive voice in Latin, by the variations throughout of the verb itself; thus, *Legeram,* I had read; *Che-wä'-ge-yä-go*, I had shot; *Legero*, I shall have read; *A-wä-ge'-yä-go,* I shall have shot. In this manner, the conjugation not only dispensed with the pronouns I, thou, and he, with their plurals, but also with the auxiliary verbs, which have introduced such prolixity into modern languages. The Iroquois verbs are conjugated with great regularity and precision, making the active and passive voices, all the moods, except the infinitive, and all the tenses, numbers, and persons, common to the English verb. Some part of the optative mood can also be made.

But the participles are wanting. It is difficult to determine upon what principle the absence of this part of speech, which in a written language would be a serious blemish, shall be accounted for; and much more difficult to ascertain the nature of the substitute in a verbal language. A substitute for the infinitive mood is found in the present tense of the subjunctive mood, together with a pronoun, as in the following passage : "Direct that *He'-no* may come and give us rain" (see the invocation entire, Vol. I. p. 189); instead of saying, "Direct *He'-no* to come, and give us rain." In correctly translated Indian speeches this form of expression will frequently appear, from the influence which this idiomatic peculiarity of all Indian languages will exercise upon the translator.

The origin of the dual number has been adverted to. In the active voice of Iroquois verbs, the dual number is well distinguished ; but in the passive voice, the dual and the plural are the same. The presence of this number is indicative of the intricate nature of their conjugations.

To convey a distinct notion of the mutations through which an Iroquois verb passes in its conjugation, and to furnish those who are curious, as linguists, with a specimen for comparison with the conjugations of other languages, one of their verbs, with its inflections, is subjoined in Appendix A, No. 2. Its great regularity, even harmony of inflection, conveys a favorable impression of the structure of the language ; but it does not, nor would it be expected to possess the elegance and beauty of the Greek, or the brevity and solidity of the Latin conjugations. The principal parts of a few verbs are given as specimens.

ACTIVE VOICE.

Pres. Indic.	Future Indic.	Perfect Indic.	
Ge'-yäse,	Eh-ge'-yäke,	Ah-ge'-yä-go,	To shoot.
O-gee'-a,	Eh-ge'-a,	Ah-ge'-a-go,	To die.
Gä-geh',	Eh-gä-geh',	Ah'-gä-geh,	To see.
Ga-go'-ace,	Eh-gä-go'-ake,	Ah-gä'-go-a-go,	To strike.
Ah-got'-hun-da,	Eh-gä'-ouk,	Ah-ga'-o-geh,	To hear.
Kna-ga-hä',	Enk-na'-ga-ă,	Kna-ga'-huk,	To drink.

It has been laid down as a maxim, that " the more simple any language is in its composition, the more complex it must be in its declensions and conjugations, and on the contrary, the more simple it is in its declensions and conjugations, the more complex it must be in its composition." The position is thus illustrated : when two people, by uniting or otherwise, blend their languages, the union always simplifies the structure of the resulting language, while it introduces a greater complexity into its materials. The Greek, which is uncompounded, and is said to have but three hundred primitives, is extremely intricate in its conjugations. On the other hand, the Latin, which is a compound language, laid aside the middle voice and the optative mood, which are peculiar to the Greek, and also the dual number. This simplified its conjugations. In its declensions, the Latin, although it has an additional case in the ablative, is yet much more simple than the Greek, as it has no contract nouns. The English, which is a mixture of several languages, is more simple than either in its declensions, which are made by the aid of prepositions alone ; and in its conjugations, which are made by other verbs. With this principle in mind, the regularity, fulness, and intricacy of the Iroquois conjugations are not particularly remarkable. Its primitive words, as before remarked, are few, and the language has been formed out of them by a complex and elaborate system of combinations.

The language of the *Ho-de'-no-sau-nee* has the substantive or neuter verb, *E-neh'-ga*, I am, although imperfect in some of its tenses. This verb is regarded by philologists as extremely difficult of invention, as it simply expresses being. Impersonal verbs are also very numerous in the language, as *O-geon'-de-o*, it snows ; *O-nä'-yose'-don-de-o*, it hails ; *Gä-wä'-no-däs*, it thunders. It is supposed by those who have inquired into the formation of language, that most of the verbs in primitive tongues originally took the impersonal form, for the reason that such a verb expresses in itself an entire event, while the division of the event into subject and attribute, involves some nice metaphysical distinctions.

Before closing upon this subject it will be proper to notice a few of the peculiarities of the language. In the first place. it has no labials, consequently the Iroquois, in speaking, never touch their lips together. This fact may be employed as a test in the pronunciation of their words and names. Their language possesses the numerals firstly, secondly, thirdly, &c., also the numbers one, two, three, ascending, by various contrivances, to about one hundred. For sums above this, their mode of enumeration was defective, as mathematical computation ceased, and some descriptive term was substituted in its place.

The voices of the *Ho-de'-no-sau-nee* are powerful, and capable of reaching a high shrill key. In conversation its natural pitch is above the English voice, especially with the female, whose voice, by a natural transition, frequently rises in conversation an octave above its ordinary pitch, and sounds upon a tone to which the English voice could not be elevated and retain a distinct articulation. It also passes up and down, at intervals, from octave to octave, the voice retaining upon the elevated key a clear and musical intonation.

In verbal languages the words appear to be literally strung together in a chain, if the one under inspection may be taken as a specimen. Substantives are mingled by declension with pronouns, and sometimes with the substantive verb, or compounded with the adjective, thus forming a new word. Particles are then conjoined, varying or adding to the signification of the compound, until the word, by the addition of the verb, becomes so far extended as to embrace a perfect sen-

75

tence. The principles upon which these combinations are effected are too much involved to be systematized or generalized. The most which can be said is, that the general result is accomplished by conjugations and declensions, which, although regular in general, are diversified and intricate. To illustrate the manner in which words are made up, the following example may be given. *Nun-da-wä-o*, the radix of the name of the Senecas, signifies " a great hill; " by suffix- ing *o-no*, which conveys the idea of " people at," *Nun-da-wä'-o-no*, results literally, " the people at the great hill." Next, by adding the particle *ga*, itself without significance, but when conjoined, con- veying the idea of " place " or " territory," it gives the compound *Nun-da-wä'-o-no-ga'*, " the territory of the people at the great hill." A more perfect speci- men of the language, as a whole, may be found in the following version of the Lord's Prayer in the Seneca dialect.

Gwä-nee' gă-o-yä'-geh che-de-oh'; sä-sa-no-do'-geh- teek; gä-o' ne-dwa na' sa-nunk-tä; na-huk' ne-yä-weh' na yo-an'-jä-geh ha'ne-sä-ne-go'-dă ha ne-de-o'-da na' gă-o-yä'-geh. Dun-dä-gwä-e'-wä-sä-gwus na' ong-wi- wä-na-ark-seh' na' da-yä'-ke-wä-sä-gwä'-seh na' onk- ke-wä-na'-ä-ge. Dä-ge-o'-na-geh'-wen-nis'-heh-da na' ong-wä-quä'. Să-nuk' na-huh' heh'-squä-ä ha' gä-yeh na' wä-ate-keh' na-gwä' na' dä-gwä-yä-duh'-nuh-onk ha' gä-yeh na' wä-ate-keh'; na' seh-eh' na ese' sä-wă na' o-nuk-ta' kuh' na' gä-hus-ta-seh' kuk' na' da-gä-ă- sä-uh'. Na-huh'-ne-yä-weh.[1]

---

[1] If an attempt should be made to give a literal translation of each word, or phrase, it would render transposition necessary, and

Names of places as well as of persons, form an integral part of their language, and hence are all significant. It furnishes a singular test of their migrations, for accurate descriptions of localities become in this manner incorporated into their dialects. The Tuscaroras still adduce proof from this source to establish a common origin with the Iroquois, and pretend to trace their route from Montreal, *Do-te-ä'-co*, to the Mississippi, *O-nau-we-yo'-kä*, and from thence to North Carolina, out of which they were driven in 1712. The era of their separation from the parent stock, and of this migration, they have entirely lost; but they consider the names of places on this extended route, now incorporated in their language, a not less certain indication of a common origin than the similarity of their languages. Indian languages are exceedingly tenacious of traditionary facts intrusted to their preservation.

change the formation of the words in some respects, as the following will exhibit.

Gwä-nee', che-de-oh' gă-o'-yä-geh, gä-sa-nuh', ese' sä-nuk-tä' gä-oh'
Our Father, which art in   heaven, hallowed be thy name, thy   kingdom   come,
ese' sne'-go-eh ne-yä-weh' yo an-jä'-geh ha' ne-de-o'-deh   gä-o'-yä-geh.
thy   will   be   done   on   earth   as   it is   in   heaven.
Dun-dä-gwä-e'-wä-să-gwus   ong-wä-yeh'-his-heh'   da-yä-ke'-a wä-
         Forgive us   our   debts   as we   forgive
sä-gwus-seh' ho-yeh'-his.   Dä-ge-oh' ne' na-geh' wen-nis'-heh-deh e' na-hä-
     our   debtors.   Give   us   this   day   our
da-wen-nis'-heh-geh o-ä'-qwa.   Hă-squä'-ah   e'   să-no'   ha'   wä-ate-keh',
     daily   bread.   Lead   us   not   into   temptation,
na-gwä' dä-gwä-yä-dan'-nake ne' wä-ate-keh', na-seh'-eh nees'   o-nuk'-tä
but   deliver from   us   evil,   for   thine is the kingdom,
na-kuh' na gä-hus'-tes-heh, na-kuh' da-gä-ă-sä-oh'.
and   the   power,   and   the glory.

Na-huh'-se-yä-weh.

Chapter III

OUR Indian geography is a subject of inquiry
peculiar in its interest and in its character.
Many of the names bestowed by our predecessors having become incorporated into our language, will be transmitted to distant generations, and
be familiar after their race, and perhaps ours, have
passed away. There is still attainable a large amount
of geographical information pertaining to the period
of Indian occupation, which, estimated at its true
value, would amply remunerate for its collection ; and
which, if neglected, must fade, ere many years, from
remembrance. The features of nature were first
christened by the red man. These baptismal names,
the legacy of the Indian, it were prodigality to cast
away. To the future scholar this subject will com-
mend itself, when, perchance, the dusky mantle of
obscurity has enshrouded it, and research itself cannot penetrate the covering.

In an antiquarian aspect, it may be considered
fortunate, that as the villages and settlements of the
Ho-de′-no-sau-nee disappeared, and the cities and villages of the succeeding race were reared upon their
sites, all of these ancient names were transferred to

these substituted habitations. Yielding step by step, and contracting their possessions from year to year, the Iroquois yet continued in the constant use of their original names, although the localities themselves had been surrendered. If a Seneca, for example, were to refer to Geneva, he would still say *Gä-nun'-dä-sa'-ga;* and the Oneida in like manner would call Utica, *Nun-da-dä'-sis.* All of these localities, as well as our rivers, lakes and streams, still dwell in the memory of the Iroquois by their ancient names, while such places as have sprung up on nameless sites, since they surrendered their domain, have been christened as they appeared. These names, likewise, are significant, and are either descriptive of features of the country, the record of some historical event, or interwoven with some tradition. From these causes their geography has been preserved among them with remarkable accuracy.

The Iroquois method of bestowing names was peculiar. It frequently happened that the same lake or river was recognized by them under several different names. This was eminently the case with the larger lakes. It was customary to give to them the name of some village or locality upon their borders. The Seneca word *Te-car-ne-o-dï',* means something more than "lake." It includes the idea of nearness, literally, "the lake at." Hence, if a Seneca were asked the name of lake Ontario, he would answer, *Ne-ah'-gä Te-car-ne-o-dï',* the lake at *Ne-ah'-gä.*" This was a Seneca village at the mouth of the Niagara river. If an Onondaga were asked the same question, he would prefix *Swa-geh'* to the word lake, literally,

"the lake of Oswego." [1]   The same multiplicity of
names frequently arose in relation to the principal
rivers, where they passed through the territories of
more than one nation.   It was not, however, the
case with villages and other localities.

The principal villages of the Iroquois, in the days
of aboriginal dominion, were connected by well-beaten
trails.   These villages were so situated that the
central trail, which started from the Hudson at the
site of Albany, passed through those of the Mohawks
and Oneidas ; and, crossing the Onondaga valley and
the Cayuga country, a few miles north of the chief
settlements of these nations, it passed through the
most prominent villages of the Senecas, in its route
to the valley of the Genesee.   After crossing this
celebrated valley, it proceeded westward to lake Erie,
coming out upon it at the mouth of Buffalo creek, on
the present site of Buffalo.

Since this Indian highway passed through the
centre of the Long House,   as well as through the
fairest portions of New York, it is desirable to commence with this trail on the Hudson, and trace it
through the State.   It will furnish the most convenient method of noticing such stopping-places as were
marked with appropriate names in the dialects of the
Iroquois, and also the Indian villages which dotted
this extended route.

Albany, at which point the trail started from the

---

[1] Lake Ontario was known at an early day among the English as lake
Cataraque.   The root of this word, *Ga-dai'-o-que* in Onondaga, *Gä-dä'-
loque* in Oneida, and *Gä-da-o'-ka* in Seneca, signifies " A fort in the
water."

Hudson, owes its Iroquois name to the openings which lay between that river and the Mohawk at Schenectady. Long anterior to the foundation of the city, this site was well known to our predecessors under the name of *Skä-neh'-tä-de*. The name is given in the Seneca dialect, and signifies " beyond the openings." [1] Out of this name originated that of the Hudson, *Skä-neh'-tä-de Ga-hun'-da*, " the river beyond the openings."

Leaving the Hudson at the site of Albany, the trail took the direction of the old turnpike north of the capitol, and proceeded, mostly on the line of this road, to a spring which issued from a ravine about six miles west. From thence it continued towards Schenectady, and descending the ravine through which the railway passes, it came upon the Mohawk at the site of this city, and crossed the river at the fording-place, where the toll-bridge has since been erected. Schenectady has not only appropriated the Indian name of Albany, but has, by inheritance, one of the most euphonious names in the dialects of the Iroquois, as given by the Oneidas. It was christened *O-no-al'-i-gone*, which signifies " in the head," a somewhat fanciful geographical name.

From this fording-place, two trails passed up the Mohawk, one upon each side. That upon the south was most travelled, as the three Mohawk castles, as they were termed, or principal villages, were upon

---

[1] In the Seneca dialect this word is compounded of *Gä-neh'-tä-yeh*, " openings," and *Se'-gwä*, " beyond." In the same manner *Skai'-dä-de*, " beyond the swamp," is a compound of *Gai'-tä-yeh*, " a swamp," and *Se'-gwä*, " beyond."

that side. Following the valley, and pursuing the windings of the river, the trail crossed the Schoharie creek, *Ose-ho-kar'-lä*, and entered *Te-hon-dä-lo'-ga*, the lower castle of the Mohawks, situated upon the west side of this creek, at its junction with the river. At a subsequent day Fort Hunter was located near the site of this Indian village. From thence the trail, continuing up the valley nearly on the line subsequently pursued by the canal, crossed the Canajoharie creek near its junction with the river, and led up to Canajoharie, *Ga-nä-jo'-hä-e*,[1] or the middle Mohawk castle. This favorite and populous village occupied a little eminence upon the east bank of the *Ot-squä'-go* creek, and overlooking the present site of Fort Plain. From Canajoharie, the trail followed up the river to *Gä-ne'-ga-hä'-ga*, the upper Mohawk castle, which was situated in the town of Danube, Herkimer county, nearly opposite the mouth of the East Canada creek. Leaving this Indian village, the last in the territory of the Mohawks, the trail pursued the bank of the river without passing any other stopping-place, until it reached the site of Utica, in the country of the Oneidas.

Near this city, on the east side, the trail passed around the base of a hill, in such a manner as to be noticeable for its singularity. Hence, *Nun-da-dä'-sis*, signifying " around the hill," was bestowed upon this locality, as a name descriptive of the course of the trail. When Utica at a subsequent day sprang up

---

[1] This word signifies " washing the basin." In the bed of the Canajoharie creek there is said to be a basin, several feet in diameter, with a symmetrical concavity, washed out in the rock. Hence the name *Ca-nä-jo'-hä-e*. One would naturally have expected to have found the Indian village upon this creek, instead of the Ot-squä'-go.

YA-WA-O-DÄ-QUÄ or PIN CUSHION.

near this spot, the name was transferred, according to the custom of the Iroquois, to the city itself.

From Utica, the trail proceeded up the river, and crossing the Whitesboro creek, at Whitesboro, *Che-gä-queh*, and the Oriskany creek, *Ole-his'-ka*, at Oriskany, it continued up the bank of the Mohawk to Rome, where this river turns to the north.

The site of Rome was an important stopping-place with the Iroquois, both as the terminus of the trails upon the Mohawk, and as a carrying-place for canoes. A narrow ridge at this point forms a division between those waters which flow through the Mohawk and the Hudson, and those which flow through lake Ontario, and the St. Lawrence. The portage from the Mohawk to Wood creek, was about a mile. In the days of aboriginal sovereignty, the amount of navigation, in bark canoes, upon the large lakes, as well as upon the smaller lakes and rivers, was much greater than we would be apt to suspect. Birch-bark canoes would find their way from Detroit, and even beyond to Rome and Schenectady. Others from Kingston, would make their way into the Cayuga[1] and Seneca lakes, and on to the old trading-post at the mouth of the Niagara river. Such was the facility of transportation, owing to the lightness of the vessel, that the portage made but a slight obstruction. In an hour

---

[1] In 1793, a canoe laded with twelve hundred pounds of fur started from Kingston in Canada ; and having coasted the lake to the Great Sodus bay, *Seo-dose'*, and been transported from thence over the portage to Clyde river, it made its way into the Cayuga lake and up to Aurora, *De-ä-wen'-dote;* where the furs were transhipped in a bateau for Albany. The canoe was owned for some years afterwards by Col. Payne, one of the first settlers of Aurora.

after drawing out the canoe from Wood creek, it was floating again upon the Mohawk; and the cargo having also been carried over, the frail vessel was soon re-laded, and under weigh upon the descending stream.[1] The aboriginal name of this locality, *Da-yä-hoo-wä'-quat*, which signifies a "place for carrying boats," has been bestowed upon Rome.

The trail upon the north bank of the Mohawk ascended the river from Schenectady nearly upon the line since pursued by the turnpike. At Tribes Hill, nearly opposite the lower Mohawk castle, a branch trail crossed the country to Johnstown, *Ko-lä-né'-kä*, a few miles north from the river. This was the name bestowed upon the residence of Sir William Johnson, the Indian superintendent. From the period of the settlement of this distinguished personage in the country of the Mohawks, and more especially after the battle of lake George in 1755, he acquired and maintained, until his death in 1774, a greater personal influence over the Iroquois than was ever possessed by any other individual, or even by any government. A careful scrutiny of his intercourse with the Iroquois shows that he exercised a watchful care over their welfare, and that his conduct was gov-

---

[1] For many years after the commencement (about 1790) of the settlement of Western New York, the greater part of the supplies of merchandise from the east, as well as the immigrants who flocked thitherward, with their household goods and farming implements, ascended the Mohawk in bateaus or small river boats as far as Rome. Having drawn out their vessels at this portage and unladed them, they carried them over the ridge and launched them into Wood creek. Descending to the Oswego river, which is formed by the outlets of the principal inland lakes of the State, the whole lake country was open before them. Like the Iroquois, they made use of the natural highways of the country.

erned by the most enlightened principles of rectitude
and benevolence. To this fact he owed his personal
popularity, and the affectionate respect with which the
Iroquois ever regarded him. His house at *Ko-lä-ne´-
kä* was a favorite place of Indian resort; and the Mohawk and the Seneca, the Oneida and the Cayuga felt
as much at ease under the roof of the baronet as beneath
the wide-spread shelter of their own forests.

Leaving Johnstown, the trail came down again upon
the Mohawk at the small Indian village of *Gä-no´-
wau-ga*, near the site of Fonda, where it intersected the
river trail. Continuing up the Mohawk, and crossing
the East Canada creek, *Date-car´-hu-har´-lo*, and over the
site of Little Falls, *Tä-lä-que´-ga*, it came next upon the
West Canada creek, *Te-uge´-ga*, and from thence led
up to the portage at the site of Rome.

As with lake Ontario, the Mohawk river was known
under a multiplicity of names. It is difficult now to
determine whether it had any general name running
through the several dialects by which it was known to
all the nations of the League. Among the Senecas,
the West Canada creek was considered the true head
of the river, and this stream, together with the Mohawk from Herkimer to the Hudson, was known as
one river under the name of *Te-uge´-ga*, while the
Mohawk from the junction of the West Canada creek
to its source was regarded as a branch under the name
of *Da-yä-hoo-wä´-quat*. With the Oneidas and Onondagas it was known under the last name, or the word
which, in their respective dialects, signifies the same
thing.

From Rome, the main trail, taking a south-west

direction, passed through Verona, *Te-o-na-täle'*, and finally came out at Oneida castle. This was the principal village of the Oneidas, called in their dialect *Gä-no-ä-lo'-häle*, which is rendered " a head on a pole." In this beautifully situated Indian village, burned the council-fire of one of the nations of the League. The Oneidas were fortunate in the location of their territories, embracing as they did not only some of the finest agricultural districts of the State, but the most attractive localities in its central parts.

Fording the Oneida creek at the Indian village, the trail, continuing west, passed near the site of Canestota, *Kä-ne-to'-tä*, crossed the Canaseraga creek, *Kä-nä-so-wä'-ga*, near the site of the village of the same name, the Chittenango creek, *Chu-de-näng'*, at the site of Chittenango, and from thence led up to the Deep Spring near Manlius, on the boundary line between the territories of the Oneidas and Onondagas. This spring was known under the name of *De-o-sä-dä-ya'-ah*, signifying " the spring in the deep basin," and was a favorite stopping-place of the Iroquois in their journeys upon the great thoroughfare.

Leaving this locality, and continuing west, the trail forded the Limestone creek, *De-ä-o-no'-he*, at the site of Manlius, and proceeding mostly on the line since pursued by the turnpike, it crossed the Jamesville creek, *Gä-sun'-to*, at the site of Jamesville, and from thence descending into the Onondaga valley, it crossed the Onondaga river, *O-nun-dä'-ga*, and entered the Indian village of *Gis-twe-ah'-na*, which occupied the site of the present village of Onondaga Hollow.

The Onondagas made this picturesque and fertile

valley their chief place of residence. Here was the Council-Brand of the confederacy, which rendered it the sylvan seat of government of the League. In the estimation of the Iroquois, it was a consecrated vale. Their eloquence, their legendary lore, and their civil history, were all interwoven, by association, with this favorite valley. Here their sachems gathered together in the days of aboriginal supremacy, to legislate for the welfare of the race. Here they strengthened and renewed the bonds of friendship and patriotism, indulged in exultation over their advancing prosperity, and counselled together to arrest impending dangers, or repair the mischances of the past. As it was upon the northern bank of the Onondaga lake that the League was formed, the united nations habitually turned to the Onondaga valley as the place to brighten the chain of brotherhood.

Upon the Onondaga river, *O-nun-dä'-ga*, were the principal villages of the Onondagas. There were but three of any note; one of them has been mentioned as on the line of the great trail. The chief village was Onondaga castle, *Kä-nä-tä-go'-wä*, situated upon both sides of the river, about four miles above *Gis'-twe-ah'-na*. It was quite a populous village in the days of their highest prosperity. Around the council-brand which burned in this secluded place, the sachems of the League were wont to meet. About three miles farther up the river, and upon the west side, the Indian village of *Nan-ta-sä'-sis* was situated near the skirts of the hill. There was another considerable village on the uplands about four miles east of Onondaga castle, called *Tu-e-a-das'-so*. Throughout the whole length of the beautiful valley of the Onondaga, the bark houses of the people were sprinkled.

After crossing the valley, the trail passed up a small ravine to the top of the hill, where it took a north-west direction, and crossing the Nine-mile creek, *Us'-te-ka*, at the site of Camillus, *O-yä''-han*, it went up to a stopping-place where Carpenter's tavern was subsequently erected, near the site of Elbridge, *Kä-no-wä''-ya*. From thence fording the Jordan creek, *Ha-nan'-to*, and passing through the town of Sennet, the trail came upon the Owasco outlet, *Was'-co*, at the site of Auburn ; and forded this stream a short distance above the prison, at the point where the " Red Store " was subsequently erected. This locality was in the territory of the Cayugas, and its name signifies " a floating bridge."

The Cayugas had but a few small villages, as the people were scattered around the lake. Their principal village, *Gă-yä-gä-an'-ha*, was situated upon the bank of a creek three miles south of Union Springs, and about a mile and a half back from the lake. Here was the council-house of the nation. There was another village consisting of a few houses, situated upon the site of Union Springs, which was called *Ge-wau'-ga*. Steeltrap, *Hise'-tă-jee*, a celebrated Cayuga chief, was buried here. On the opposite side of the lake was the village of *Gä-no'-geh*, occupying the site of the present Cannoga. Near this village was the birthplace of Red Jacket. Along the eastern margin of the lake, the former residences of the Cayugas were indicated by the apple and peach orchards which they left behind them. Back from the lake, upon the ridge, similar but more numerous evidences of Indian occupation were to be found. In 1779, the villages of the Cayugas were destroyed by General Sullivan.

Leaving the site of Auburn, the trail proceeded nearly on the line of the turnpike, half-way to the lake, where it turned out upon the south side and came down upon the lake about half a mile above Cayuga bridge, *Wäs-gwase'*. At the precise point where the trail reached the shore, the original Cayuga ferry was established. The trail, turning down the lake, and following its bank about four miles to the old fording-place near the lower bridge, there crossed the foot of the lake, and came out upon the north bank of the Seneca river, *Swa'-geh*.[1] Following up the north bank of the river, it passed over the site of Waterloo, *Skoi-yase'*, and pursued the stream up to its outlet from the Seneca lake. A shorter route from the east bank of the Cayuga was taken by crossing the lake in canoes at the ferry, and proceeding due west to the river, which the trail came upon at the rapids a little above Seneca Falls. Ascending the river upon the south bank, the trail passed through South Waterloo, *Skoi-yase'*, and continued up the river to the lake, where, crossing the outlet, it intersected the other trail. Having run along the foot of the lake upon the beach

---

[1] There is a geographical novelty in the method adopted by the Iroquois to designate the several outlets of the lakes which, united, form the Oswego river. Descending from the Seneca lake to Oswego, the river was called *Swa'-geh* through its whole length. But ascending from Oswego, it was called the Onondaga river, *O-non-dä'-ga*, until you passed the outlet of the Onondaga lake. Then it was called the Cayuga river, *Gwä-u-gweh*, until you passed the Cayuga outlet. After that it was called the Seneca river, *Gä-nun-dä-sa'-ga*, up to the Seneca lake.

to the present site of Geneva, *Gä-nun-dä-sa'-ga*, it turned up the Geneva creek, which it ascended about one and a half miles north-west, to the Indian village of *Gä-nun-dä-sa'-ga*, the first in the territory of the Senecas.

This name, which signifies " a new settlement village," was bestowed upon the lake, the creek, and also upon the outlet. At a subsequent day it was transferred to Geneva. During the destructive inroad of General Sullivan, in September, 1779, the Indian village was entirely destroyed. No efforts were ever made subsequently to rebuild it. Many of the old trees in the Indian orchard are still standing and yield fruit, although partially girdled at the time. The artificial burial mound[1] about one hundred paces in

---

[1] There is an interesting tradition connected with this mound. The Senecas say that they once had a protector, a mighty giant, taller than the tallest trees, who split the largest hickory for his bow, and used pine-trees for his arrows. He once wandered west to the Mississippi, and from thence east again to the sea. Returning homeward over the mountains along the Hudson, he saw a great bird on the water, flapping its wings as if it wished to get out, so he waded in and lifted it on land. He then saw on it a number of men, who appeared dreadfully frightened, and made signs to him to put them back again. He did so, and they gave him a sword and a musket, with powder and balls, and showed him how to use them, after which the bird swam off and he saw it no more. Having returned to the Senecas at *Gä-nun-dä-sa'-ga*, he exhibited to them the wonderful implements of destruction, and fired the gun before them. They were exceedingly terrified at the report, and reproached him for bringing such terrible things among them, and told him to take them away again, for they would be the destruction of the Indians, and he was an enemy to their nation who had brought them there. Much grieved at their reproaches, he left the council, taking the dreaded weapons with him, and lay down in a field. The next morning he was found, from some mysterious cause, dead, and this mound was raised over his body where it lay. It is averred by the Onondagas, that if the mound should be opened a skeleton of supernatural size would be found underneath.

circuit, still remains undisturbed, and also the trenches of a picket enclosure, seventy by forty feet on the ground plan, concerning the erection and uses of which but little can be ascertained.

From *Gä-nun-dä-sa'-ga* the trail proceeded through the towns of Seneca and Hopewell, nearly on the line of the turnpike, to the Indian village of *Gä'-nun-dä'-gwa*, situated at the foot of the lake of the same name. It signifies " a place selected for a settlement." Canandaigua, the fairest of all the villages which have sprung into life upon the central trail of the Iroquois, not only occupies the site of the Indian village, but has accepted and preserved its name with unusual accuracy ; the only legacy which the retiring Seneca could bestow, save the beautiful natural scenery by which it is surrounded, and which induced him " to select it for a settlement."

Leaving Canandaigua were two trails. One turning south-west, passed through the town of Bristol, and led to the foot of the Honeoye lake, *Hä'-ne-ä-ya'*. After crossing the outlet, it continued west through the town of Richmond, going over the hill in sight of the Hemlock lake, *O-neh'-dä*, and coming out upon the Connesus, *Gä-ne-a'-sos*, near the north end. Following the shore to the foot of the lake, and fording the outlet, it proceeded west, passing over the site of Geneseo, *O-hä'-di*, and crossing the valley and the river Genesee, *Gen-nis'-he-yo*, it led into Little Beards town, *De-o-nun'-dä-gä-a*, the most populous village of the Senecas. It is worthy of remark that the root of the word Genesee was the name of the valley and not of the river, the latter deriving its name from the former. *Gen-nis'-he-yo* signifies " the beautiful valley," a name most fitly bestowed.

The other trail, which was the main highway, leaving Canandaigua, passed along the north road, over the site of West Bloomfield, *Gä-nun'-dä-ok*, and the Honeoye outlet, and proceeded to the Indian village of *Skä-hasé-gä-o*, on the site of Lima. From thence, proceeding westward nearly on the line since pursued by the State road, it passed over the site of Avon, *Gä-no-wau'-ges*, and, descending into the valley of the Genesee, crossed the river a few rods above the Avon bridge, and followed along its bank up to the Indian village of *Gä-no-wau'-ges*, about a mile above the ford. This word signifies " fetid waters," and was bestowed by the Senecas upon the sulphur springs at Avon, and upon the whole adjacent country.

Departing from the valley of the Genesee, the trail, taking a north-west direction, led to the Caledonia cold spring, *De-o'-na-gä-no*, a well-known stopping-place on the central trail through the territories of the Iroquois. Proceeding westward from thence, it came upon Allen's creek, *O-at'-kä*, at the dam near the rapids, in the village of Le Roy. This fording-place was known under the name *Te-car'-no-wän-ne-dä'-ne-o*, rendered " many falls," which is accurately descriptive of the locality. This name has been conferred upon Le Roy. After turning up the stream about a mile to avoid a marsh near the rapids, the trail again proceeded west, and crossing Black creek, *Jä-go'-o-ga*, near Stafford, it continued in a westerly direction, and finally came out upon the Tonawanda creek, *Tä'-nă-wun-dä*, about a mile above Batavia, to which it led. The ancient name of Batavia, or rather of the locality itself, was *De-o'-on-go-wä*, which signifies "the grand hearing-place." Here the rapids in the Tonawanda creek first began to be heard, and some assert that the distant roar of Niagara could be heard by the practiced ear of the Indian, at this point, in certain states of the atmosphere.

Descending the creek, the trail passed over the site of Batavia. At the point where the arsenal now stands, it turned north-west through the oak-openings to Caryville, and came again upon the creek at "Washington's fording-place," where it crossed, and led to the Indian village of *Tä'-nă-wun-dä'*, one of the present villages of the Senecas, situated upon the borders of the great swamp which stretches for many miles along the Tonawanda creek. On leaving the Indian village the trail branched. One taking a north-west direction, recrossed the creek at a short distance below the village, and passing through the swamp, out of which it emerged near Royalton, it proceeded direct to *De-o'-na-gä-no*, or the Cold Spring, about two miles north-east of Lockport, *Tä-gă'-ote*. From thence continuing north-west, it came out upon the ridge-road, where it intersected the Ontario, or ridge trail, and followed this ridge westward to *Gä-a-no'-ga*, the Tuscarora Indian village on Lewiston Heights. Here was the termination of one branch of the main trail upon the bank of the Niagara river. This was the route to Canada.

The other trail, leaving the village of Tonawanda, took a south-west direction, and having forded Murder creek, *De-o-oon-go'-at*, at Akron, and the

Eighteen-mile creek, *Ta-nun-no-ga'-o*, at Clarence Hollow, it continued west, crossing Ellicott creek, *Gă-dă-o-yä'-deh*, at Williamsville, *Gä-sko-sä-dä'-ne-o*, and leading direct to the Cold Spring, it finally came upon the site of Buffalo at the head of Main street, and descended to the mouth of the creek, within the limits of the city. Here was the western terminus of the central trail; and like its eastern terminus on the Hudson, it has become a point of great commercial importance, and the site of a flourishing city. It is not a little remarkable, that these two geographical points should have been as clearly indicated, as places of departure, by the migrations of the red race, as they have been at a subsequent day, by the migrations of our own.

We have thus followed the great Indian trail, *Wä-a-gwen'-ne-yu*, through the State, from the Hudson to lake Erie; noticing, as far as ascertained, the principal stopping-places on the route. To convey an adequate impression of the forest scenery, which then overspread the land, is beyond the power of description. This trail was traced through the over-hanging forest for almost its entire length. In the trail itself, there was nothing particularly remarkable. It was usually from twelve to eighteen inches wide, and deeply worn in the ground; varying in this respect from three to six, and even twelve inches, depending upon the firmness of the soil. The large trees on each side were frequently marked with the hatchet. This well-beaten footpath, which no run-ner, nor band of warriors could mistake, had doubt-less been trodden by successive generations from

century to century. It had, without question, been
handed down from race to race, as the natural line
of travel, geographically considered, between the Hudson and lake Erie. While it is scarcely possible to
ascertain a more direct route than the one pursued by
this trail, the accuracy with which it was traced from
point to point, to save distance, is extremely surprising. It proved, on the survey of the country, to
have been so judiciously selected that the turnpike
was laid out mainly on the line of this trail, from one
extremity of the State to the other. In addition to
this, all the larger cities and villages west of the Hudson, with one or two exceptions, have been located
upon it. As an independent cause, this forest highway of the Iroquois doubtless determined the establishment of a number of settlements, which have since
grown up into cities and villages.

There are many interesting considerations connected with the routes of travel pursued by the aborigines; and if carefully considered, they will be
found to indicate the natural lines of migration suggested by the topography of the country. The
central trail of the Iroquois, which we have been
tracing, after leaving the Mohawk valley, one of
nature's highways, became essentially an artificial road
across the drainage of the country, fording rivers,
crossing valleys, and traversing marshes and dense
forests, pursuing its course over hill and plain,
through stream and thicket, as if in defiance of nature,
without an aim and without a reason. Yet the establishment of this trail between two such points as
Albany and Buffalo, exhibits not only the extent

and accuracy of the geographical knowledge of our predecessors,[6] but also indicates the active intercourse which must have been maintained between the various races east of the Mississippi. The tide of population which has poured upon the west, in our generation, mostly along the line of this old trail of the *Ho-dé'-no-sau-nee*, and the extraordinary channel of trade and intercourse which it has become, between the north-western States and the Atlantic, sufficiently and forcibly illustrate the fact that it was and is, and ever must be, one of the great natural highways of the continent.

Having traced the main trail from the Hudson to lake Erie, it remains to notice briefly the lake and river trails, and to locate such Indian villages as were situated upon them. In pursuing this inquiry, the Ontario trail first arrests our attention. Bordering lake Ontario, from Oswego to Lewiston, there is a ridge running, for the entire distance, from three to six miles inland from the shore, and mostly a continuous level. From the shore-marks everywhere conspicuous, it is generally admitted that this ridge was anciently the shore of the lake, the basin of which has been depressed some three hundred feet, or the surrounding country elevated by subterraneous agencies. A natural road is formed by this ancient beach from Oswego to Lewiston. From the valley of Genesee to Niagara, it was extensively travelled by the Iroquois, as one of the routes to Canada.

Oswego, *Swa'-geh*, was a point of considerable importance to our predecessors, both as the terminus of the trails which descended the river from the Onondaga and Oneida country, and as the inlet of intercourse by water from lake Ontario. Commencing at the site of this place, the trail followed the ridge to the westward, until it came upon the Irondequoit bay, *Nu-dă-on'-dä-quät*, when it turned up the bay to its head. From the head of the bay, the trail turned back from the ridge, and proceeded direct to the Genesee ford, at Rochester, *Gä-skó'-sä-go*, which crossed the river at the point where the aqueduct has since been constructed. Turning down the river to the lower falls, it came again upon the ridge-road, which it followed westward to *Gä-o-nó'-geh*, the Tuscarora village near Lewiston. Here was the principal crossing-place into Canada.

Having now reached the banks of the Niagara, and the vicinity of the great cataract, the derivation of the word Niagara suggests itself as a subject for inquiry. Colden wrote it *O-ni-ag-a-ra*, in 1741,[1] and he must have received it from the Mohawks or Oneidas. It was the name of a Seneca village at the mouth of the Niagara river, located as early as 1650, near the site of Youngstown. It was also the place where the Marquis De Nonville constructed a fort in 1687, the building of which brought this locality under the particular notice of the English. The name of this Indian village in the dialect of the Senecas was *Ne-ah'-gä*, in Tuscarora *O-ne-ä'-kars*, in Onondaga *O-ne-ah'-gä*, in Oneida *O-ne-ah'-gäle*, and in Mohawk *O-ne-ä'-gä-rä*. These names are but the same word under dialectical changes. It is clear that Niagara was derived from some one of them, and thus came direct from the Iroquois language. The signification of the

[1] Colden's History of the Five Nations, ed. of 1741, p. 79.

word is lost, unless it be derived, as some of the present Iroquois suppose, from the word which signifies " neck," in Seneca *O-ne-ah'-ä*, in Onondaga *O-ne-yä'-ä*, and in Oneida *O-ne'-arle*.[1]

The name of this Indian village was bestowed by the Iroquois upon Youngstown ; upon the river Niagara, from the falls to the lake ; and upon lake Ontario, as has been elsewhere stated.

In bestowing names upon water-falls, the Iroquois custom agrees with the English. The name of the river is connected with the word " fall." In the case of Niagara Falls, however, an adjective is incorporated with the word " fall," as the idea of its grandeur and sublimity appears to have been identified with the fall itself. Thus, in Onondaga it is called *Date-car'-sko-sis*, in Seneca *Date-car'-sko-sase*, the word *Ne-ah'-gä* being understood. It signifies " the highest falls."

In the broad valley of the Genesee, the Senecas established most of their villages. Of great extent, boundless fertility, and easy cultivation, it became their favorite residence, and fully deserved the appellation of " the beautiful valley," which they bestowed upon it. Its situation in the centre of their territories, and the easily forded river which flowed through it, alike invited to its settlement. At the period of their highest prosperity, it became the most thickly peopled district in the country of the Iroquois.

From Rochester there were two trails up the Genesee, one upon each side. That upon the west side, following the bank of the river, first entered the small

---

[1] Bancroft is in error in deriving this word from the language of the Neuter Nation.

Indian village of *O-at'-kä*, upon the site of Scottsville; and continuing up the valley upon the flat, it next passed into the Indian village of *Gä-no-wau'-ges*, before mentioned.[1]   From thence the trail pursued the winding of the river up to *O-hä'-gi*, a Tuscarora village on the flat, between two and three miles below Cuylerville.   Proceeding up the river, it next led up to the Seneca village of *Gä-un-do'-wä-neh*, or " big tree," which was situated upon the hill about one mile north of Cuylerville.   Here at a subsequent day was marked off to the Senecas the " Big Tree Reservation," in the same manner as they had reserved a tract around the favorite village of *Gä-no-wau'-ges*.   Leaving this village, the trail turned a bend in the river, and entered *De-o-nun'-dä-gä-a*, or Little Beard's town, also before mentioned.   It was situated upon the flat immediately in front of Cuylerville, and on the opposite side of the valley from Geneseo.   Adjacent to this village, upon the sloping bank, was a small settlement called *Gä-neh'-dä-on-twă*.   There was also an Indian village upon the site of Moscow, *Gä-nun'-dä-sa*.   The trail, following up the river, next turned out of this valley, and led up to *Da-yo-it'-gä-o*, or Squakie Hill, opposite Mount Morris.   This word signifies " where the river issues from the hills," and it is beautifully descriptive of the emergence of the river from between its rocky barriers into the broad valley of the Genesee.

It is a singular feature of the country, geologically considered, that the valley follows the river from near Rochester to Mount Morris only.   At the latter place the river is suddenly confined in a narrow channel cut

[1] Mr. Newbold's farm embraces the site of this ancient village.

through the rock, while the valley, which at this place is about three miles wide, follows the Caneseraga creek, *Gä-nose'-gă-go*, up to Dansville, situated at its head. From Mount Morris south, up the Genesee, the valley is narrow and irregular, until at Portage the whole scenery is changed into rugged declivities and picturesque water-falls. On the Caneseraga creek, however, from Dansville down to Mount Morris, the scenery and the valley are quite the same as upon the Genesee from the latter place to Rochester. This "beautiful valley" of the Senecas, varying from one half mile to three miles in breadth, for the distance of forty miles, vies with, if it does not surpass, the more celebrated valley of Wyoming.

Leaving Squakie Hill, the trail continued up the river, crossing the outlet of the Silver lake, *Gä-na'-yät*, and entering the Indian village of *Gä-dă-o'*, situated in the town of Castile, Genesee county. Here, at a subsequent day, was the Gardow Reservation. From thence the trail continued up the river, and over the site of Portage, to the Indian village of *O-wa-is'-ki*, near the confluence of the creek of the same name with the Genesee. Having crossed this stream, the trail led up the river to *Gä-o-yä-de'-o*, or Caneadea, the last Seneca village upon the Genesee. It was situated in the town of Hume, in the county of Allegany. The name is rendered, "the heavens leaning against the earth." It appears that there was an extensive opening at this locality, on looking through which the heavens and earth appeared to meet, or the sky seemed to rest upon the earth. Subsequently, there was a large reserve retained by the Senecas around this

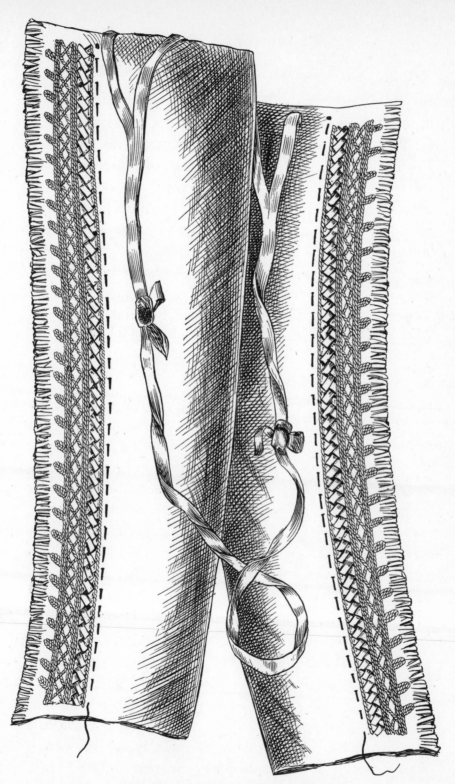

GISE-HA or DEER SKIN LEGGIN

the Blue Ridge, rendered it an important and well-known locality among the Iroquois.

From Tioga there were two trails up the Susquehanna, *Gä-wa-no-wä'-nă*. That upon the north bank ascending the river, passed over the site of Owego, *Ah-wä'-ga*, forded the Chenango, *O-che-näng'*, near its mouth, and passing over the site of Binghampton, *O-che-näng'*, continued up the river to the junction of the Unadilla, *De-u-na-dil'-lo*, where it intersected the trail coming down from the Oneida country. Continuing up the Susquehanna to the junction of the Charlotte river, the trail branched. One ascended to the junction of the Cherry Valley creek, and following up this creek, finally passed over to Canajoharie. The other trail, having ascended the Charlotte river to its head, crossed over to the Cobuskill, *As-ca-le'-ge*, and descended that stream to the Schoharie creek, where it intersected the Schoharie trail, from the lower castle of the Mohawks. From Schoharie, *Ose-ko-har'-lä*, a branch trail turned up Foxes creek, and crossing the Helderberg hills, descended to Albany. Another branch leaving the Schoharie, crossed the town of Middleburgh to the Caatskill river, and descended that river to the Hudson.

Many of the early settlers of middle Pennsylvania, and nearly all of our people who located themselves on the fertile tracts spread out upon the Susquehanna, entered the country upon these trails, which were the only roads opened through the forest. They trusted entirely for their route to the well-beaten, well-selected trails of the Iroquois. The same observation applies to the central trail, which before the opening of regular roads, was traversed by the early pioneers of western New York, with their horses, cattle, and implements of husbandry. For many years this trail was the only route of travel. It guided the early immigrants into the heart of the country, and not a little were they indebted to the Iroquois for thus making their country accessible.

There were also regular beaten trails along the banks of our inland lakes, which were used for hunting purposes, for mutual intercourse, and as routes of communication between the central thoroughfare, and the river trails which converged upon Tioga.

We have thus followed the devious footsteps of the Iroquois, for many hundred miles through their territories, and restored some of the names in use during the era of Indian occupation. Facts of this character may not possess a general interest; but they will find an appropriate place among our aboriginal remains. The trails of our Indian predecessors, indeed, have been obliterated, and the face of nature has been transformed; but all recollection of the days of Indian supremacy cannot as easily pass away. They will ever have "a share in our history."

"The Empire State, as you love to call it," said a Cayuga chief on a recent occasion, "was once laced by our trails from Albany to Buffalo, — trails that we had trod for centuries, — trails worn so deep by the feet of the Iroquois, that they became your roads of travel, as your possessions gradually eat into those of my people. Your roads still traverse those same lines of communication, which bound one part of the

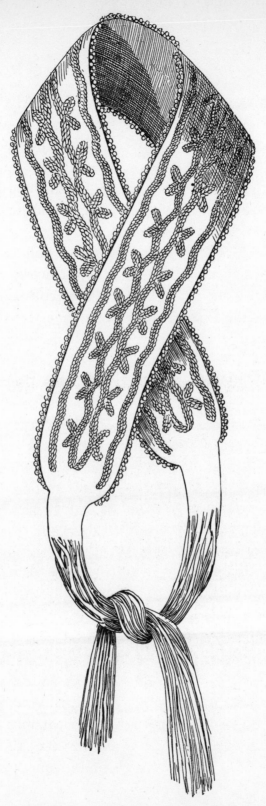

YUNT KA TO DA TA or DEER SKIN SHOULDER BELT

Long House to the other. Have we, the first hold-
ers of this prosperous region, no longer a share in
your history? Glad were your fathers to sit down
upon the threshold of the Long House. Had our
forefathers spurned you from it, when the French
were thundering at the opposite side to get a passage through, and drive you into the sea, whatever
has been the fate of other Indians, the Iroquois
might still have been a nation, and I, instead of
pleading here for the privilege of living within your
borders, I — might have had a country." [1]

A brief reference to Indian runners will not be inappropriate in this connection. To convey intelligence from nation to nation, and to spread information
throughout the Confederacy, as in summoning councils upon public exigencies, trained runners were employed. But three days were necessary, it is said, to
convey intelligence from Buffalo to Albany. Swiftness
of foot was an acquirement, among the Iroquois, which
brought the individual into high repute. A trained
runner would traverse a hundred miles per day. With

[1] "The eloquent speech, of which the above is an extract, was an
unpremeditated effort of Dr. Peter Wilson (Wä-o-wo-wă-nó-onk), an
educated chief, and was delivered at the May, 1847, meeting of the New
York Historical Society, at which he chanced to be present. The substance of the present chapter and of Chapter II. of Book I. of this work
being a paper entitled 'On the Territorial Limits, Geographical Names,
and Trails of the Iroquois,' had just been read before the society, when
under the impulse of the moment this chief accepted an invitation to
address the meeting. He spoke with such pathos and earnestness upon
his people and race — their ancient prowess and generosity — their present
weakness and dependence — and especially upon the hard fate of a small
band of Senecas and Cayugas, which had recently been hurried into the
western wilderness to perish, that all present were deeply moved by his
eloquence. He produced a strong sensation."

relays, which were sometimes resorted to, the length of the day's journey could be considerably increased. It is said that the runners of Montezuma conveyed intelligence to him of the movements of Cortes, at the rate of two hundred miles per day; but this must be regarded as extravagant. During the last war, a runner left Tonawanda at daylight in the summer season, for Avon, a distance of forty miles upon the trail. He delivered his message, and reached Tonawanda again about noon. In the night their runners were guided by the stars, from which they learned to keep their direction, and regain it, if perchance they lost their way. During the fall and winter, they determined their course by the Pleiades, or Seven Stars. This group in the neck of Taurus, they called *Got-gwär'-där*. In the spring and summer they ran by another group, which they named *Gwe-o-gä'-ah*, or the Loon, four stars at the angles of a rhombus. In preparing to carry messages they denuded themselves entirely, with the exception of the *Gä-kä'-ah*, or breech cloth, and a belt. They were usually sent out in pairs, and took their way through the forest, one behind the other, in perfect silence.

Upon the map accompanying the first volume of this work, the trails which have been traced will be found. Also the names in the several dialects of the Iroquois, of the lakes, rivers, and creeks; of the Indian villages, and ancient localities, known to our immediate predecessors; and the names of our own cities and villages, which have been christened as they appeared.[1]

1 In Appendix A, I, will be found a schedule containing all the names upon the Map, with the signification of each, arranged under their respective counties.

This map is newly designed, to exhibit the Home Country of the *Ho-dé-no-sau-nee.*

The Iroquois were the master spirits of the north. Fortunate in their geographical position, and powerful from the concentration of their strength through the League, the lesser tribes scattered over these vast territories could offer but slight obstruction to their combined attack. Large masses, like the Sioux of the west, or the Cherokees of the south, were alone able to withstand their valor, or resist their invasions. In comparison with other Indian nations, the Iroquois might well exult in the superiority of their institutions; and felicitate themselves upon the high destiny which seemed to await the full development of their civil institutions.

Chapter IV

THE future destiny of the Indian upon this continent, is a subject of no ordinary interest. If the fact, that he cannot be saved in his native state, needed any proof beyond the experience of the past, it could be demonstrated from the nature of things. Our primitive inhabitants are environed with civilized life, the baleful and disastrous influence of which, when brought in contact with Indian life, is wholly irresistible. Civilization is aggressive, as well as progressive — a positive state of society, attacking every obstacle, overwhelming every lesser agency, and searching out and filling up every crevice, both in the moral and physical world; while Indian life is an unarmed condition, a negative state, without inherent vitality, and without powers of resistance. The institutions of the red man fix him to the soil with a fragile and precarious tenure; while those of civilized man, in his highest estate, enable him to seize it with a grasp which defies displacement. To uproot a race at the meridian of its intellectual power, is next to impossible; but the expulsion of a contiguous one, in a state of primitive rudeness, is comparatively easy, if not an absolute necessity.

The manifest destiny of the Indian, if left to himself, calls up the question of his reclamation, certainly, in itself, a more interesting and far more important subject than any which have before been considered. All the Indian races now dwelling within the Republic have fallen under its jurisdiction ; thus casting upon the government a vast responsibility, as the administrator of their affairs, and a solemn trust, as the guardian of their future welfare. Should the system of tutelage and supervision, adopted by the national government, find its highest aim and ultimate object in the adjustment of their present difficulties from day to day ; or should it look beyond and above these temporary considerations, towards their final elevation to the rights and privileges of American citizens? This is certainly a grave question, and if the latter enterprise itself be feasible, it should be prosecuted with a zeal and energy as earnest and untiring as its importance demands. During the period within which this question will be solved, the American people cannot remain indifferent and passive spectators, and avoid responsibility ; for while the government is chiefly accountable for the administration of their civil affairs, those of a moral and religious character, which, at least, are not less important, appeal to the enlightened benevolence of the public at large.

Whether a portion of the Indian family may yet be reclaimed and civilized, and thus saved eventually from the fate which has already befallen so many of our aboriginal races, will furnish the theme of a few concluding reflections. What is true of the Iroquois, in a general sense, can be predicated of any other portion of our primitive inhabitants. For this reason the facts relied upon to establish the hypothesis that the Indian can be permanently reclaimed and civilized, will be drawn exclusively from the social history of the former.

There are now about four thousand Iroquois living in the state of New York. Having for many years been surrounded by civilization, and shut in from all intercourse with the ruder tribes of the wilderness, they have not only lost their native fierceness, but have become quite tractable and humane. In addition to this, the agricultural pursuits into which they have gradually become initiated, have introduced new modes of life, and awakened new aspirations, until a change, in itself scarcely perceptible to the casual observer, but in reality very great, has already been accomplished. At the present moment their decline has not only been arrested, but they are actually increasing in numbers, and improving in their social condition. The proximate cause of this universal spectacle is to be found in their feeble attempts at agriculture; but the remote and the true one is to be discovered in the schools of the missionaries.

To these establishments among the Iroquois, from the days of the Jesuit fathers down to the present time, they are principally indebted for all the progress they have made, and for whatever prospect of ultimate reclamation their condition is beginning to inspire. By the missionaries they were taught our language, and many of the arts of husbandry and of domestic

GÄ·YÄ·AH or WORK BAG

life ; from them they received the Bible and the precepts of Christianity. After the lapse of so many years, the fruits of their toil and devotion are becoming constantly more apparent : as, through years of slow and almost imperceptible progress, they have gradually emancipated themselves from much of the rudeness of Indian life. The Iroquois of the present day is, in his social condition, elevated far above the Iroquois of the seventeenth century. This fact is sufficient to prove, that philanthropy and Christianity are not wasted upon the Indian ; and further than this, that the Iroquois, if eventually reclaimed, must ascribe their preservation to the persevering and devoted efforts of those missionaries, who labored for their welfare when they were injured and defrauded by the unscrupulous, neglected by the civil authorities, and oppressed by the multitude of misfortunes which accelerated their decline.

There are but two means of rescuing the Indian from his impending destiny ; and these are education and Christianity. If he will receive into his mind the light of knowledge and the spirit of civilization, he will possess, not only the means of self-defence, but the power with which to emancipate himself from the thraldom in which he is held. The frequent attempts which have been made to educate the Indian, and the numerous failures in which these attempts have eventuated, have, to some extent, created a belief in the public mind, that his education and reclamation are both impossible. This enterprise may still, perhaps, be considered an experiment, and of uncertain issue ; but experience has not yet shown that it is hopeless.

There is now, in each Indian community in the State, a large and respectable class who have become habitual cultivators of the soil ; many of whom have adopted our mode of life, have become members of the missionary churches, speak our language, and are in every respect discreet and sensible men. In this particular class there is a strong desire for the adoption of the customs of civilized life, and more especially for the education of their children, upon which subject they often express the strongest solicitude. Among the youth who are brought up under such influences, there exists the same desire for knowledge, and the same readiness to improve educational advantages. Out of this class Indian youth may be selected for a higher education, with every prospect of success, since to a better preparation for superior advantages, there is superadded a stronger security against a relapse into Indian life. In the attempted education of their young men, the prime difficulty has been to render their attainments permanent, and useful to themselves. To draw an untutored Indian from his forest home, and, when carefully educated, to dismiss him again to the wilderness, a solitary scholar, would be an idle experiment ; because his attainments would not only be unappreciated by his former associates, but he would incur the hazard of being despised because of them. The education of the Indian youth should be general, and chiefly in schools at home.

A new order of things has recently become apparent among the Iroquois, which is favorable to a more general education at home and to a higher cultivation in particular instances. The schools of the missionaries, established as they have been, and are, in the heart of our Indian communities, have reached the people directly, and laid the only true and solid foundation of their permanent improvement. They have created a new society in the midst of them, founded upon Christianity; thereby awakening new desires, creating new habits, and arousing new aspirations. In fact they have gathered together the better elements of Indian society, and quickened them with the light of religion and of knowledge. A class has thus been gradually formed, which if encouraged and strengthened, will eventually draw over to itself that portion of our Indian population which is susceptible of improvement and elevation, and willing to make the attempt. Under the fostering care of the government, both state and national, and under the still more efficient tutelage of religious societies, great hopes may be justly entertained of the ultimate and permanent civilization of this portion of the Iroquois.

It is, indeed, a great undertaking to work off the Indian temper of mind, and infuse that of another race. It is necessary, to its accomplishment, to commence in infancy, and at the missionary school, where our language is substituted for the Indian language, our religion for the Indian mythology, and our amusements and mode of life for theirs. When this has been effected, and upon a mind thus prepared has been shed the light of a higher knowledge, there is not even then a firm assurance that the Indian nature is forever subdued and submerged in that superior one which civilization creates. In the depths of Indian society there is a spirit and a sentiment to which their minds are attuned by nature; and great must be the power, and constant the influence which can overcome the one, or eradicate the other.

In the education of the Iroquois, New York has recently made a commencement. Prior to 1846 our Indian youth were excluded from the benefits of the common school fund; their want of preparation for such schools, furnishing, to some extent, a sufficient reason. At that time schools were first opened among them under appropriations from the public fund. These schools have not met with encouraging success; but their efficiency would have been much greater if they had been organized upon the boarding-school or missionary plan, instead of that of the common school. The former is the more practicable and successful system of Indian education; and it is greatly to be hoped that it will soon be adopted. To meet the growing demand for a higher education, the State Normal School, within the past year, has not only been opened to a limited number of Indian youth, but a sufficient appropriation made for their maintenance while improving its advantages. These two important events form an interesting era with the modern Iroquois. It remains only to give them permanent boarding-schools at home for the instruction of the mass of their youth, with access to the Normal School for their advanced scholars, and in a few years they will rise in the scale of intelligence, as far above their present level, as their fathers raised themselves, in the days of aboriginal sovereignty, above the level of cotemporary nations.

GOT-GWEN-DÄ OR POCKET BOOK

In addition to the special claim which the residue of the Iroquois have upon the people of the State, every principle of philanthropy pleads for the encouragement of their young men in their efforts to obtain a higher course of instruction than the limited earnings of Indian husbandry can afford. The time has come, in their social progress, when they are capable of a thorough intellectual training, and are able to achieve as high and accurate a scholarship as many of their white competitors. The time has also arrived when academical attainments will prove a blessing to themselves and to their families. By the diffusion of knowledge among them the way will be facilitated for the introduction of the mechanic arts, and for their improvement in agricultural pursuits. A small band of educated young men in each Indian community would find sufficient employment for their acquired capacities, in the various stations of teacher, physician, mechanic, and farmer; in each and all of which they would greatly promote the general welfare. If the desire for improvement, which now prevails among them, is met and encouraged, it will require but a few years to initiate them into the arts of civilized life, and to prepare them eventually for exercising those rights of property, and rights of citizenship, which are common to ourselves. How much more noble for the State to reclaim and save this interesting and peculiar portion of her people, than to accelerate their extinction by injustice; or to abandon them to their fate, when they are struggling to emancipate themselves by taking into their hands the implements of agriculture, and opening their minds to the light of knowledge.

There is no want of sympathy for their welfare among the people of New York ; on the contrary, there is a wide-spread and deep-seated interest in their future reclamation. Whatever can be done to ameliorate their condition, and encourage that portion who have commenced the work of their own improvement, would receive the warmest commendation. If the Indian puts forth his hand for knowledge, he asks for the only blessing which we can give him in exchange for his birthright, which is worthy of his acceptance.

The education and christianization of the Iroquois is a subject of too much importance, in a civil aspect, to be left exclusively to the limited and fluctuating means of religious societies. The schools established and sustained among them by private benevolence, are, to the Indian, almost the same as common schools to our own people ; and without them the Indian would, in times past, have been denied all means of instruction. These schools bring together the youth for elementary tuition, as a necessary preparation for moral and religious training. While there, they adopt, in all respects, the habits of civilized life, are taught our language, and the more simple elementary studies. In so far, it would be but a just act of public beneficence to allow those pupils to draw the same share of public money which falls to the other children of the State. A system of public Indian education, upon such a plan as their circumstances demand, should either be adopted by the State ; or a portion of the public money, bearing some proportion to the number of Indian pupils, should be placed at the disposal of the local missionary, to be expended with an equal portion contributed by private benevolence, or by the Indians themselves. It is time that our Indian youth were regarded, in all respects, as a part of the children of the State, and brought under such a system of tutelage as that relation would impose.

The vast extent of the religious enterprises of the present day has tended to draw the attention of the Christian world away from the Indian, into fields more distant, and perhaps more attractive. During the past sixty years, the Iroquois have received but a small share of the Christian watchfulness to which their wants entitled them. Faithful and zealous missionaries, it is true, have labored among them, producing results far greater than is generally believed ; but the inadequate scale upon which these missions were organized, and the fluctuations in their efficiency, which were inseparable from their irregular and limited supplies, have prevented them from carrying forward their work to its full completion. But whatever has been done, is chiefly to be ascribed to them, and to the denominations which they represent.

Too much cannot be said of the teachableness of the Indian, and of his aptitude to learn, when subjected to systematic discipline. If the same means and the same influences which are employed to educate and elevate the mass of our own people, and without the constant application of which, they them-

selves would soon fall into ignorance, were brought
to bear upon our Indian population, they would rise
under it with a rapidity which would excite both surprise and admiration. Instances are not wanting,
among the present Iroquois, of attainments in scholarship which would do credit to any student. To give
employment to those Indian youth whose acquired
capacities would enable them to fill stations of trust
and profit among ourselves, is another species of encouragement which commends itself to the generous
mind. Both in our civil and social relations with
the red men, we regard them as a distinct and separate class; when in each of these relations they should
not only be regarded as our fellow-men, but as a part
of our own people. Born upon the soil, the descendants of its ancient proprietors, there is no principle
which should make them aliens in the land of their
nativity, or exclude them from any of those advantages which are reserved to ourselves. So far as they
are able to appreciate and enjoy the same privileges
which pertain to the mass of the people, the claim
for participation which their situation silently puts
forth should not be disregarded.

The lands of the Iroquois are still held in common,
the title being vested in the people. Their progress
towards a higher agricultural life has rendered this
ancient tenure a source of inconvenience; although
they are not as yet prepared for their division among
the people. Each individual can improve and enclose
any portion of their common domain, and sell or retain such improvements, in the same manner as with
personal property; but they have no power to transfer

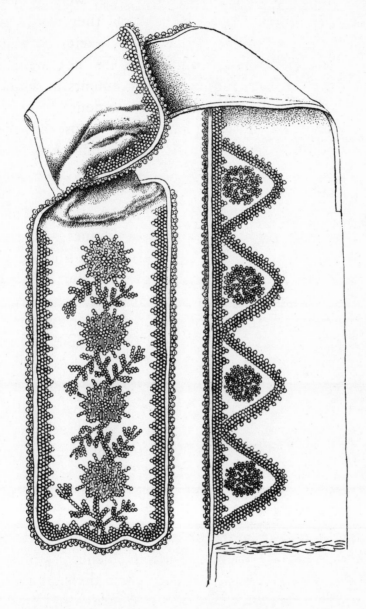

GÄ-SWÄ-HOS-HĂ or BABY FRAME BELT.

mination. This sentiment, which is so wide-spread as to have become a general theme for school-boy declamation, is not only founded upon erroneous views, but it has been prejudicial to the Indian himself. If, then, public opinion and the national policy are both wrong upon these great questions, or if there are even strong grounds for suspecting them to be so, it becomes an act of justice, as well as of duty, to correct the one, and change the other. Our Indian relations, from the foundation of the Republic to the present moment, have been administered with reference to the ultimate advantage of the government itself; while the reclamation of the Indian has been a secondary object, if it ever entered into the calculation in the slightest degeee. Millions of money, it is true, have been expended, and some show of justice preserved in their complicated affairs; but in all prominent negotiations the profit has been on the side of the government, and the loss on that of the Indian. In addition to this, instances of sharp-sighted diplomacy, of ungenerous coercion, and of grievous injustice, are to be found in the journal of our Indian transactions — a perpetual stigma upon the escutcheon of our Republic. If references are demanded to the paragraphs, the reader may turn to that upon the Seminoles, or to the Georgia Cherokee treaty, executed by the government, or to the more recent treaties with the Iroquois themselves, in which the government bartered away its integrity, to minister to the rapacious demands of the Ogden Land Company.

Jefferson made the civilization of the Indian a

subject of profound consideration, and a favorite element of the national policy during his administration. Washington, at a still earlier period, regarded the future welfare of the Indian with deep solicitude. In founding the first system of intercourse and superintendence, he was guided by the most enlightened principles of justice and benevolence; and to such a degree were the Iroquois, in particular, impressed with the goodness and beneficence of his character, that they not only bestowed upon him, in common with other Indian nations, the appellation of *father*, but to this day he is known among them as " the Great American." The aggressive spirit of the people, however, in connection with the slight estimation in which Indian rights were held, has ever been found too powerful an element to be stayed. It has had free course during the last sixty years, until the whole territory east of the Mississippi, with inconsiderable exceptions, has been swept from the Indian. This fact renders any argument superfluous, to show that within this period the reclamation and preservation of the red man has formed no part of the public policy.

But with the same period the moral elements of society have been developed and strengthened to such a degree as to work a change in public sentiment. A kindlier feeling towards the Indian is everywhere apparent, joined with an unwillingness to allow him to be urged into further extremities. He has been sufficiently the victim of adverse fortune, to be entitled to a double portion of the interest and assistance of the philanthropist ; and a new day, it is to be hoped, has already dawned upon his prospects.

It cannot be forgotten, that in after years our Republic must render an account, to the civilized world, for the disposal which it makes of the Indian. It is not sufficient, before this tribunal, to plead inevitable destiny ; but it must be shown affirmatively, that no principles of justice were violated, no efforts were left untried to rescue them from their perilous position. After all has been accomplished which the utmost efforts of philanthropy, and the fullest dictates of wisdom can suggest, there will still be sufficient to lament, in the unpropitious fate of the larger portion of the Indian family. It is the great office of the American people, first, to shield them against future aggression, and then to mature such a system of supervision and tutelage, as will ultimately raise them from the rudeness of Indian life, and prepare them for the enjoyment of those rights and privileges which are common to ourselves.

To the Indian Department of the national government, the wardship of the whole Indian family is, in a great measure, committed ; thus placing it in a position of high responsibility. If any discrimination could be made between the several departments of the government, this should be guided by the most enlightened justice, the most considerate philanthropy. Great is the trust reposed, for it involves the character of the white race, and the existence of the red. May it ever be quickened to duty by a vivid impression of its responsibilities, and never violate, for any consideration, the sacred trust committed to its charge.

The profoundly truthful sentiment of Cicero, " without the highest justice a republic cannot be governed," furnishes a text eminently worthy of being studied in this connection. It would form an apt inscription, to be written over the doorway of the Indian Department —

" Sine summa justitia Rempublicam regi non posse."

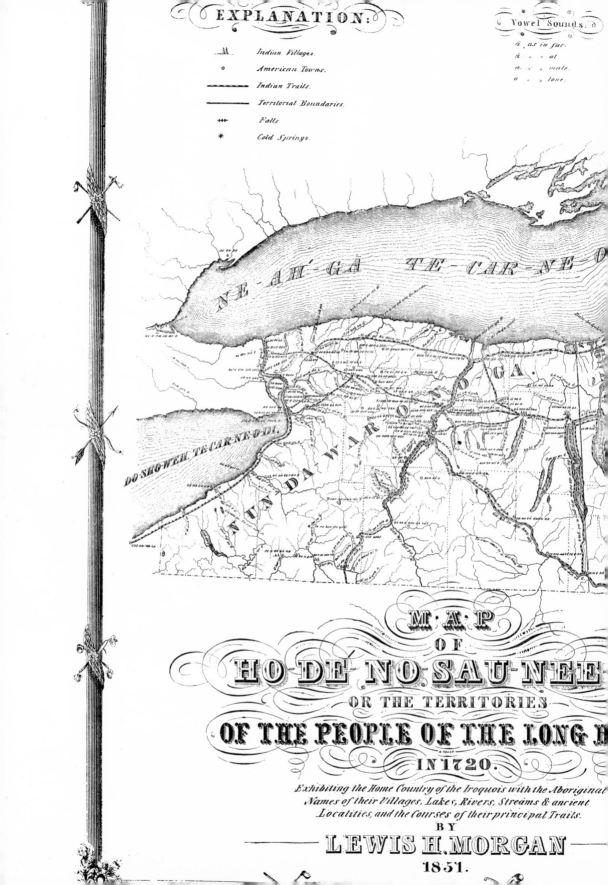

EXPLANATION:

- ⋔   Indian Villages.
- ○   American Towns.
- ‒‒‒   Indian Trails.
- ───   Territorial Boundaries.
- ⧓   Falls
- ✳   Cold Springs.

Vowel Sounds.

ä , as in far.
ă .. „ at
a.. „ „ mate.
o .. „ , low.

NE·AH′·GA TE·CAR·NE·O

DO·SHOWEH TE·CAR·NE·O·DI.

O·NUN·DA·WAR·O·GA.

MAP

OF

HO·DE′·NO·SAU·NEE

OR THE TERRITORIES

OF THE PEOPLE OF THE LONG H

IN 1720.

Exhibiting the Home Country of the Iroquois with the Aboriginal
Names of their Villages, Lakes, Rivers, Streams & ancient
Localities, and the Courses of their principal Trails.

BY

LEWIS H. MORGAN

1851.